The Vulnerable Years:
The United States, 1896–1917

The Vulnerable Years:
The United States, 1896–1917

Irwin Unger
New York University
Debi Unger

New York • New York University Press • 1978

To Our Children With Love:
Anthony, Brooke, Elizabeth, Miles, Paul

Contents

The Vulnerable Years:
The United States, 1896–1917

Chapter One

The Republic Becomes Republican

It was election day, November 3, 1896, and the United States had reached a watershed in its political history. Across the nation, millions of men—factory hands, salesclerks, wheat farmers, storekeepers, civil servants, construction workers, lawyers, bankers—took time off from their busy chores to drop a ballot into a polling station box. The weather was good in most parts of the country, and the turnout was particularly heavy. Some 14 million male citizens, more than in any previous presidential election, managed to perform their civic duty that day.

As the returns came in to the two modest Midwestern homes where the presidential candidates awaited the results of the great national poll, the drift of the public will became clear early in the evening. At Canton, Ohio, crowds gathered on the scuffed lawn of ex-Governor William McKinley's gingerbread home. With each encouraging bulletin, the spectators roared out their delight that the "Major," the town's most eminent citizen, was on his way to becoming the first citizen of the land. Inside it was quieter, though as the Canton factory whistles began to shriek, the noise penetrated into the library where McKinley and his associates were receiving the latest returns by phone and telegraph. Several times the Republican candidate went into the dining room to speak to his wife. Despite her chronically bad health and her inability to meet the demands of her husband's public life, Ida Saxton McKinley this evening had chosen to join the ladies to await the returns. The Major inquired about her comfort and after a few cheerful words returned to the exuberant circle of friends and political associates in the smoke-filled room where the latest bulletins were arriving.

On "D" Street in Lincoln, Nebraska, the atmosphere was more subdued. There, in equally modest surroundings, William Jennings Bryan impassively read the discouraging returns that the three telegraph operators were recording. Dressed jauntily in a velvet jacket with a pink carnation in his buttonhole, the "Great Commoner" refused to show his disappointment even to his solicitous wife whose heart ached as she watched her husband face the certain prospect of defeat. Late that night the Democratic candidate went up to his room, convinced that he had lost, and quickly fell into an exhausted sleep. He later professed to be glad that he had been spared the crushing responsibility of the presidency, but a newspaper friend said that before Bryan had gone to bed, his youthful face had become drawn and aged.

The nature of an American presidential campaign dictates that one man wins and another loses. Victory or defeat is total and unequivocal. Yet on its face the McKinley victory of 1896 was not an overwhelming triumph for the Republicans. The Ohioan had carried twenty-three states with an electoral vote of 271; Bryan had taken twenty-two states with an electoral vote of 176.[1] In the popular vote, the Democrats had won 46.7 percent (6.49 million) and the Republicans 50.8 percent (7.1 million), a difference only a little greater than usual in the two-candidate races of the nineteenth century. When Bryan wrote his history of the campaign, *The First Battle*, he noted that his 6.5 million votes had exceeded Democrat Grover Cleveland's total in 1892 by almost a million and that the change of just a few thousand ballots in several key states would have given him an electoral majority. Other observers noted that John M. Palmer, candidate of the National Democratic party, had drawn off enough supporters from Bryan to push several states into the Republican column.

Yet the close results on that November evening in 1896 concealed some important underlying political developments. For twenty-five years following the Civil War, the two great parties had fought each other to a national standoff. In northern New England, the Republicans clearly dominated both local and national elections. In the lower South, once Reconstruction ended, the Democrats seldom had to worry about their Republican opponents. But elsewhere in the nation, the two parties had waged annual battles for local office, biennial ones for Congress, and quadrennial ones for the presidency that neither could regularly count on winning.

For only four years between 1875 and 1897 did one party or the other simultaneously control the presidency and both houses of Congress. Though voter turnouts were extremely high in this period—reaching to well over 80 percent of the eligible voters in national elections—and campaigns were marked by tremendous fervor, Democrats and Republicans time and again fought one another to a near draw. Victory or defeat did not always hinge on defections from one party to the other. Disappointed or disgruntled voters of one side might stay home on election day because they disliked their party's candidate, were angry over some local issue, or were disgusted with party squabbling. If enough of them stayed away from the

---

[1] In two states, California and Kentucky, the electoral vote was split, though in each the majority went to McKinley.

polls—and it did not take many—they gave the victory to their opponents.

No doubt the closeness of the contests contributed to the extraordinary turnouts. Like a modern major league baseball pennant race, where interest and enthusiasm are in direct proportion to the uncertainty of the outcome, a political contest during the Gilded Age created intense personal involvement among participants. The simile is apt in more ways than one. American politics in the Gilded Age was a major form of entertainment. One newspaper reporter described a political rally in Cambridge City, Indiana, in 1876 as a "spectacle no foreign fiesta could equal." Even though most of the people could not hear the speaker, General Benjamin Harrison, they were perfectly content, for it was "the holiday diversion, the crowds, the bravery of the procession, the music and the fun of the occasion they came chiefly to enjoy." Another observer of the late nineteenth-century American political process wrote: "What theatre is to the French, or the bullfight or fandango to the Spanish, the hustings and the ballot box are to *our* people."

And yet politics, like religion, was a more serious enterprise than bullfights and fandangos—or major league baseball games. Party affiliations reflected the deepest level of personal identification and loyalty in these years. Men were Democrats or Republicans—and consistently so—for more than recreational reasons, a fact that helps to explain the constant failure of third party efforts.

These loyalties are not, however, based primarily on pocketbook concerns before the 1890s. Most Americans in these years did not vote along class or economic lines. It is true that, outside the South, big businessmen were more apt to be Republicans than Democrats and that urban workers were more likely to be Democrats than Republicans, but these were tendencies, not fixed divisions. Many business magnates, particularly those associated with banking and commerce, were attracted to the Democrats; thousands of wage earners, particularly skilled craftsmen, voted Republican.

Far more important than these economic distinctions were the cultural ones. For more than half a century preceding 1896, the United States had been developing into a culturally diverse society. In the 1840s and 1850s, millions of Irish and Germans had poured into the country, bringing with them their customs, religion, prejudices, and historical memories. The Civil War discouraged immigration, but after Appomattox the influx of foreigners resumed. Thousands of newcomers from Ireland, Germany, and Great Britain were joined by a flood of Canadians, Scandinavians, Poles, and Czechs. During the 1890s the stream broadened to include throngs of Hungarians and Slavs from the Austro-Hungarian Empire, Jews and more Poles from Russia, and Italians from the southern portion of the newly unified Kingdom of Italy. Thousands of others—Greeks, Syrians, and Armenians—soon deserted the Turkish dominions for America.

These immigrants did not constitute a single voting bloc. The newest ones, those from the Austrian, Russian, and Turkish empires, were not yet numerous enough or politically aware, and their votes were not important in the Bryan-McKinley contest. The acclimated north Europeans and their children, along with the Canadians and some of the earlier Slavic groups, did count in 1896, but they failed to unite behind a single party and instead divided their vote in complex ways.

To begin with, religion was more important than national origin in affecting how voters cast their ballots. Members of liturgical churches that emphasized "right belief" over personal regeneration—regardless of nationality—tended to be Democrats. The largest group of these was the Catholics. Ever since the 1830s, if not in fact since the days of Jefferson, the Democratic party had provided a political home for the Catholic voter. Led by men of tolerant and pragmatic temper, it welcomed the Catholic Irish and Germans before the Civil War and catered to their needs. These needs were in part material and practical, and the Democratic political machines in the cities provided the immigrants with jobs, handouts, and legal aid.

But this was a game that both parties could play, and often did. A more difficult task for the Republicans—and for their Whig and Federalist predecessors—was to confer cultural boons. Catholics wanted more than the material advantages of America; they also wanted freedom to pursue their religion and their customs. This meant not only formal freedom to worship —something which neither party would refuse—but also the right of Catholic parochial schools to share in local taxes; it meant the right of Catholic chaplains to serve in state hospitals and penal institutions; it meant the right of Catholics to buy and publicly consume wine, beer, and whiskey; it meant the right of Catholic citizens to enjoy a "continental Sunday," unharassed by puritanical blue laws that gave many American cities and towns a funereal aspect on the Sabbath. Many of these preferences were uniquely Catholic, but Catholic voters shared with the members of other churches that emphasized ceremony, ritual, and a well-defined set of dogmas, such as Lutherans, Jews, and Episcopalians, a desire for government hands-off in matters of morals and personal behavior. Yet the Catholics retained their individuality and remained the largest single bloc of "liturgical" voters in the country.

Republicans and their Whig and Federalist forebears could not support these cultural and religious demands. From the outset of the American party system, the more aristocratic party had also been the party of puritanism. It had rejected both Catholics and nonbelievers and had forced them to seek refuge among the Jeffersonian Republicans. The Federalists, Whigs, and Republicans, each in its own day, had represented evangelical, "pietistic" America. Their supporters were drawn heavily from among members of churches that placed inner regeneration, personal reformation, and "right behavior" ahead of outward forms and correct dogma as did Catholics and other "liturgicals." Pietists were mostly native Baptists, Methodists, Congregationalists, and Presbyterians, but they also included Norwegian Haugean Lutherans, Netherlanders of the Dutch Reformed Church, and other foreign groups who, like native evangelicals, tended to consider politics a vehicle for attaining public virtue.

In the 1850s these pietistic attitudes helped create the Republican party, dedicated to the containment and eventual extinction of sinful slavery. Through much of the remainder of the century, the zeal of Republican voters for public and private virtue took such forms as enforcing Sabbath business closings, enjoining Sabbath sports and recreation (blue laws), imposing prohibition measures, and requiring compulsory reading of the Protestant bible in the public schools. These actions offended Catholics and many Lutherans and Episcopalians, who took a more relaxed view of personal behavior and, in the case of the Catholics, objected to Protestant domination of the public schools.[2]

If political puritanism had stopped at such mild expressions as these, it might not have had such a polarizing effect on the voters. But it did not. In the 1880s the American Protective Association (APA), organized around hostility to foreigners and Catholics, demanded the exclusion of noncitizens from American political life, attacked "the diabolical works of the Roman Catholic church," and pledged its members to fight for the "cause of Protestantism." During the 1890s the APA insinuated itself into as many local political campaigns as it could, usually as an unacknowledged ally of the Republicans and a champion of "true Americanism" against "aliens" and "papists." However restless with their traditional party or tempted by an attractive Republican candidate, most liturgical voters were disturbed deeply by this virulent nativism and anti-Catholicism, and it confirmed their allegiance to the Democrats.

Religion formed the basis for party identification primarily in the North. In the South, race and a shared sectional experience transcended all other forces, including religion, in determining party affiliation. Below the Mason-Dixon line and the Ohio River, almost all white voters were Democrats. Native-born Protestants overwhelmingly, their allegiance to the Democratic party was a heritage of the sectional antagonisms of the 1850s, the divisive slavery controversy, and the traumatic experiences of the Civil War

---

[2]My conclusions regarding the cultural basis for political affiliation outlined in the preceding paragraphs draws heavily on the following works: Paul Kleppner, *The Cross of Culture: A Social Analysis of Midwestern Politics, 1850–1900* (New York: The Free Press, 1970); Richard Jensen, *The Winning of the Midwest: Social and Political Conflict, 1888–96* (Chicago: University of Chicago Press, 1971); Samuel McSeveney, *The Politics of Depression: Political Behavior in the North East, 1893–1896* (New York: Oxford University Press, 1972); and Ronald Formisano, *The Birth of Mass Political Parties: Michigan, 1827–1861* (Princeton: Princeton University Press, 1971).

and Reconstruction. This allegiance cut across class, religious, and cultural lines, so that planters, industrialists, farmers, wage earners and sharecroppers—those who were white—voted alike and voted Democratic. People of Southern origin also voted Democratic in the North. In the lower counties of Ohio, Indiana, and Illinois, transplanted Southerners lived in large numbers, and constituted a pool from which the Democrats drew strong support. In effect, men of Southern heritage, with their memory of the antislavery agitation and their special attitudes toward race, wherever they lived, found the ethical laissez-faire of the Democrats more to their taste than the moral zealotry of the Republicans. The converse of this response was that black men in the North, and wherever in the South they still retained the franchise, voted almost to a man for the party of Lincoln and, incidentally, of the old-time, evangelical religion.

II

Normally the cultural-religious bases for politics overshadowed the economic ones, but bread-and-butter issues were never entirely absent from politics and in bad times strongly intruded into the country's political life. In the difficult period 1873–79, grangerism and greenbackism competed with the cultural issues on the political firing line. But the depression of the 1870s, though long, was rather shallow and did not seriously challenge the customary basis for political behavior. Then in 1893 the nation was struck by a severe panic that ushered in five years of bitterly hard times. By the end of the first year, the unemployment rate was over 13 percent of the labor force, a figure representing over 3 million men out of work.

The economic distress percolated all through the country. In more normal times, the Milwaukee County poor list contained the names of 600 or 700 families. In 1894 it listed over 3,400, and as late as 1897, more than 2,700 poor families were still registered with the city. Other cities also felt the cold chill of hard times. A police poll of New York in the winter of 1893–94 tabulated over 67,000 unemployed. In Chicago more than 100,000 were jobless, a figure swollen by the thousands drawn to the city by the World Columbian Exposition. As far west as Denver, where the mining industry's collapse shattered the local economy, the problems of idle men consuming their small savings and falling back on the authorities for relief strained the meager economic and social resources of the country's urban communities.

If the wage earners of the cities suffered, so did the farm population of the countryside. As unemployment figures climbed, farm commodity prices tumbled. In 1890, corn was selling for 50 cents and wheat for 84 cents a bushel, and cotton for 8.6 cents per pound. By 1895, corn was down to 25 cents, wheat to 50 cents, and cotton to 7.6 cents.

In both urban and rural America, hard times generated disorder and discontent. Through the Mississippi Valley and out to the Pacific Coast, armies of unemployed men set out for Washington to force Congress to help the jobless. The largest force—the Commonweal Army—was led by Jacob Coxey, a prosperous businessman with a strong social conscience. Coxey and his lieutenants, Carl Browne and Christopher Jones, considered the march a "petition to Washington with boots on" for their scheme to issue $500 million in paper money for roads to put the unemployed back to work. Today we would consider such a public works program financed by deficit spending a valid way to deal with serious unemployment. But in March 1894, when Coxey's army began its march on the capital from Massillon, Ohio, it seemed like a crackpot nostrum—a "sham crusade," *Harper's Weekly* called it—and the public and the press greeted it with ridicule. When the small ragged band of surviving marchers arrived at the Capitol building, they were blocked by the police. Coxey, Browne, and Jones tried to approach the Capitol steps but were arrested. On May 21 the Washington court convicted the three men of carrying banners on the Capitol grounds and Coxey and Browne of walking on the grass. The forces of law and order had turned an intelligent and compassionate undertaking into slapstick comedy.

The growing labor discontent soon posed more serious threats to public stability as the economy continued its downward spiral. Where employers did not respond to declining sales by discharging workers, they slashed wages. Workers bitterly resented these cuts, but unfortunately they could respond only with sullen resentment or extemporized and poorly financed strikes. By April 1894 the business magazine *Bradstreet's* reported that a "wave of industrial unrest" had enveloped the country with some thirty strikes in progress affecting as many as 750,000 workers. Many of these bore the earmarks of bitter class warfare, with riots, clashes with police, and general mayhem marking their course.

The culmination of the labor strife was the blowup in 1894 in Pullman, Illinois, location of the Pullman Palace Car Company, the nation's chief manufacturer of railroad sleeping cars. The town itself had been conceived as a model community by George Pullman, the company's founder, and for over a decade the attractive little city of tree-lined streets, cream-colored brick houses, parks, and gardens had sheltered Pullman's thousands of employees. Most of the Pullman workers were grateful for being spared the decrepit housing of the urban slum neighborhoods and the depressing factory towns where industrial workers usually lived during these years. But as time passed, it became clear that all was not well in George Pullman's paradise either. Pullman not only wanted an attractive town but also a moral, obedient, and paying one. He outlawed liquor, spied on his employees, discharged workers for running against his own candidates for school board offices—the only elective ones in the town—and squeezed excellent profits from high rents and utility charges. Pullman considered himself a benevolent man, but he acted like a feudal baron entitled to treat the town's residents as his serfs.

In mid-July 1893, in response to decreasing orders from the railroads, Pullman began to dismiss workers, reduce hours, and cut wages. In self-defense Pullman Palace Car workers began to join the newly formed American Railway Union led by a tall, slender Indianan, Eugene Victor Debs. On May 11, 1894, over three thousand Pullman employees walked off the job and appealed to the American Railway Union for support in their previously unsuccessful efforts to have grievances redressed by negotiation. Though reluctant to take on the Pullman Company, the ARU agreed to approach the company's management on behalf of the strikers. When this conciliation effort failed, Debs reluctantly ordered ARU switchmen not to attach Pullman cars onto trains. The railroad operators, hostile to the ARU and fearful of its growing strength, in turn refused to operate passenger trains without the normal complement of Pullman cars and dismissed the recalcitrant switchmen. By July 1 the twenty-four railroads operating out of Chicago had shut down, idling thousands of men.

Without question the strikers were angry and excited, but most labor historians agree that at first they conducted themselves circumspectly. On June 23 a South Chicago crowd held up trains for a few hours; in fact, a number of derailings occurred in the Chicago area. In the West, where ARU members obeyed Deb's order to refuse to inspect, switch, or run trains with Pullman cars, some minor trouble took place. But on the whole the men remained calm.

Yet from the outset, the dispute frightened the operators, the press, and the middle-class American public in general, all of whom were convinced that it threatened the principle of private property and the very foundation of the social order. *The Nation*, noting the disorderly episodes out West, exclaimed: there "does not seem to be a voice raised there in favor of law and civil government." *The Chicago Herald* excitedly charged that "if the strike should be successful the owners of the railroad property . . . would have to surrender . . . future control to the class of labor agitators and strike conspirators who have formed the Debs Railway Union."

Hoping simultaneously to break the strike and smash the union, the General Managers Association, representing the twenty-four Chicago railroads, swung into action. Offices were set up in New York, Philadelphia, Cleveland, and Baltimore to hire men to replace ARU members. In all, twenty-five hundred strikebreakers were enrolled. The association also disseminated scare stories recounting the extremism and violence of the strikers. Their trump card, however, was the federal government. In the person of Attorney General Richard Olney, the railroads had a friend at court. A former railroad attorney and a man of truculent and irascible temper, Olney despised and feared labor agitators and sympathized with the railroads. At the behest of the managers, he authorized the hiring of federal marshals ostensibly to protect the mails, which he claimed were being held up by the strike. On July 2 his deputy in Chicago, Edwin Walker, applied for and got from the federal court an injunction against the union on the specious grounds that its actions violated the Sherman Antitrust Act. If ARU officials did not desist from blocking the movement of trains into and out of Chicago, they would be found in contempt of court. The next day Walker wired President Cleveland urging him to protect federal property, prevent interference with the mails, and enforce the court ruling. Cleveland quickly responded by dispatching the entire garrison at Fort Sheridan, infantry, artillery, and cavalry, to Chicago.

The president's action infuriated Governor Altgeld, a man sympathetic to labor. Under the Constitution, he insisted, federal troops could be called in to put down domestic disorder only by a request of a state governor. He had not made such a request because there had been no need to; the men had been orderly and law-abiding. The governor's complaint was ignored.

The strike did not long survive the injunction and the arrival of federal forces. Among the five thousand federal marshals that Olney had recruited were hundreds of loyal railroad employees, as well as some roughnecks and criminals. The presence of these elements antagonized the strikers, touching off far more violence than had yet taken place. Debs tried to prevent his resentful men from expressing their anger and frustration, but in the next few days, the railroad yards were swept by a wave of shootings, rioting, and arson. The federal authorities then cracked down. On July 17, Debs and other ARU officials were arrested for violating the injunction. Deprived of leadership, the strike soon petered out. The ARU officials were eventually tried, and Debs was sent to prison for six months for violating the injunction.

The experience of Pullman was a chastening one to many laboring men. To some it proved the futility of labor organizations; to others it underscored the iniquity of the Cleveland administration; to still others, Debs among them, it demonstrated the failure of capitalism. During his six months in federal prison, Debs read widely and pondered the lessons of the strike. In the end he concluded that American working men could not hope to get a fair break within the capitalist system and that socialism was the only real answer to labor's discontents. In 1897 Debs helped organize the Socialist Party of America, and in 1900 became its presidential candidate.

However, Debs's conversion to socialism was not a typical response to the depression and its labor difficulties. During the first decade and a half of the twentieth century, socialism appealed strongly to thousands of foreign-born and native American wage earners and even to some farmers. But during the 1890s, Marxist parties that questioned the traditional institution of private property attracted only a handful of Americans. Before 1900, such groups as the Anarchists, the Socialist Laborites, and Edward Bellamy's Nationalists were largely debating societies that argued endlessly about the proper roads to a "cooperative commonwealth" of common ownership and universal brotherhood with little action to implement their vision. The single exception was the Anarchists, mostly immigrant German intellectuals, who endorsed violence to overthrow the system and whose rabid rhetoric, even more than their occasional violent deeds, did much to convince middle-class Americans that all socialists and indeed all labor leaders were dangerous bomb-throwers, no better than common criminals.

All things considered, American wage earners showed a surprising amount of faith in capitalism during the hard years following 1893. To understand this we must make some careful distinctions among the elements comprising the labor force, and we must separate short-term discontents from long-term satisfactions. First, let us remember that a large proportion of the lowest paid wage earners were foreign born. Generally, these men and women found America to their liking. Though they worked hard and long for what they got, they recognized that American conditions were better than they could expect in Europe. At every level of skill and in almost every industry, real wages in the United States exceeded those of Europe. Along with free land, this fact, more than political democracy or religious freedom, explained why millions of Europeans had for generations crossed the Atlantic to America.

Except in times of unusual stress, people like these did not make willing recruits for revolution or even for labor unions. Aside from their general satisfaction with American wages, many immigrants were unattached males anxious to save money so that they could pay boat passage for wives, parents, and children. Strikes and lockouts, not to speak of revolution, were scarcely thinkable to men looking forward to reunion with their families and worried about depleting their savings or losing their jobs. Moreover, people so unfamiliar with America, so unused to the new urban environment in which they now found themselves, and so beaten down by the heritage of powerlessness that characterized European peasants could scarcely be expected to challenge openly the predominant institutions they had to deal with day by day. At times of great frustration or special injustice, the foreign-born miner or factory worker might make some desperate, spontaneous gesture of defiance. But these occasions were rare. Rather than forming a volatile, dangerous component of the population, the foreign-born working class contributed fundamentally to social stability in the United States of the late nineteenth century.

Nor were native-born wage earners especially anxious to challenge the economic and social order in a systematic way. By and large, native American workers filled the ranks of the skilled crafts—the carpenters, printers, plumbers, bricklayers, blacksmiths, telegraphers, and machinists. These were the better-paying trades, and men experienced and skilled enough to work at them could earn a decent living for themselves and their families.

These labor aristocrats were, if anything, staunch supporters of the overall status quo.

Moreover, from the native-born Americans the expanding middle class recruited many of its members. Social mobility was an important fact of life in late nineteenth-century America. Sociologists tell us that relative freedom to move out of one class into a higher one has been common to all industrializing societies. Although no conclusive proof exists—at least by the crude indices employed by sociologists—that social mobility was greater in the United States than, for example, in Britain, Germany, or Sweden at comparable stages of economic development, the American social experience was clearly more open than the European. Americans, for one thing, did not stay put geographically: the United States was a nation of nomads. Stephen Thernstrom estimates that about a quarter of Boston's population at any given time between 1837 and 1921 had arrived in the city only a year previously. Rapid movement into and out of communities was obviously not conducive to the development of class solidarity or to cooperative effort among laboring men.

Cultural values and ideology also blunted the edge of class distinctions and class resentment. Even if the United States was not uniquely open to movement up and down the social ladder, it did have an unusually egalitarian set of values that refused to penalize people for their origins. Any man who raised his income or moved up in his job was accepted as an equal by those already there. Not only was mobility possible, but the belief in its certainty as a reward for hard work, sobriety, and intelligence was even more common. One of the most potent social myths of nineteenth-century America was that rich men were once poor boys and that every American, certainly every native-born white American, began at the same starting line in the race of life. This combination, then, of reality and belief produced an acceptance of the system and a tolerance of it, except in extreme cases, that reinforced the normal acquiescence of men in whatever social order existed.

But not all Americans who worked with their hands were urban wage earners. As late as the 1890s, over 40 percent of the labor force was engaged in agriculture. These 10 million husbandmen felt the ill effects of the 1893–97 depression, but like other economic groups, they did not all suffer equally. Least affected by the depression and the deflationary trend that had long preceded it were those farmers who had abandoned the great American staples—wheat, cotton, and corn—and planted various sorts of specialty crops. In the Northeast and older Midwest, these included the fruit and vegetable growers and the dairymen, who supplied the swelling markets of the large cities. They also included the farmers of the Illinois and Iowa prairies who, in the decades immediately preceding and immediately following the Civil War, moved from raising wheat for bread to raising corn as fodder for hogs and cattle. The corn belt farmers, like the truck gardeners and dairymen, produced primarily for domestic or local markets and did not experience the erosion of income that afflicted the staple producers, especially the growers of wheat and cotton, who sold much of their output abroad.

Of these last two, the cotton farmers were, by 1890, in the more distressed state. In addition to a steady fall in the price of their chief commodity, they labored under an intolerable social regime, an outgrowth of the Reconstruction effort to readjust both the social and labor systems of the South to the fact of black emancipation. To most white Southerners, the prospect of a black yeomanry consisting of independent farm owners was inconceivable. Where would the land come from? Who would provide the capital and the managerial skill? The federal government, which might have helped with these problems, was reluctant to violate the American tradition of laissez faire in agriculture. The conservative white South, which only reluctantly accepted the emancipation of the slaves, would not help. Not only would such aid be expensive but it would disturb profoundly the essential social relations between the races by elevating the black man above his "proper place."

If the white South had had its way, the Negro, though formally free, would have been virtually reenslaved. During the months immediately following Appomattox, while President Andrew Johnson was in full control of the Reconstruction process, the ex-Confederate states were given a free hand to decide exactly how far freedom for the former slaves would extend. Each of the states adopted a Black Code that in almost every case relegated the freedmen to second-class citizenship by law. At the same time, the labor system that initially replaced slavery closely resembled it. Blacks were worked in gangs by drivers in the fields just as they had been before the war; the only difference was that now they received a small wage instead of shelter, clothing, and subsistence rations. The improvement did not seem great.

Blacks detested the wage system, and they balked at fulfilling labor contracts. The freedmen yearned for land as the landless have always done. In the end, by a process of trial and error, a bargain was struck with the white South, one that left the black man few economic advantages but at least gave him some basic personal freedoms. In return for his labor, the black farmer would be allowed rent of a house, generally a squalid shack, and a share of the crop, usually one-third. If he could also provide animals, seed, and tools, his share would be greater. But at no time would he own the land; it would remain in the legal hands of the white landlord.

Theoretically, with luck and hard work, the sharecropper might make enough of a profit to save money and buy the land for himself under this arrangement. With cotton prices steadily declining, however, this proved a rare occurrence. But the sharecropper faced another hurdle to success. Superimposed on sharecropping was a credit system that made it nearly impossible for him to accumulate any cash surplus. Under this system the cropper bought seed, tools, cloth, clothing, even food at a store often run by the landlord from whom he rented. These purchases were on credit, and to secure the loan on these goods, the storekeeper received a lien—a kind of mortgage—on the tenant's crop. At harvest time when the crop was sold, usually through the storekeeper, the account was settled. If the proceeds were sufficient, the debt was canceled and the remainder given in cash to the cropper. If the proceeds were too little, as was usually the case, the cropper remained in debt to the storekeeper.

All credit systems have their drawbacks, but the crop-lien scheme was particularly pernicious. Buying at the store was expensive, as credit buying generally is. In addition, once the sharecropper fell behind, he was forced to buy on the same credit arrangement and could not shop for good prices elsewhere; he remained a captive customer of the storekeeper. Furthermore, since the tenant was often illiterate, he was at the mercy of the storekeeper when it came to keeping accounts. The opportunity for cheating was enormous, and given the racial values of the post–Civil War South, few black men had the temerity to dispute the records of the storekeeper even when they had reason to believe that they were being swindled.

The system posed hardships for the former slaves particularly but generally was a curse to the South as a whole. Eventually thousands of white farmers found themselves reduced to tenantry along with the freedmen. More important, the system wedded the South firmly and unhappily to cotton, since storekeepers and landlords preferred cotton. Unlike vegetables, pork, or fruit, it was not perishable and could be marketed readily. And confining the tenant exclusively to cotton made him that much more dependent on the storekeeper for everything else he consumed.

A one-crop economy is always vulnerable. But if cotton prices had risen over the years, or at least had remained stable, the South's commitment might have been tolerable. Unfortunately, cotton prices declined steadily after 1875, falling to half the level of that year by the end of the century. This trend was the consequence of constantly increasing output not only in the American South but also in Brazil, India, and other countries that poured millions of bales every year into the world cotton market. Had it been possible to lower the costs of production substantially, the lower price per pound that the American grower received might have been offset. But as the system was arranged in the South, simple hand labor continued to be used and there was relatively little change over the years in the output per man.

Migration out of the region or its farm areas might have mitigated Southern rural distress. Some movement of rural folk, black and white, to the South's towns and cities did occur. Toward the end of the century, cotton mills began to spring up in the Piedmont region of the Carolinas, Georgia, and Virginia, and many rural whites came to work in them, but for blacks there was little escape. Race prejudice kept them out of the new Southern mills, and even in the North, as long as millions of European immigrants took the factory, mining, and construction jobs, black workers had no place. Locked into a system of cotton monoculture combined with tenantry, victims of ignorance and racial prejudice, the black farmers of the South constituted a depressed peasantry that weighed down the region and the nation.

The other great staple-growing area of the country—the wheat belt of the plains—also faced trouble toward the end of the century. In the generation following the Civil War, the wheat region had moved ever westward from Indiana, Illinois, Wisconsin, and Iowa into Kansas, Minnesota, Oklahoma, Nebraska, the Dakotas, eastern Montana, Washington, and Colorado. Much of this area was a semiarid, rolling, treeless plateau characterized by a fine, deep soil but a harsh climate with long, cold winters and frequent droughts. During good years farmers could raise bumper wheat crops on the plains and harvest them efficiently with the new horse-drawn machinery developed during the mid-nineteenth century. But the good years were often followed by bad ones of light rainfall, parching winds, cinch bugs, and locusts. Many farmers who moved cheerfully into western Kansas during the 1880s crawled back during the 1890s after a decade of drought with the sides of their wagons inscribed: "In God we trusted, in Kansas we busted."

Nature was not the only obstacle to profitable farming in the plains. A host of human impediments also seemed to bedevil the wheat farmer. First there were the railroads. For producers living thousands of miles from their final markets in the East and in Europe, the railroads were indispensable. In fact, successful commercial agriculture was inconceivable on the plains without railroad connections to market. Plains farmers had moved west only with the advent of railroads (or at least following the promise that they would shortly arrive), and many plains communities had offered substantial sums of cash to railroad promoters to induce them to build their lines nearby.

Yet the very indispensability of the railroads made them a problem. In the plains region where population was sparse, a single road ordinarily served a large area. If the local railroad company chose to charge high rates, the farmer could do little: he had no alternative. High rates per ton mile for the plains farmer constrasted, moreover, with low rates for others. Between Chicago and Omaha, for example, goods could be shipped a given distance for far less than where the rail net was less dense and the traffic lighter. The railroad companies justified this policy on the ground of necessity. They had to cut rates on competitive routes or lose business, they explained, but then they had to make up their losses by charging all the traffic would bear everywhere else. The principle might be harsh, but it was unavoidable.

Whatever the rationale for this "long haul–short haul" abuse, to plains farmers the practice seemed like insufferable discrimination. Why should they be forced to make up the railroads' losses? They were incensed further at rebates whereby the railroads secretly and selectively reduced their rates to large shippers. They complained that the railroads misgraded wheat at their grain elevators, monopolized the best lands of the West, and engaged in corrupt dealings with venal politicians. In sum these allegations formed a strong agrarian indictment against the men who managed the Western railroad system.

Still other characters were included in the western farmer's book of villains. Manufacturers, agrarian critics charged, had used the government for their selfish purposes for years. If the railroad promoters had finagled Congress into handing them enormous chunks of the national domain, manufacturers had extracted special favors in the form of protective tariffs. Ever since the Civil War, the barriers behind which American industry could hide from European competition had risen higher and higher. These tariffs had been at the expense of the American consumer, including farmers, and had enabled the manufacturers to charge high prices and supply shoddy goods without fear of losing customers. Tariffs also had contributed to the formation of monopolies. Farmers especially resented the tariff because European nations, offended by American protectionist policies, discriminated against American wheat, cotton, and other farm products.

A final major offender of the plains farmer's sense of justice and fair play was the dispenser of credit. In a new, rapidly growing region like the trans-Mississippi West, abundant credit was sorely needed. Fencing, livestock, plows, harvesters, windmills, barns, silos, construction materials all cost money. Even to acquire land, farmers needed capital, since much of the West's best acreage was originally in the hands of railroads or speculators, and only a moderate amount came free of cost from the federal government under the Homestead Act of 1862. In addition, farmers often needed credit during the growing or harvesting season before their crop was sold. Unfortunately, credit charges were high in the West. National banks were not allowed to lend on the security of land, the only asset the farmer usually had. State-chartered banks and eastern-based mortgage companies could and did lend on real estate, but many plains farmers were convinced that these institutions charged exorbitantly high interest rates and were quick to foreclose when farmers were unable to keep up their payments.

In the minds of many western and southern farmers, the credit problem was closely linked with the issues of farm commodity prices and money. Why, they asked, were farm prices remorselessly sinking while at the same time the cost of borrowing money remained high? The answer for many was that a sinister "money power" existed, composed of bankers and financiers who deliberately had restricted the money supply of the country. Though the economy was steadily growing and the amount of business in the country was rapidly expanding, the money stock had actually declined. Sitting in their offices on Wall Street and on London's Threadneedle Street, the international financiers had issued orders that money should be kept tight and dear. Dear dollars meant cheap corn, wheat, and cotton because the first measured the value of the others. And it also meant high interest charges, since interest was the "cost" of money. Both together meant distress for the farmers while the creditors of the nation and the world grew rich from farm mortgages and cheap farm prices.

Over the years this belief in a money monopoly was incorporated into several distinct movements aimed at restoring a balance between debtors and creditors. Immediately after 1865, greenbackism emphasized the dangers of withdrawing from circulation the paper money that the federal treasury had issued to help finance the Union cause during the Civil War. By the late 1870s, the focus had shifted to the issue of silver and its function in the nation's monetary system.

In one of their more melodramatic formulations, agrarian proponents insisted that dropping the old-weight silver dollar from the list of United States coins in 1873 was a "crime" perpetrated by a group of clandestine conspirators for the purpose of hurting the "producing classes." The elimination of silver from the country's circulation and the recourse to an exclusive gold-based money system had effectively reduced the money stock; the remedy was to resume silver coinage on the old basis of sixteen ounces of silver to one of gold. The more adamant silverites hoped that this action would devalue the dollar, raise prices, and scale down all debts in quick succession. The bimetallists argued that by "remonetizing" silver the world's rapidly growing stock of silver would be added to its static stock of gold, thereby augmenting the whole money supply. Although some increase in prices and some decline in the real value of fixed debts might result, bimetallists explained, this was not the primary purpose of "remonetization"; rather, the goal was to prevent the constant appreciation of the dollar and the remorseless depreciation of all prices imposed by the gold standard.

For thirty-five years after the Greenbackers of 1865, silverites, bimetallists, and gold standard advocates (gold bugs) battled over national finance. At times the arguments were temperate and rational; often they were angry and emotional. Extremists at both ends of the spectrum were convinced that far more was at stake than some technical details of money and banking, or even the simple question of group benefits or losses. "Soft money men" (and silverites, curiously, were considered soft money men), as we have seen, held that the gold standard was a device of the money power to oppress the producers and reduce them to utter bondage. Gold bugs, on the other hand, were convinced that the gold standard was the very basis of civilization and that the silverites, Greenbackers, and even the bimetallists were fit candidates for either prison or the madhouse. The money question incorporated a remarkable amount of the social conflict of the day, generating some of the most bitter and overwrought rhetoric that has ever been displayed in American political life.

The heart of the soft money country was the staple-growing Plains, the

South, and the silver-mining Mountain states. Here and there among Eastern working men small pockets of greenback or silver sentiment thrived. But the East, and the older Midwest, was largely hard money—or "honest money"—territory, and here most people feared the derangement of prices and of credit relationships that might follow the overthrow of the gold standard.

For a generation the battle between these groups seesawed back and forth. In 1878 the silver forces won a partial victory when Congress passed the Bland-Allison silver purchase bill over the veto of President Hayes. Dissatisfied with the small amount of silver that the measure required the Treasury to buy and coin into dollars (between $2 million and $4 million annually), the silver forces soon resumed the attack and in 1890 procured the Sherman Silver Purchase Act. This measure increased the amount of silver to 4.5 million ounces per month at the market price but still fell short of the "free and unlimited coinage of silver" that the most ardent silverites wanted.

Nevertheless, the ever-growing silver circulation soon threatened to topple the gold standard. Ever since the late 1870s, the Treasury had maintained a gold reserve as backing against the remaining greenbacks. When silver became part of the country's money stock after Bland-Allison, this same reserve was used to back the new silver dollars. By the early 1890s, however, the reserve had declined relative to the ever-expanding volume of paper and silver it was supposed to redeem. As the public lost confidence in the ability of the Treasury to convert paper and silver into gold on demand, it began to insist on that very thing. At an ever faster pace, people began presenting paper money and silver coins at the banks to be converted into gold. As the gold reserve fell, still more people, worried that the Treasury would be forced off the gold standard, began to ask for gold. As the reserve dwindled, it soon began to look as if the extreme silverites would get the devaluation of the dollar that they wanted.

The situation worsened after the panic struck in 1893. President Grover Cleveland, blaming the Sherman Silver Purchase Act for both the gold drain and the panic itself, called Congress into special session to repeal the measure. Eventually the president got his way, but the bitter debate pitting the Eastern wing of the Democrats against its Western wing tore the party apart.

Meanwhile, the drain continued. By January 1894 the gold reserve had fallen to $69 million. At this point Cleveland and Treasury Secretary John G. Carlisle took steps that further alienated the Western and Southern wing of the party. To replenish the gold reserve, the Treasury began to sell gold bonds. The first issue was in January; second and third issues followed soon after. These brought gold back to the Treasury, but the relief was temporary. The public bought the bonds but then promptly presented more paper and silver for redemption. Gold went into the Treasury at one end and out the other. By January 1895 the gold reserve touched $45 million, the lowest point ever.

Hoping to stop this endless circular process, the president then turned to the international bankers, the very men whom the silverites blamed for oppressing the nation's producing classes. A fourth loan, placed with J. P. Morgan and Company and August Belmont, the American representatives of the Rothschilds, brought gold from Europe. Finally, after still another foreign bond issue, the gold drain was stopped. But the political price Cleveland paid was high. Few Western and Southern Democrats credited the president for his achievement. In the House of Representatives, Bryan prefaced his attack on the Morgan sales by reading Shylock's bond from *The Merchant of Venice.* Senators Morgan of Alabama and Vest of Kentucky accused Cleveland of allowing the bankers to hold the government for ransom. Cleveland had saved the gold standard but had split the Democratic party irrevocably along ideological and sectional lines.

III

These, then, were the pocketbook issues that increasingly dominated politics in the mid-1890s. Farm distress, wage cuts, strikes, deflation, unemployment—all the ugly consequences of the hard times following 1893—intruded massively into the normal political patterns of American politics during the 1896 election year. The party in power was certain to bear the onus for hard times, but could the blame be confined to the Eastern, Cleveland wing, or must the whole party suffer? And how could the Democratic silverites prevent the nomination of a gold bug and secure the nomination for one of their own?

An unusual piece in the puzzle of presidential politics in 1896 was the uncertain role of a third party, the Populists. Organized in 1892, the People's party (or Populists) was the culmination of more than a decade of farmer discontent. This discontent had grown rapidly during the early nineties from isolated rural grumbling into a "religious revival, a crusade, a pentecost of politics in which a tongue of flame sat upon every man." An outgrowth of the National Farmers' Alliance (Northern Alliance) and the National Farmers' Alliance and Industrial Union (Southern Alliance), the new political organization also gathered into its embrace a mixed bag of disgruntled politicians, third party men, and maverick, often self-taught, intellectuals and ideologues.

At first glance, the Populists appeared to offer the American people a broad and truly progressive program. Their rhetoric was infused with the traditional moral indignation of the oppressed against their oppressors. In the words of the party platform adopted at Omaha in 1892, the nation had been "brought to the verge of moral, political and material ruin" by the political events of the preceding years. Corruption dominated national life, the people were demoralized, the newspapers were muzzled, labor impoverished, the people's homes mortgaged, business prostrate, and the land itself controlled by the capitalists: "The fruits of the toil of millions are boldly stolen to build up colossal fortunes for a few . . . and the possessors of these, in turn despise the republic and endanger liberty. From the same prolific womb of governmental injustice we breed the two great classes—tramps and millionaires."

The Populist antidote to these fearful conditions, as expressed by the Omaha platform, was the expansion of federal power. The government should take possession of the railroads and also of the telegraph and telephone systems; they recommended a graduated income tax to reduce the tax burden on the common people and favored giving the government, rather than the banks and private institutions, the power to issue the circulating medium of the nation. At the same time, the Omaha platform endorsed new political machinery to improve the processes of democratic control. Such reforms as the initiative and referendum, popular election of United States senators, and the secret ballot would help the people to bypass unresponsive officials and legislators and guarantee that government would listen to the discontented and aggrieved.

In various forms most of these measures were taken seriously by later generations of Americans, and the Populists have been hailed as the precursors of the Progressives and the New Deal. There is much to be said for this view. As we shall see, the Progressives would indeed borrow much of the Populist program. Nevertheless, one side of populism did not stand the test of time and was considered by later generations of reformers as crankish and eccentric. Though the Omaha platform and other Populist statements strongly endorsed the rights of labor to organize and proclaimed that the farmer and the city wage earner were allies in the struggle for social and economic justice, the tone of Populist rhetoric was decidedly agrarian. Even in 1892 a strong monetary emphasis characterized the People's party platform. Admittedly, a few labor leaders and labor intellectuals toyed with soft money solutions to labor's problems, but at no time did a majority of American working men accept monetary answers to their problems. Yet the financial question was the core of populism. The money power above all the rest, the Omaha platform proclaimed, was the source of the people's distress. "A vast conspiracy against mankind has been organized on two continents," declared Ignatius Donnelly, a Populist politician and theoretician who wrote the 1892 platform. The conspiracy was "rapidly taking possession of the world," and if it were "not met and overthrown at once," it would produce "terrible social convulsions, the destruction of civilization or the establishment of an absolute despotism." To head off these disasters, it was necessary to increase the circulating medium to fifty dollars per capita and, still more urgently, to authorize the free and unlimited coinage of silver at sixteen to one.

The appeal of the Omaha platform and the People's party was limited outside the South, the Plains, and the mining states of the Rocky Mountain region. The 1892 Populist ticket of James Weaver and James Field carried Kansas, Idaho, Colorado, and Nevada, while several Populist electors were also chosen in North Dakota and Oregon. But the Populists claimed few, if any, votes in the eastern cities, and in such western states as Kansas and California, the labor planks of the platform attracted relatively few working-class voters. The Western hard-rock miners voted for Weaver, but obviously many wage earners considered the Populists a farmer's party that had little to offer them.

The Populist explanation for falling prices and an appreciating dollar did have some truth to it. Modern economists such as Milton Friedman have concluded that linking the nation's money system to gold did indeed reduce the growth rate of the money supply and exert a steady downward pressure on prices.[3] Yet however valid in fact, the Populist monetary analysis of economic distress and inequality had a highly abstract quality to it that reduced its appeal to urban workers. Perhaps more importantly, to the extent that ordinary wage earners understood the significance of Populist monetary principles, they had good reason to fear it, for at the very best, it meant that the downward trend of prices would be stopped; at the very worst, that falling prices and the falling cost of living would give way to higher prices and a growing struggle to make ends meet.

Another quality of populism that made it suspect to many voters as well as to later reformers was its obsession with conspiracy. Populists were always seeing plots and nefarious schemes in the country's political life. Mrs. Sarah Emery, a Populist from Lansing, Michigan, described at least seven horrendous "financial conspiracies" from the Civil War to the mid-1870s that together had "enslaved the American people." Ignatius Donnelly wrote an apocalyptic novel in which the world of the future is controlled by a small inner council of ruthless, unprincipled plutocrats. To William "Coin" Harvey, the American people toiled at the mercy of the bankers of England, who could "dictate the money of the world" and "thereby create world misery."

The nation undoubtedly has had its share of behind-the-scenes scheming for advantage by one group or another, but these maneuvers almost always have been for private gain. At no time, Watergate excepted perhaps, has there ever been a serious plot to subvert the American system as a whole, as Donnelly, Mrs. Emery, and many other leading Populists seemed to think. Most middle-class and educated people were offended by these con-

---

[3]See Milton Friedman and Anna Schwartz, *A Monetary History of the United States, 1867–1960* (Princeton, N.J.: Princeton University Press, 1963), pp. 89–134.

spiracy theories and believed that the plots were figments of naive and deluded imaginations.

A strain of bigotry and intolerance in populism also repelled many contemporaries. Some historians have depicted the Populists as tolerant toward ethnic minorities and unusually willing to support their aspirations.[4] C. Vann Woodward has said that Georgia leader Tom Watson was among the few Southern white politicians who upheld the civil rights of the Southern black man and tried to guarantee him access to a decent life.[5]

Actually, the facts regarding Populist racial and ethnic attitudes also point in the other direction. Some Populists were indeed anti-Semites. Donnelly, for one, believed that the Jews were "the owners of all the great Trusts and Combines." They owned the whiskey ring completely. "They are," he insisted, "all gold bugs; opposed to government paper money and free silver; for the scarcer the money the richer they are, and the poorer the rest of mankind." Populists were also skeptical of city people and often expressed fear of the alien population of the nation's metropolises: Harvey claimed that "cities do not breed statesmen"; C. W. McCune's *National Economist* charged that "the masses of the people in great cities are volatile and unstable, lacking in patriotism and unfit to support a wise and pure government"; a famous Populist cartoon showed a transcontinental cow feeding on the prairies while being milked in New York.

It has been said that Populist anti-Semitism boils down to little more than conventional remarks about "shylocks" and the "Rothschilds" and, in any case, was no worse than the elitist anti-Semitism of Henry Adams and Henry James or the proletarian anti-Semitism of the New York Irish immigrant. Populist anti-Semitism, it could be argued, was merely the converse of urban antiruralism. Yet the Populist strain of intolerance had its own peculiar virulence and in various forms persisted until recent times as an indictment of the supposedly unproductive elements in American society.

As for the Populist efforts to achieve racial justice and reconcile whites and blacks in the South, the facts are contradictory. In Louisiana, apparently, white Alliance men and Populists were among the few political friends of the black man.[6] On the other hand, in Georgia Tom Watson was not the ardent champion of blacks that Woodward claims. According to Charles Crowe, Watson was a transparent opportunist whose racial liberalism was designed to win votes and was fragile and short-lived at best.[7] In Tennessee,

---

[4]See, for example, Walter T. K. Nugent, *The Tolerant Populists: Kansas Populism and Nativism* (Chicago: The University of Chicago Press, 1963).

[5]See C. Vann Woodward, *Tom Watson: Agrarian Rebel* (New York: Oxford University Press, 1963).

[6]See William Warren Rodger, *The One-Gallused Rebellion: Agrarianism in Alabama, 1865–1896* (Baton Rouge: Louisiana State University Press, 1970), pp. 141–46, 332–33.

[7]Charles Crowe, "Tom Watson, Populists and Blacks Reconsidered," *The Journal of Negro History* (April 1970).

the Farmers' Alliance was an enthusiastic ally of the Democrats' efforts to disenfranchise the state's remaining black voters in 1890.[8]

Obviously one major impediment to evaluating the Populists is their incredible variety. The agrarian movement varied widely from state to state, hence the diverse racial attitudes just noted. It also varied from person to person. Donnelly, a self-taught intellectual given to spinning out elaborate, ill-supported fantasies, had very different ideas about the money problem than did the cultured Columbia College graduate Henry Demarest Lloyd. Populist Governor Davis Waite of Colorado was a sincere friend of the laboring man and at times sounded like a flaming social radical, but Alliance Governor John P. Buchanan of Tennessee sent the state militia into the Cumberland coal field to force striking miners to submit to competition from convict labor.

In all likelihood we shall never be able to sum up precisely what Populism really was because the movement was too variegated for any simple descriptive formula. The difficulty of evaluating it is compounded by the fact that it evokes modern political and ideological echoes. Urbanites and political conservatives tend to find it retrograde, bigoted, and backward looking. People of the political left and scholars whose origins are small town or rural tend to view it as both progressive and tolerant.[9] It is difficult to see how there can ever be a consensus on the subject. Far more likely, scholars of differing persuasions, like the three blind men estimating the shape of the elephant in the Indian parable, will continue to have their own opinions—and each of these will contain some part of the truth.

IV

However modern ideologues and historians may evaluate the Populists, the attempted coalition of Western and Southern farmers with urban wage earners clearly was unsuccessful in 1892. With the 1893 panic and the depression, however, Populist prospects suddenly improved. Hard times promised to loosen all party ties, while Cleveland's dealings with the international bankers threatened to drive many Democrats into the new party.

In the end the Populists did not reap the expected harvest. Both major parties had a silver and a gold wing. The most prominent Republican silverite was Senator Henry Teller of Colorado. In the Democratic camp, Richard Bland of Missouri, Benjamin Tillman of South Carolina, and the young,

---

[8]Roger L. Hart, *Redeemers, Bourbons and Populists: Tennessee, 1870–1896* (Baton Rouge: Louisiana State University Press, 1975), pp. 266 ff.

[9]See Irwin Unger, "Critique of Norman Pollack's 'Fear of Man,' " *Agricultural History* 39, no. 2: 75–80.

eloquent Nebraska congressman, William Jennings Bryan, led the silver faction. In the case of both Democrats and Republicans, the party machinery was in the hands of the Eastern, sound money wing, though the silver Democrats were stronger proportionately than their Republican counterparts.

In the battle over party control, the Western and Southern silver Democrats had the advantage over their Eastern opponents as the election of 1896 approached. The depression and Cleveland's association with Morgan had hurt the party as a whole but had hurt the sound money groups within it even more. By the opening of the presidential campaign, Western Democrats could charge that the bungling in Washington had already badly damaged the party. After Cleveland's spectacular victory in 1892, everything had gone downhill. In 1893 the Democratic vote had declined in the state elections. Then in the 1894 congressional contest, the voters had repudiated Cleveland's party in record numbers although the APA, by noisily supporting the Republicans, had handed the Democrats a ready-made issue. Matters had come to a sad state when the party could no longer count on the traditional cultural and religious allegiances of the voting public!

For months before the Democratic convention in Chicago, the various Democratic candidates jockeyed for position. Though not himself a candidate for reelection, Cleveland sought to head off the silverites through his use of patronage and influence. His efforts were not successful. Both the leaders and the rank-and-file members of the party in the West and South considered Cleveland and his position death to the chances of party success and refused to heed him. Instead they mounted a campaign of their own to capture the party leadership. At a series of meetings in 1895, the silver Democrats set up the National Democratic Bimetallic Committee pledged to impose a free silver platform on the party in 1896 and, although this was unspoken, to seize the nomination for one of their own.

One of the most active participants in these meetings was the congressman from Nebraska. William Jennings Bryan was an intelligent young lawyer who had made himself master of the highly technical subject of national finance. Yet in many ways he was a provincial who had cast his lot with rural, small town America and whose values and limitations—as well as virtues—were very much those of the people among whom he lived. Though a Democrat, he was not typical of his party. He himself was a native-born Protestant of evangelical background, educated at a small, pious college in downstate Illinois. His Democratic politics, inherited from his father, may be ascribable to the family's Southern origins. In any event Bryan continued the family tradition in the midst of the heavily Republican part of Nebraska where he set down roots after marriage and law school.

Despite his maverick political views, the young lawyer was sent to Congress in the Democratic sweep of 1890. In 1892 he was reelected in another good Democratic year. Meanwhile, in the House of Representatives, Bryan joined the silver bloc and established a reputation as an effective champion of silver. From 1894, when he ran unsuccessfully for the United States Senate, to the time of the Democratic convention in 1896, Bryan kept his name before the public as editor of an Omaha newspaper and as a frequent speaker before Democratic groups and on the Chautauqua lecture circuit. Wherever he appeared, he sounded the same moralistic and apocalyptic note as the Populists in his defense of the silver position. In his House speech attacking Cleveland's effort to repeal the Sherman Silver Purchase Act, Bryan likened the financial struggle to the momentous battle of Tours in the eighth century when Charles Martel had stopped the forces of Islam and saved Christian Europe from destruction.

At this point Bryan was not, however, a one-issue man. He supported a graduated income tax to help equalize wealth; he favored peaceful settlement of international disputes by arbitration; he defended a low tariff. But as the campaign for the Democratic nomination advanced, free silver came to loom ever larger in his rhetoric and plans.

The reason for this narrowing process is clear. In the buffeting of political attack and counterattack that characterizes American election campaigns, politics almost inevitably tend to reduce themselves to single issues. In 1860 it was slavery; in 1868 it was Reconstruction; in 1888 it was the tariff. This reductionism often misrepresented the candidates, their parties, and their platforms, but it was difficult to avoid, and it was doubly difficult when, as in 1896, a third party with considerable voter support was in the field with a strong position on a single issue.

As the Chicago Democratic convention approached, free silver came to symbolize the fundamental conflict within the Democratic party and, to many people, the fundamental conflict within the country as a whole. When the delegates arrived in the Windy City in July, a major battle over the two monetary standards was expected. Bryan arrived in Chicago in a fourteen-car train decorated with free silver slogans and jammed with enthusiastic partisans. "Silver Dick" Bland chose to stay home in Missouri, ostensibly to gather in the hay on his farm. Hundreds of his supporters, however, came to the convention bearing literally tons of pro-Bland, free-silver literature and huge portrait posters of their favorite, which they plastered over hotel walls. Tillman and Governor Horace Boies of Iowa were other contenders on the silver side. Behind the scenes was Governor John Peter Altgeld of Illinois, disqualified from nomination by his German birth. Considered by conservatives a dangerous radical for his stand on the use of federal troops during the Pullman strike and his pardoning of several anarchists convicted of complicity in the 1886 Haymarket riot, Altgeld controlled the Illinois delegation and was an influential supporter of Bland.

The gold standard people, led by William C. Whitney, Navy secretary in Cleveland's first administration, also came, though without much hope that they could carry the convention. They were right. The nomination of silver-ite Senator John Daniel of Virginia as temporary party chairman signaled the power of the silver bloc. This was confirmed soon after by the packing of the convention committees with silver majorities. The majority on the Resolutions Committee promptly submitted a free silver platform. The gold bugs countered with their own resolutions, but they did so without much spirit. The South-West steamroller had too much momentum, and the gold bugs could only look on helplessly while it rode over everything in sight. The fight obviously would be among the various silver candidates, not between the silver and gold men.

It used to be said that Bryan, an obscure Nebraska politician, came out of nowhere in Chicago to seize the nomination by a brilliant display of oratory. This is not true. The Nebraskan was an acknowledged leader of the Western silver forces and already had been spoken of prominently for the nomination. He and his friends had prepared the ground well among leading silver Democrats and he had considerable support among the silver delegates at Chicago even before he rose to speak in defense of the prosilver platform. Yet it is also true that his electrifying address, one of the most brilliant political orations of our history, helped secure the nomination.

"The humblest citizen in all the land," Bryan began, "when clad in the armor of a righteous cause is stronger than all the hosts of error. I come to speak to you in defense of a cause as holy as the cause of liberty—the cause of humanity."

For the next half an hour, he held the delegates spellbound as his sonorous and powerful voice rolled out the praises of the silver crusade. "If they ask us why it is that we say more on the money question than we say upon the tariff question, I reply that, if protection has slain its thousands, the gold standard has slain its tens of thousands. If they ask us why we do not embody in our platform all the things that we believe in, we reply that when we have restored the money of the Constitution, all other necessary reforms will be possible; but that until this is done, there is no other reform that can be accomplished."

The cause of silver, he continued, was the cause of the struggling masses, and in embracing silver, the Democrats were endorsing the concept "that if you make the masses prosperous, their prosperity will find its way up through every class that rests upon them."

Easterners might not agree with this, but they were wrong. He did not wish to offend the people of the East, he declared, but the "pioneers" also deserved consideration. "You come to tell us that the great cities are in favor of the gold standard; we reply that the great cities rest upon our broad and fertile prairies. Burn down your cities and leave your farms, and your cities will spring up again as if by magic; but destroy our farms and the grass will grow in the streets of every city in the country."

With the delegates damp and hoarse from cheering, he then moved into his soaring conclusion. Defying the anglophiles of the country, who insisted that the United States must imitate England's gold standard, he trumpeted that the silver forces would fight the gold bugs "to the uttermost": "Having behind us the producing masses of this nation and the world, supported by the commercial interests, the laboring interests and the toilers everywhere, we will answer their demand for a gold standard by saying to them: You shall not press down upon the brow of labor this crown of thorns, you shall not crucify mankind upon a cross of gold."

For some five seconds, Bryan held his arms outstretched as if transfixed on a cross as his last words echoed through the Chicago Colosseum. Then he lowered his arms and stepped quietly off the platform. For a moment the audience sat in silence and then a great roar went up accompanied by a blizzard of hats, handkerchiefs, umbrellas, and newspapers sailing through the air. For a full twenty-five minutes pandemonium reigned.

Had the Bryan forces wished, observers believed, their candidate might have been nominated that evening. But they decided to delay until the following day to clinch the result. Though the Cross of Gold speech probably guaranteed the final victory, the delegates went through five roll calls before giving Bryan the two-thirds majority party rules required for nomination at this time. Soon after, in an effort to conciliate the East, the convention selected a silverite Maine businessman, Arthur Sewall, as Bryan's running mate.

Despite this attempt to heal the sectional breach, reporters noted ominously that hundreds of delegates had quietly slipped out of the convention hall shortly after the Bryan nomination. Two months later a group of gold Democrats nominated a separate ticket headed by John M. Palmer of Illinois and Simon Buckner of Kentucky. Thus the Democrats entered the campaign crippled by deep inner divisions.

Bryan's nomination had followed the June Republican convention in St. Louis. There also an East-West split had developed. But the Republicans proved less susceptible to the silver virus than the Democrats and consequently were damaged far less by disunity. Senator Teller and a handful of Western delegates walked out of the convention when it adopted a weak silver plank, and these dissenters eventually endorsed Bryan; but most delegates agreed with the platform emphasis o n the blessings of tariff protection.

The nominee himself, William McKinley of Ohio, had earned a reputation as a tariff expert and protectionist and also as a fighter against the political bosses. A man of limited interests and education, he was nonetheless popular personally and upright and honest in a stuffy Victorian way. Above all he looked like a president—or so, at least, thought Mark Hanna, a forceful Cleveland industrialist who had become McKinley's close friend and confidant. A plainspoken man in a mealymouthed age, Hanna had been planning to put McKinley in the White House ever since 1888, not because he wished to control the national government from behind the scenes, as his enemies said, but because he genuinely liked and respected McKinley and believed him capable of spreading the blessings of a rich, productive society to the entire country. Hanna was scarcely a reformer. It was he who first used the phrase "stand pat" to describe a hard line, antireform position. Yet Hanna was a strange personality. The Democrats in 1896 pictured him as a "bloated plutocrat" and an enemy of the common people, but he was actually an unusually enlightened industrialist who favored labor unions and despised the typically stubborn hostility of fellow businessmen to organized labor.

In 1895 Hanna had retired from business to devote himself full time to advancing McKinley's career. During the next two years, he used his talents as an organizer first to secure the nomination for his friend and then to insure that the Republican candidate was firmly ensconced in the White House. Though his motives were probably more disinterested than those of most American politicians, like most president-makers he aroused suspicion and suffered historical ignominy.

The last of the important conventions in 1896 was that of the People's party. Meeting shortly after the Bryan nomination, the Populists found themselves in a quandary. How could they endorse the Democratic nominee and not betray their principles? The dilemma was particularly acute for the party's left wing. Bryan was not a Populist in either the formal or ideological sense. He was particularly out of step with the Populist left wing, which often was indistinguishable from moderate socialists. Although unable to convince the People's party to endorse collective ownership of business and industry, they favored a sharp break with political tradition and placed their hope for change on a clear-cut victory for the third party. These "middle-of-the-roaders"[10] considered the one idea of free silver a feeble attack on the status quo and demanded a separate People's party ticket.

These feelings were reinforced among Southern Populists by the conviction that merging with the Democrats was equivalent to surrendering to the enemy. In the West, Populists sometimes formed coalitions with Democrats against the common Republican opposition, but in the one-party "Solid South," the enemy always had been the very group that Populists were now being asked to embrace as a close ally. The *Southern Mercury*, in a typical caveat, warned its fellow Populists not to be "deceived" by Democratic blandishments and advised that "experience should teach us to 'fear the Greeks even when bearing gifts.' "

Opposing the "middle-of-the-roaders" were those conservative Populists who either agreed with Bryan that free silver would open the

---

[10]So-called because they opposed fusion with the Democrats on one side of the road and the Republicans on the other.

door to all other needed reform or who were tempted by the political loaves and fishes that success might bring under Bryan. Though recent partisans of populism have been critical of the fusionists, the People's party leaders understandably convinced themselves that a victory for Bryan would be a victory for populism. The Democratic platform, besides favoring free silver, also condemned Cleveland for sending troops to Pullman and selling bonds to J. P. Morgan, endorsed the income tax, and advocated tighter federal control over railroads. All of these were consistent with populism after all. It is also hard to condemn their desire for the recognition and influence that their support of Bryan would give them if he won.

At their St. Louis convention, a heterogeneous assemblage of heavily bewhiskered delegates fought it out (a newspaper reporter noted that there seemed to be "some mysterious connection between Populism and hair"). In the end the fusionists won, and the convention endorsed Bryan. But something had to be done to appease the middle-of-the-roaders, and rather than accept the Eastern businessman Sewall as their vice-presidential candidate, the convention nominated Tom Watson. The result was curious: two parties supporting the same presidential candidate, but each with its own choice for his running mate!

V

The presidential campaign that now ensued was one of the most intense and emotional on record. Contemporaries saw it as a momentous struggle of two distinct principles, philosophies, and views of the American future. Today we can see that less was at stake than Americans of the day believed. Both parties were well within the American tradition of political democracy and private property, and in all likelihood, the nation's fundamental characteristics would not have been altered drastically if the result had been a Bryan victory. In the context of American politics, however, the choice placed before the voters in 1896 was unusually sharp, and the outcome did more to change the American political scene than any election since 1860.

The two parties and the two candidates adopted widely differing strategies. The Republicans campaigned on the issue of the economy. Flush with money raised by Hanna through his fellow business magnates, they flooded the country with pamphlets and speeches describing the dangers of free silver and the virtues of the tariff. Over 200 million copies of Republican campaign literature costing over half a million dollars were sent to every part of the country and every segment of the voting population. One hundred full-time campaign workers staffed the mailing room of the Republican literary bureau in Chicago alone. Hanna also allotted thousands of dollars more to dispatching hundreds of McKinley people, including a trainload of former union generals, to every city, county seat, and rural hamlet to speak for the Republican candidate and his principles.

Meanwhile, McKinley himself stayed at home in Canton, conducting a dignified front-porch campaign almost as if he were an incumbent. Of course, he was politically active. Through the months of September and October, the candidate received hundreds of delegations, each of which addressed him with a speech carefully edited by McKinley's staff to avoid the same sort of political blunder that had hurt James G. Blaine in 1884 when one of his visitors had called the Democrats the party of "Rum, Romanism and Rebellion." Knowing in advance what the address contained, McKinley was able to respond carefully and effectively. In all, over three-quarters of a million visitors came to Canton to greet, meet, and "serenade" the candidate and to be served refreshments on his well-trampled front lawn.

The Republicans were intent on avoiding many of their past mistakes. This campaign would emphasize pocketbook issues: McKinley would be touted as the "Advance Agent of Prosperity," who would bring good times to the nation through the Republican protective tariff. Bryan, on the other hand, would be decried as a dangerous adventurer who would undermine the dollar that the wage earner received, shake the credit of the nation, and set loose the forces of anarchy and revolution. This time the Republicans would stay away from divisive cultural issues and positions that offended the good folk of the liturgical churches. All groups would be welcome under the broad Republican banner of a restored prosperity; none would be kept from its shelter.

Bryan took a different tack. Unable to tap the full purses of Eastern bankers and industrialists and disappointed by the unexpectedly begrudging response of the Western silvermine owners, the Democratic candidate was forced to carry much of the campaign's burden on his own broad shoulders. No dignified front-porch campaign for him. The Democratic nominee set off soon after the convention on a peripatetic one-man crusade for the common man against his oppressors. Bryan traveled over 18,000 miles and delivered some 570 speeches in every cranny of the country. In these he attacked the plutocrats, the "interests," the large corporations, and the bankers and demanded that the country be returned to the people from whom it had been stolen.

On the face of it, Bryan too was running on the economic issue. But actually he did not emphasize pocketbook issues. To many who watched it, his campaign seemed indistinguishable from a traveling revival meeting. The Democratic candidate did not waste much time on the intricacies of national finance. However well he understood them himself, he recognized that they were too abstruse for the public. The great political issues, he declared, were in their final analysis "great moral questions," and it required "no extended experience in the handling of money to enable a man to tell right from wrong." Wherever he spoke his audiences responded not as people attending a political rally but as participants at a camp meeting where some eloquent preacher was execrating the forces of darkness and calling them and the nation back to virtue. To his partisans the Great Commoner seemed less a politician than a sublime religious teacher preaching a new doctrine of salvation. "No matter what may be the result," wrote one of his supporters, "you will be greater than any other man since Christ." In a word, whether intentionally or not, Bryan made his party trade positions with the Republicans: under his leadership, the Democratic party gave up its traditional posture of ethical laissez faire and stole the "God and morality" position of the Republicans.

The strategy, if deliberate strategy it was, did not work. In the end the Republican tack—and Republican cash—paid off. Bryan's evangelism won over some of the pietists who had formerly favored the Republicans, but these gains were more than offset by defectors among the liturgical groups. German voters, both Catholic and Lutheran, were especially offended by Bryan's moralizing.

Nor did he succeed in convincing the country that silver would bring good times. To the extent that the Democratic campaign was aimed at the economically discontented, it fell far short of the Democrats' expectations. Eastern working men, Midwestern farmers, and the middle class were frightened more by the prospect of a profound unsettling of the national finances by a free-silver victory than they were by the alleged injustices of the gold standard. Bryan carried the silver miners of the Far West and garnered votes among Populist wheat and cotton farmers, but he failed to carry either the urban wage earners or the Midwestern and Eastern farmers who had never taken to agrarianism. In the cities of the Northeast, the defection from the party's old stock Episcopalian supporters and other middle- and upper-class voters was greater than among the working-class Irish. But even among the intensely loyal sons of Erin, free silver as an answer to hard times proved ineffective.

The Bryanites later charged that the Republicans had stolen the labor vote. At Hanna's behest, they claimed, employers had intimidated their workers by telling them that if Bryan won, they need not return to work. Republican manufacturers had made these threats convincing by telling suppliers that they would cancel new orders for parts and materials if the Democrats succeeded. Most scholars do not take these claims seriously. Businessmen did support McKinley, but few actually made the threats ascribed to them by the defeated Democrats. And those who did anticipate disaster were not serving merely as Hanna's minions. In many cases their fears expressed a sincere and possibly valid view that Bryan's victory would disturb business and touch off another panic. In any event few historians now believe that pressure from employers changed very many votes.

VI

The Republican crowds at Canton and elsewhere around the nation who cheered the news of McKinley's triumph could not have recognized the scope or full significance of the election results. The 1896 presidential contest was one of those "critical elections," along with 1800, 1828, 1860, and 1932, that have changed the nation's political configuration for an extended period.

Bryan's defeat ushered in a generation of Republican ascendancy. After 1896 the close contests of previous years yielded to a succession of Republican landslides, punctuated by Wilson's two narrow victories, one of which (1912) was in a three-sided race where the Republican vote was split between Theodore Roosevelt and William Howard Taft. The Republican years did not end until 1932, when the deep social traumas of the Great Depression produced a normal Democratic majority. The 1896 results also were followed by a sharp decline of voter interest in national and local elections. Instead of the heavy Gilded Age turnouts of eligible voters that often reached well over 80 percent, the proportion of those voters who actually cast their ballots following the McKinley-Bryan contest dropped to 60 percent or less. After 1896, apparently, the voters wearied of the predictable Republican majorities and started to stay away from the polls. Finally, the election marked the beginning of independent voting on a large scale. After 1896, party loyalties declined as more and more people abandoned their fervent partisan attachment to the major parties and began to support reform groups, especially on the local level. Although the 1896 election was neither a revolution nor a counterrevolution, McKinley's victory did open a new era in American party history.

Chapter Two

Outward Thrust

As the Republicans had promised, prosperity returned with McKinley's election. Through 1895 and well into 1896 the depression had worsened. Just before the presidential contest, farm prices and new railroad construction dropped to their nadir for the decade; unemployment, severe for three years, reached its worst point during the election year. After November, however, conditions began to improve. Wheat and corn quotations rose sharply as short grain harvests in France, Germany, Russia, and Hungary created worldwide shortages. Grain from America at good prices for the farmer soon began to flow across the Atlantic in great volume to ease the European deficit. With more cash jingling in the pockets of Midwestern and Plains wheat growers, business in many parts of the nation picked up; unemployment leveled off and then dropped.

The good times that immediately followed 1896 can be explained in part, no doubt, by such lucky events and also by the normal rebound of a free market economy after a severe depression. But the rising prices and full employment of the next two decades require some deeper explanation. Republicans, of course, were happy to explain it as the natural outcome of Republican ascendancy: first the Dingley Tariff of 1897 elevated duties to new highs and helped produce "that tranquility and confidence which are so necessary for the development of business." Then there was the healthy effect of the Gold Standard Act of 1900. By confirming the gold basis of United States currency, this law settled the money question once and for all.

This political analysis is to some extent true. Republican ascendancy did contribute to recovery. McKinley proved to be the competent, if unspectacular, leader that his former career in Congess and the Ohio state house foreshadowed. He supported the moderate rate increases of the Dingley Tariff while the bill was being debated in Congress but unsuccessfully resisted the greedy "exclusionists" who sought to raise some rates so high that they shut off entirely the importation of particular goods. The president eventually signed the Dingley bill, hoping that its provisions allowing him to reduce rates up to 20 percent in return for foreign concessions for American goods (reciprocity) would make it possible to offset some of its failings. The Dingley law remained in force for twelve years and in all likelihood gave business a much needed shot in the arm.

The other side of the Republican economic program, sound money, also helped to revive the economy. The 1896 Republican platform had not been completely unfriendly to bimetallism. McKinley himself was willing to accept silver as an adjunct to gold if the major nations of the Atlantic world could reach an accord on a fixed international ratio between the two metals. To implement this conservative bimetallism, the United States attempted to talk Britain, France, and other European countries into accepting some joint policy, but with little success. Britain resisted every attempt to modify the gold standard, and the French, angered by higher American duties on wines and other French products, also proved to be stubborn. The monetary negotiations collapsed, and having demonstrated their good faith to the bimetallists, the Republicans put bimetallism on the shelf. When Congress passed the Gold Standard Act in 1900, silver was put aside as a serious political issue until the New Deal. Settlement of the controversial money question restored business confidence, a necessary ingredient for prosperity in this era of high capitalism, thereby helping to turn the economy around.

But the upward trend of the economy for most of the decade following 1897 also owed much to several unplanned and unforeseen changes in the international economy that had long-term impact. Toward the end of the 1890s, the world gold stock began to grow at an accelerated rate as a consequence of more efficient gold refining methods and the opening of new mines in the Klondike and South Africa. Soon golden streams from the far north and the far south began to flow into the Western nations' treasuries and central banks to become the basis for expanded credit and currency issues. Though not all historians accept a monetary explanation for the rising prices and economic buoyancy after 1896, the growing money stock probably contributed substantially to the good times of the succeeding years.[1]

Another component of the new prosperity was the rapid, long-term expansion of foreign and domestic markets for the products of American fields and factories. At home, population soared. In 1897 it was 72 million; ten years later it was 87 million; and ten years after that it zoomed to 103 million. In 1903, for the first time in our history, the number of immigrants arriving on our shores exceeded eight hundred thousand. In 1905 the figure reached over a million, and for five of the next nine years it again exceeded

---

[1]On this point see Milton Friedman and Anna Schwartz, *A Monetary History of the United States, 1867–1960* (Princeton N.J.: Princeton University Press, 1963), pp. 133 ff.

a million annually. At the same time, thousands of American-born rural people moved to the cities, where they received higher money incomes than on the farms. Population also burgeoned in Europe under the influence of rising standards of living. All of this meant more mouths to feed, more backs to clothe, and more personal wants to supply. American manufacturing, farming, mining, and construction all felt the pull of rapidly expanding demand for their output both at home and abroad.

II

The Republicans welcomed prosperity, of course. But from the beginning of the new administration, domestic concerns took a back seat to foreign affairs. As McKinley and Cleveland drove together to the Capitol on inauguration day for the formal oath-taking ceremony, the two men discussed public affairs. Between greetings to the crowds lining both sides of Pennsylvania Avenue, they talked about the past and the responsibilities of high office. In a prescient remark, the outgoing president told his successor that he regretted leaving him with a war with Spain. Cleveland was not speaking literally, for war was still over a year away, but he was putting his finger on the single most important event of McKinley's five years in office.

The war with Spain was not an isolated or aberrant occurrence in American foreign affairs. It was part of a pattern of expansion that was rooted deep in the American past. How deep is a matter of interpretation. Some historians would say that America had been an expansionist society from the days of the first colonial settlements. In a sense this is true. As the child of European expansion, the American community had grown rapidly in both geographical extent and in population. For centuries the country expanded into contiguous territory at the expense of the Indian tribes. But early in the nineteenth century, the United States purchased or seized French, Spanish, and Mexican territory and would have annexed Canada in 1812 if not for British power.

Much of this pre–Civil War outward thrust was defended as the fulfillment of America's manifest destiny. The United States, according to this doctrine, had the God-given right, if not indeed the responsibility, to extend its government, its culture, its institutions over the whole of the North American continent. This right was conferred by the superiority of American free institutions and the innovative and enterprising energies of the American people.

This assertion of a divine mandate struck foreigners, especially Canadians and Mexicans, as an arrogant and self-serving rationalization for American economic and strategic interests. And it certainly was this in part, but it was also something more complex. Much of the continent was thinly populated. Even the northern provinces of the Mexican Republic were settled sparsely by Indians and a few thousand Spanish-speaking soldiers, officials, ranchers and friars. This does not justify the Mexican war and the subsequent annexation of a gigantic block of Mexican territory by the United States, but it is easy to see that the power vacuum that existed at our borders could not fail to tempt a people as aggressive and energetic as the Americans.

The logic of geopolitics aside, manifest destiny had a truly benevolent component. Americans did not see their country as an enslaver or exploiter of subject peoples. Only the old, autocratic nations of Europe deserved such labels. The United States would bring the rest of the continent the benefits of democracy, respect for law, and the blessings of material plenty. No doubt all imperialists profess such humane goals, but the American claim was more than rhetoric. By the policy first developed in the 1780s, the United States conferred complete equality on the new states of the West that joined the Union and successfully transplanted to these newer communities the high American standard of living and the blessings of democratic political institutions. If nothing else, this commitment to republican institutions and to a rough equality of social and economic status served—and would continue to serve—as a restraint on American policy toward neighbors and other weaker peoples. The United States would resist seizing densely populated regions inhabited by impoverished alien peoples with alien ways, since such areas promised to be incompatible with, and threatened to distort, American institutions and values. Better to let them alone, most Americans felt, no matter how tempting. The apparent absence of this limiting factor in relation to Canada, a European-settled and prosperous land, has made the United States at times a serious threat to its northern neighbor's autonomy.

But territorial expansionism, however motivated, halted during the Civil War. Then, in the later 1860s, it resumed under the aegis of Secretary of State William Henry Seward. A prominent antislavery leader and an early Republican party organizer, Seward had been Lincoln's choice for the State Department. From 1861 to 1865, he had guided the Union through highly dangerous shoals, successfully avoiding serious confrontations with Britain and France that would have helped the Confederacy and gravely endangered the Union. After Appomattox, Seward, now serving under Andrew Johnson, went on a territorial acquisition spree that represents the first instance of American overseas expansion, if we exclude the halfhearted attempt to buy Cuba during the 1850s.

Seward's expansionist motives were mixed. The secretary was a sincere believer in American manifest destiny; he remarked in a diplomatic note to the American minister in France that the "advance of civilization in this hemisphere seem to us . . . likely to be secured when the other American states assimilate to our own." Like the antebellum expansionists, he contemplated extending full citizenship and the equal blessings of the American republic to those people who could be induced to join themselves politically to the United States. This attitude linked Seward with the more generous version of expansion that had characterized the antebellum years. But Seward's aggressiveness also foreshadowed the more blatantly selfish expansionism of the 1890s. Impressed by the disastrous wartime experience of the United States with Confederate sea raiders, he was anxious to acquire bases and coaling stations for the navy. He was attracted also by the "China market," that supposedly vast and insatiable outlet for American raw materials and manufactured goods that would intrigue Americans for several generations.

The China market was one of the most persistent myths that have influenced our foreign relations. As far back as the 1840s, American merchants, journalists, and politicians were drawn to the possibility of extensive trade with China and the Far East. An important component of the demand for Oregon in that decade was the desire to acquire ports on the Pacific to expedite the latent Chinese trade. Even though the China market proved elusive, for the rest of the century Americans continued to posit an enormous potential outlet for their goods among the teeming millions of the Celestial Empire.

Beginning in 1867 Seward began to convert these assorted concerns into action. In that year he was able to pick up Alaska from Russia for some two cents an acre. He also took possession of Midway Island in the Pacific and opened negotiations for the purchase of the Danish West Indies (the Virgin Islands).

Under Seward's successor, Hamilton Fish, the United States abandoned the purchase talks with the Danes but then tried to acquire the Dominican Republic or some substantial part of it. This scheme foundered when Congress refused to honor the agreement concluded owing to the unsavory character of the negotiators on both American and Dominican sides.

Soon after the breakdown of negotiations with the Dominicans, the expansionist impulse abated, and the nation returned to the isolationist mood that periodically seized it. But expansionism never fully disappeared. From the end of the 1870s until the early 1890s, the United States made agressive gestures at moments towards other nations that suggested that it was not fully reconciled to staying within its national boundaries. One expression of this bellicose disposition was the decision in the mid-1880s to replace the decrepit wooden fleet of the Civil War period with a new steel navy. Despite such rumblings, as late as 1889 the young historian Henry Cabot Lodge remarked that "our relations with foreign nations today fill but a slight place in American politics, and excite generally only a languid interest." In the same year, the *New York Sun* suggested abolishing the diplomatic service, as it was "a costly humbug and sham . . ." which "does no good to anybody. Instead of making Ambassadors, Congress should wipe out the whole service."

But even as Lodge wrote, American attitudes were changing. The reasons

for the turnabout form one of those indestructable "problems" that historians love to debate. As is usual with such controversial issues, expansionism
is associated with conflicting political ideologies among historians themselves. On one side are the politically left scholars who emphasize the
economic element in the revived expansionist impulse. Borrowing from
V. I. Lenin, the Bolshevik leader and Marxist theorist, and J. A. Hobson,
a nineteenth-century British economist, these scholars identify the inner
"contradictions" of late capitalism as the force behind nineteenth-century
colonialism. Compelled to find markets abroad when they had already
exhausted those at home and to find new outlets for profitable investment
when domestic ones had dried up, capitalists, in their desperate battle to
survive, inevitably turned abroad. Foreign markets would offset periodic
economic crises and the severe social tensions and dislocations inherent in
mature capitalist societies and postpone the day of reckoning. Applying this
thesis directly to the United States of the late nineteenth century, Hobson
concluded that "it was Mssrs. Rockefeller, Pierpont Morgan and their
associates who needed Imperialism and who fastened it upon the shoulders
of the great Republic of the West."[2]

More recent versions of the economic interpretation are somewhat different from the Lenin-Hobson kind. As developed by the diplomatic historians
Walter LaFeber and William A. Williams, these theories acknowledge that
the United States was generally uninterested in the actual seizure of foreign
territory. But this made little practical difference. The aggressive trade
expansion policies of the American government were not essentially different from the more blatant political conquests of the British, French, or
Germans in this period, and in the end, commercial ambition even induced
the United States to seize small parcels of overseas territory.

While LaFeber and Williams both accept the commercial urge as both the
American embodiment and the force behind expansion, they differ over its
source. According to LaFeber, the expansionist impulse of the years following 1890 arose first from "the general consensus reached by the American
business community and policy makers in the mid-1890s that additional
foreign markets would solve the economic, social, and political problems
created by the industrial revolution"; and, second, from "the growing belief
that, however great its industrial prowess, the United States needed strategic bases if it hoped to compete successfully with government-supported
European enterprises in Asia and Latin America."[3] Williams, on the other
hand, believes that "the expansionist outlook that was entertained and acted
upon by metropolitan American leaders during and after the 1890s was
actually a crystallization in industrial form of an outlook that had been

---

[2]J. A. Hobson, *Imperialism* (London; George Allen and Unwin, Ltd., 1938), p. 77.
[3]Walter LaFeber, *The New Empire* (Ithaca N.Y.: Cornell University Press, 1963), p. 412.

developed in agricultural terms by the agrarian majority of the country between 1860 and 1893." In a word, the "roots of the modern American empire" lay primarily in the need for American farmers to find overseas markets for their surplus wheat, corn, and cotton.[4]

How valid is the economic interpretation? After about 1880, farmers and businessmen, and especially politicians talked much about the need to expand American foreign trade. Whether this explains American expansionism is dubious. The issue breaks down into several parts. The first is whether the United States really *depended* upon foreign trade or foreign investment to survive or to maintain its internal stability. Here the conclusion is clear. In 1897, American investments abroad totaled about $700 million, a small sum in an economy that produced a gross output of goods and services (GNP) of about $17 billion annually. As for trade, American exports and imports represented a declining, not a growing, proportion of the country's gross output in the period 1880–1900, as compared with the years before 1860. In a word the Lenin-Hobson thesis that capitalism, or American capitalism in any case, could survive only by expanding overseas is a weak argument.

Another question raised by the economic interpretation is whether the United States *used* overseas trade and investment as an instrument of colonialism. Here again the assertion by the left scholars is questionable. How this country's foreign economic connections could have been used to further its foreign ambitions, even if Americans had wished to, is unclear. Most American overseas trade and investments involved advanced nations, not backward ones. Trade with Europe was far more extensive than with the whole rest of the world together. Moreover, much more European money was invested in the United States as late as 1908 (about $6.4 billion) than American money in all other countries combined (about $2.5 billion). Using the argument of the left revisionist historians, we could conclude from this that the United States was really a disguised colony of Europe! This is, of course, nonsense; America was not converted into a colony by foreign investment. Similarly, with the plausible exception of Mexico, none of the nations with which the United States had its most important economic connections was incapable of defending its interests against the American colossus.

It does not seem likely, then, that the U.S. *needed* overseas expansion to preserve its capitalist institutions. Nor is it easy to see how it could have used its economic power to coerce its major trading partners. But what about the hypothesis of Williams and LaFeber that the yen for overseas markets was the fuel for America's outward thrust after 1865? No one will

---

[4]William Appleman Williams, *The Roots of the Modern American Empire* (New York: Vintage Books, 1969), pp. xvi–xvii.

deny that in these years Americans were interested in finding outlets for surplus commodities and capital. But is this synonymous with imperialism? The left revisionists equate the desire for expanded foreign trade with colonialism. They are mistaken. Most international trade is a free exchange between countries where both sides benefit. Though trade between a developed and an undeveloped nation may produce distortions in the latter's economy, this is not necessarily the purpose of the former, and certainly it is not the same as imperialism. True, both farmers and businessmen talked of the need for overseas markets, but they seldom, if ever, endorsed the acquisition of colonies. The same cannot be said of politicians, who, especially after 1898 prated much of imperial glory but even a close reading of LaFeber and Williams uncovers few explicit demands by economic interest groups that the United States emulate the European powers and build an overseas empire. If the desire for expanded overseas markets is imperialism, it is imperialism of such a diffuse and abstract kind as to be unrecognizable.

American expansionism in the generation straddling 1900 is not completely unrelated to the economic interests of certain groups and individuals, however. Scarcely any scholar denies that once Americans tasted a little imperial grandeur, some became convinced that it could be turned to profitable account. As we shall see, this proved illusory. But for a while, a few Americans had visions of vast captive markets for American grain and industrial goods.

Nor can we deny that strategically placed American businessmen with foreign trade interests at times were able to use the American government for their own acquisitive purposes. Typically these men were planters, mine operators, bankers, and merchants with investments in Latin American countries who found their property endangered by the policies of the local government or by the actions of some European power. As a matter of course at such times, they turned to the local American consul or minister for help, and as a matter of course, the consul appealed to Washington. Usually a diplomatic protest was enough to ease the pressure, but on occasion during this period, the American government resorted to force or threats of force to protect American citizens against what it judged to be a violation of their economic rights. Such actions in defense of specific American business interests often impaired the sovereignty of weaker Latin American or oriental countries and constituted a kind of imperialism, but it was unimportant in the aggregate and did not loom large in the American economy as a whole. Most certainly it does not support those views, whether Marxist or New Left, which hold either that overseas possessions were essential to American capitalist survival or that the major thrust behind American expansionism was fear that American capitalism had to expand or die.

If we reject the Marxists and New Left scholars, how do we account for the expansionist impulse of the 1890s that led to America's first overseas colonies? Historians unimpressed with the economic explanations have suggested a number of alternatives. Most of these rely on some theory of altered public perception or shifts in the climate of opinion during the last years of the nineteenth century.

This approach is expressed in several distinct ways. One version ascribes the change to social Darwinism, which sought to justify strong nations dominating weak ones by analogy with the struggle for existence in nature's realm. This struggle for survival explained the forward and upward thrust of evolution in the world of living creatures and by analogy sanctioned vigorous nations like the United States imposing their wills on weaker ones.

A second interpretation stresses the influence of naval historian Admiral Alfred Thayer Mahan and social philosopher-historian-prophet Brooks Adams. The laws of history, these two thinkers contended, required that the United States expand outward to avoid decay. Mahan's conclusion was derived from a reading of naval history, as befitted a man whose life had been spent as a career naval officer. Great nations were made by great navies, for national power was an outgrowth of sea power. Sea power in turn depended on naval bases and coaling stations and, in the case of the contemporary United States, required a canal across the Isthmus of Panama to connect the two oceans that washed the nation's coasts. Adams, the scion of the distinguished Massachusetts family that had given the country two presidents, had a quasi-mystical theory about the rise and fall of civilizations. Every society, he believed, must capture new sources of social "energy" to prosper and achieve greatness. These could be attained by the United States only if it expanded westward across the Pacific.

Still another explanation that emphasizes the intellectual milieu updates manifest destiny. Americans it says, had always accepted implicitly the idea that their nation was commissioned to bring the blessings of Western civilization to other peoples. Before the Civil War, the American mission was "continental" and secular. In the 1880–1900 period, its scope broadened to include the non-European world, especially Asia, and assumed a religious coloration.

The new sense of American mission could be explained by two changes. Globalism was a reaction to the experience of establishing the nation's continental boundaries. Unable, practically speaking, to add additional contiguous American territory, the country could only look overseas. The religious tone was a response to the growth of Protestant missions abroad. By the end of the century, Protestant missionary groups, financed by societies in the United States, had developed vital interests in the Far East and the Pacific and were hopeful of replacing the "heathen" religions of the Orient with a "purer" form of worship. Although most of the clergymen who left the seminaries for distant shores were imbued by the most self-sacrificing and most spiritual of motives, their work, nevertheless, created an important American presence in non-Christian lands. Inevitably they became the agents, unwitting ones usually, of Western influence and power among the peoples they came to "save."

A final hypothesis combines cultural, psychological, and political elements. Late nineteenth-century American imperialism, this theory holds, was imitative. The closing decades of the nineteenth century witnessed the last burst of European colonialism. In these years the European powers divided Africa and grabbed the remaining islands of the Pacific, while France gobbled up hitherto independent portions of the Southeast Asia mainland. All the great European powers and newly emerged modern Japan nibbled at China, a feeble, ungainly giant. Only the western hemisphere, under the protection of the United States, was immune toEuropean acquisitiveness, and as time would show, even the Monroe Doctrine could not automatically protect Latin America against European aggression.

In the West's final push to dominate the world, the United States was nowhere to be seen. Already the nation had achieved preeminence economically. By the last decade of the century, it was the richest and most productive country in the world, but it did not loom large in international affairs. Few European nations considered the United States a power to reckon with except in the affairs of the western hemisphere, and few assigned full ambassadors to Washington, being content instead with ministers and lesser diplomatic representatives. American opinion leaders, the argument runs, assumed that a colonial empire would end this inferiority and propel the United States into the ranks of the world powers where it clearly belonged. Strongly influenced by the ideas of a new school of British neoimperialists, these men, says Professor Ernest May, considered America's aloofness from the imperialist race a foolish and cowardly mistake.[5]

None of the explanations which ascribe overseas expansion solely to an intellectual change is fully convincing; cumulatively they add up to more. American perceptions of the appropriate role of the United States did indeed have to change for the country to venture out of its continental shell. Even those Americans who came to favor an aggressive pursuit of foreign markets had to be convinced at some point that such markets were needed if they and their nation were to prosper. Still more did the average American need to be convinced that his personal well-being depended on a new departure in the country's international relations.

But part of the argument is still missing. How do we explain the chronological grouping of such ideas and the apparent willingness of the public to take them seriously towards the closing years of the century? The best explanation of this phenomenon has been provided by Richard Hofstadter. According to Hofstadter, the decade of the 1890s had been one of unusual personal frustration and anxiety for many Americans. The depression, the

---

[5]See Ernest May, *American Imperialism: A Speculative Essay* (New York: Atheneum, 1968).

growth of trusts, the Bryan campaign, and the end, supposedly, of the open frontier (which Frederick Jackson Turner and others claimed had supplied a buoyancy to American society and the American economy)—together produced a feeling of crisis, a sense that the times were out of joint. Aggressiveness, suitably softened and rationalized by these social theories, was an oblique expression of this anxiety and frustration, especially among the political leaders of the country. As if to get their minds off their fears, Americans turned to the rest of the world for distraction and developed an aggressive stance toward other nations and peoples that produced an unprecedented imperialist interlude for the country.

III

Whichever of these competing explanations for late nineteenth-century American expansionism we choose, we must recognize that each decade produces a new crop of hypotheses that are popular for a while and then recede. The economic explanation for the American outward thrust is not currently as convincing as the cultural and psychological ones. But a distinction must be made here. If cultural and psychological considerations were the most important factors predisposing the American people to expansionism through 1898, the emphasis changed once the United States had experienced the euphoria of victory in the Spanish-American War. As we shall see, the war altered American attitudes by seeming to open up new vistas of economic opportunity. Thereafter, in the guise of Dollar Diplomacy, the lust for profit abroad competed seriously with national pride, international emulation, missionary zeal, social Darwinism, and manifest destiny as an impelling force behind America's intense new concern with the non-European world.

Whatever the reasons, Americans began to display a new interest in overseas expansion during Cleveland's second administration. The first step in the revival proved to be an abortive one, however. The strategic value of the Hawaiian Islands, two thousand miles off the coast of California, had been recognized ever since their discovery by Captain James Cook in 1778. In the early nineteenth century, they were visited by American merchants trading with China. In 1820 the first American missionaries arrived intent on bringing the Christian faith to the native Polynesian peoples. Whalers came still later, and the whaling crews, hungry for female companionship, helped to undo much of the missionaries' efforts to Christianize Hawaiian morals.

The sons of missionaries, along with other American settlers attracted to the islands, made sugar production rather than the saving of souls their chief concern and eventually came to own much of the land. In 1875 the United States adopted a reciprocity treaty with the Hawaiian kingdom allowing

Hawaiian sugar to enter the United States duty-free. The islands experienced a tremendous economic boom and soon became dependent on the American market. The Hawaiian government meanwhile came under the influence of the American planters and businessmen who had helped bring prosperity to the kingdom.

Then suddenly the situation changed. In 1890 all sugar imported into the United States was put on the free list, ending the tariff advantage that Hawaii had previously enjoyed. The boom abruptly collapsed. Almost simultaneously Queen Liliuokalani came to the Hawaiian throne determined to restore the royal power surrendered to American advisers by her predecessor. American businessmen and planters, who at first had opposed annexation on the grounds that it would threaten their contract labor system, now had both political and economic reasons for seeking annexation to the United States.

In 1893 the American residents of Hawaii organized a Committee of Safety and staged a revolution or, more precisely, a coup d'état. With the connivance of the American minister, John L. Stevens, who brought in marines from the cruiser *Boston* then conveniently stationed at Honolulu, they forced the queen to abdicate. Stevens immediately proclaimed the islands an American protectorate and triumphantly wrote the State Department at home: "The Hawaiian pear is now fully ripe and this is the golden hour for the United States to pluck it." Soon after, the American residents formed a provisional government and applied for annexation to the United States.

President Benjamin Harrison's secretary of state, John W. Foster, favored the application and the president signed an annexation treaty with representatives of the new provisional government. Unfortunately for the annexationists, Cleveland succeeded to the presidency before the Senate could act on the treaty. The new president was a figure from an older America, upright, conscientious, and principled, at least where public matters were concerned. Reluctant to involve the country in a new policy of acquisition and suspicious of the moral standing of the American residents' coup, he withdrew the treaty from the Senate and sent a personal representative, James Blount, to the islands to investigate the circumstances of the queen's overthrow.

The Blount report attacked Minister Stevens for interfering in Hawaii's internal affairs and convinced Cleveland that annexation would be unjust. Cleveland tried to restore the queen to her throne but discovered, to his dismay, that she intended to behead the revolutionists when restored to power. Faced with the prospect of authorizing a bloodbath of Americans, Cleveland declined to help the queen and the provisional government remained in power. Cleveland recognized the Hawaiian Republic, as did the other powers, but did not press for a reconsideration of annexation.

The Hawaiian affair illustrates the continuing importance of the unaggressive, "little America" side of public opinion. But another event of the Cleveland administration suggests that the jingoistic and assertive side of the public mood was fast growing in strength. Venezuela, a South American republic on the Caribbean, long had disputed its boundary with the colony of British Guiana. The Venezuelans had appealed for American sympathy and support, picturing the British as callous aggressors against a weaker nation.

Americans naturally sympathized with the Venezuelans. Ever since the first announcement of the Monroe Doctrine in the 1820s, the United States had set itself up as the guardian of Latin American independence against European encroachments. Admittedly we had not always respected the sovereignty of the Latin American republics, but we had in fact successfully thwarted European attempts to establish control south of the Rio Grande. To the American government, Great Britain appeared to be asserting territorial claims that would expand its influence and interests in the western hemisphere. Combined with other British moves in Central America and French maneuvers in Brazil, the Venezuela boundary dispute aroused real fears that, unless reinforced, the Monroe Doctrine would become a dead letter and Europe would begin to consider Latin America a possible field for colonial intrusion. The traditional American policy probably was strengthened by fears that British control of the mouth of Venezuela's Orinoco River would give her commercial priority in the large area of the continent that the river drained.

Early in 1895 the American Congress passed a resolution declaring that the United States opposed British claims in Venezuela. In July Secretary of State Richard Olney, a blunt and forceful man, sent a letter to the American minister in London transmitting the official American view of the boundary dispute. The letter, like the man, was brusque and aggressive. After a brief review of the historical roots of the controversy, Olney asserted that the concern of the United States in the dispute was a legitimate one founded both on the precedent of the Monroe Doctrine and on simple self-interest. He then proceeded to defend the right of the United States to guarantee that none of the independent republics of the Americas fell under the sway of a non-American power. On this point Olney was expressing only what American political leaders had said many times before. But hoping to startle the British, he then launched into a blunt and pugnacious declaration of American power:

Today the United States is practically sovereign on this continent, and its fiat is law upon the subjects to which it confines its interposition. Why? It is not because of the pure friendship or good will felt for it. It is not simply by reason of its high character as a civilized state, nor because wisdom and justice and equity are the invariable characteristics of the dealings of the United States. It is because, in addition to all other grounds, its infinite resources combined with its isolated position render it master of the situation and practically invulnerable as against any or all other powers.

Olney concluded by demanding that the issue be arbitrated and that the British submit an answer before Congress met in December.

The British were offended by this peremptory and arrogant note and in their reply firmly rejected both the arbitration and the applicability of the Monroe Doctrine to the dispute. The tone of Lord Salisbury, the British prime minister, was as condescending and unfriendly as Olney's had been challenging, and it irritated the American people and government. When Cleveland sent a bellicose message to Congress declaring that if Britain would not arbitrate, the United States would impose a boundary line and then defend it, he was cheered wildly by members of both houses.

Many Americans supported this aggressive position. Congress unanimously appropriated $100,000 for a boundary commission. Among the public, the professional anti-British, the jingoes, and the generally belligerent felt exhilarated at the prospect of a war with Great Britain. The ever-combative Theodore Roosevelt, ready as always to test the country's strength, wrote his friend Henry Cabot Lodge: "Personally, I rather hope that the fight will come soon. The clamor of the peace faction has convinced me that this country needs a war."

But the peace faction, whatever its impact on Roosevelt, proved more effective with other Americans. In a few days, the protest of clergymen, financiers, publishers, and educators against Cleveland's truculent stand cooled the public's enthusiasm for a fight. In Britain, after it became clear that a war with the United States over a few thousand square miles of jungle might result from intransigence (and at a time when Britain was facing difficulties with Germany), the government decided to accept the American boundary commission. Eventually Britain and Venezuela agreed formally to accept arbitration, and by the time the arbitrator's decision was delivered in 1899, the whole incident had been virtually forgotten.

IV

The Cleveland administration represented a transitional phase in the emerging expansionist commitment. McKinley brought the commitment to fruition.

As the retiring president had suggested to his successor on inauguration day in March 1897, the big foreign policy issue that McKinley would face was Cuba. That rich island, along with Puerto Rico, had remained Spanish long after the rest of Spain's once great empire in the New World had broken away. But the Cubans were not happy with their continued subordination to a decaying Spain. In 1868 they rose in revolt and for ten years fought a bitter war for independence. During the insurrection Cuban rebels, some of them naturalized American citizens, attempted to embroil the United States on the side of the insurrectionists. But despite a number of minor clashes with Spain, the United States had been able to remain neutral.

After seventeen years of peace, harsh Spanish rule, magnified by a severe crisis in the Cuban sugar industry, brought the Cuban people once more to the boiling point. Cuba again rose in revolt. The Cuban rebels this time not only attacked Spanish soldiers and officials but also put the island's sugar plantations and cattle ranches to the torch in hopes that Spain would surrender the island if nothing of value was left. Cuban patriots residing in the United States simultaneously organized various juntas to aid the rebels and stir up trouble between Spain and the United States.

The Spanish authorities used even harsher methods to put down the revolt. Under General Valeriano Weyler, they gathered up large numbers of suspected rebels and rebel sympathizers, including women and children, and herded them into wire-encircled concentration camps. Weyler, despite the name "Butcher" given him by Cuban sympathizers, did not intend mass murder, but the inefficiency of the Spanish health and sanitation services and rebel interference with the food supply systems turned the concentration areas into death camps. The American consul general in Havana, Fitzhugh Lee, vividly described the horrors of the camps to the American public:

> I have the honor to state ... that the "reconcentrado order" of General Weyler ... transformed about 400,000 self-supporting people, principally women and children, into a multitude to be sustained by the contributions of others, or die of starvation, or of fevers resulting from a low physical condition and being massed in large bodies, without change of clothing and without food. Their homes were burned, their fields and plant beds destroyed and their livestock driven away or killed.
>
> I estimate that probably 200,000 of the rural population in the province of Pinar del Rio, Havana, Matanzas, and Santa Clara have died of starvation or from resultant causes; and the deaths of whole families almost simultaneously, or within a few days of each other, and of mothers praying for their children to be relieved of their horrible sufferings by death, are not the least of the many pitiable scenes which were ever present. ...

Lee was a biased observer, who had favored American intervention from the moment he arrived in Cuba. But he was not wrong. Spanish policies *were* harsh. On the other hand, both sides had been brutal and destructive; yet the American people came to sympathize completely with the rebels. The reasons for this partisanship were rather complex. Our sympathies were not determined by our economic interests in the island. Even if we accept the economic interpretation of the expansionist impulse after 1880 it cannot explain our specific intervention in Cuba. Some Americans had an economic stake in the island. By 1895 about $50 million of American capital was invested in Cuba, mostly in sugar and tobacco plantations and in iron mines. Businessmen who had investments in Cuba or who traded with Cuba generally desired American intervention to restore order. If Spain had been some inconsequential "banana republic," their voices might have been heeded. But though a shadow of its former self, Spain was still a nation of consequence, and it would have required more than a few petty capitalists to make the country willing to risk war.

But in any event most American businessmen vociferously opposed United States involvement in Cuba. Some distrusted the Cuban rebels. The larger group, however, believed that a war with Spain just as the depression was finally receding was the last thing the country needed. As relations with Spain over Cuba worsened, the business press expressed its unequivocal opposition to any disturbing foreign adventure that would, in the words of one eastern trade journal, "impede the march of prosperity and put the country back many years." Professor LaFeber argues that business opinion did shift to favor war, but a close examination of his evidence suggests that he is talking primarily about a few individual businessmen whose jingoist dander was aroused by Spanish intransigence, and a few groups that preferred to end the suspense when war became imminent.

And in any case, there were other economic groups besides bankers, merchants, railroad owners, and manufacturers in the country. Most Americans, after all, were farmers and wage earners, rather than businessmen. A study of the opinions of these interest groups makes the case for economic causation still murkier. Some farm spokesmen and part of the agricultural press took a strong prointerventionist stand, but not for economic reasons. Even if we concede that farmers wanted overseas markets and were willing to support an aggressive foreign policy generally, what advantage they would have gained from a war with Spain over Cuba is difficult to see. As far as working men were concerned, many of them shared the same attitudes as their employers. If a war with Cuba was apt to be bad for business, it seemed likely to hurt labor also.

And yet by April 1898, most American—farmers, businessmen, wage earners, and others—favored intervening in Cuba at the risk of war with Spain. Obviously these people were not acting primarily as members of occupational or economic interest groups. In fact they were acting on their feelings as citizens. It is important to remember that in the public realm, people function not only as doctors, machinists, bankers, dairy farmers, teachers, and so forth; they also act as voters, taxpayers, and citizens.

Keeping this in mind, we are still left with the question: what made Americans interventionists in 1898? One explanation for pro-Cuban sentiment emphasizes the effects of pro-Cuban propaganda. According to historian Joseph Wisan, the war took place because the sensational press, particularly the supersensational "yellow press" of New York City, convinced the public that Spanish policies in Cuba were indescribably brutal and the Cuban insurgents all noble patriots. Spurred on by an intense circulation war between William Randolph Hearst's *Journal* and Joseph

Pulitzer's *World*, the New York press, he notes, provided readers with a daily diet of scare headlines and atrocity stories that kept Cuba and its plight constantly before the public's view. "From March, 1895, until April, 1898," Wisan writes:

> There were fewer than a score of days in which Cuba did not appear in the day's news. The newspaper reading public was subjected to a constantly increasing bombardment, the heaviest guns booming for "Cuba Libre." The effect was cumulative. The average reader, naturally sympathetic to the cause of freedom and critical of monarchies, became convinced that Spain was arrogant, insulting, vindictive, cruel, [and] that Weyler and his cohorts were brutes in human form.... So thoroughly convinced was ... [the reader] of Spanish guile and deceitfulness that he completely agreed when the newspapers brushed aside Spanish promises to end hostilities....[6]

Wisan undoubtedly exaggerated the influence of the yellow press of New York City on American public opinion. How could the New York press have had much effect on Western or Southern public opinion? Expanding the Wisan thesis to include the press elsewhere makes the case for a newspaper-manufactured war somewhat better. We know the Cuban junta supplied provincial papers and religious journals with prepackaged atrocity stories which these organs of opinion were happy to use. But there are other objections to the Wisan hypothesis as well. Expansionist sentiment already had begun to infect the American people before the Cuban issue raised its head. Moreover, having themselves fought a war for independence, Americans were almost certain to sympathize with the Cuban rebels and despise the Spanish colonialists, with or without the yellow press. Finally, Spain was in fact brutal in its treatment of the Cubans and did much to create its own bad press. Yet from whatever source derived, by early 1898 American public opinion was violently inflamed against Spain and strongly in favor of intervening in the island to secure a just solution to Cuba's problems.

V

Despite the growing public disgust with Spanish policy, the possibility of a war over Cuba seemed remote when McKinley took office in March 1897, especially since the new president was strongly opposed to war. In his inaugural address, McKinley declared that "war should never be entered upon until every agency of peace has failed; peace is preferable to war in almost every contingency."

But he could not control events. By this time many Americans were demanding that the president end Spanish brutality in Cuba. Some, includ-

---

[6]Joseph Wisan, *The Cuban Crisis as Reflected in the New York Press* (New York: Columbia University Press, 1934), p. 460.

ing Lodge, Roosevelt, and Mahan, actually were clamoring for war. Early in 1898 a key group of Republican congressmen caucused and agreed to tell the president that unless he introduced a war resolution they would join with the Democrats and sponsor one themselves.

While the dispute over intervention raged, the Spaniards seemed at times to be their own worst enemies. The Spanish minister to the United States was Señor Enrique de Lôme, a cynical gentleman of strong and aristocratic views. In December 1897 de Lôme wrote to a friend in Cuba expressing his contempt for President McKinley as "weak and a bidder for the admiration of the crowd, besides being a would-be politician who tries to leave a door open behind him while keeping on good terms with the jingoes of his party." The letter was intercepted by a Cuban patriot at the Havana post office and sent to William Randolph Hearst, who promptly published it. As Hearst intended, it produced a sensation. De Lôme's insult to the American president was an outrage, the public cried. De Lôme's usefulness had ended, and he had to be sent home. In the words of a popular jingle:

> Dupuy de Lôme, Dupuy de Lôme, what's this I hear of you?
> Have you been throwing mud again, is what they're saying true?
> Get out, I say, get out before I start a fight.
> Just pack your few possessions and take a boat for home.
> I would not like my boot to use but—oh—get out, de Lôme.

The Spanish minister instantly resigned in hopes of mending the situation, but it was already too late. The American people now had one more reason to suspect Spain of duplicity and deceit.

The scandal of the de Lôme letter was followed six days later by an even bigger blow to Spanish-American relations. In January 1898 the American government sent the battleship *Maine* to Havana harbor, supposedly as an act of "friendly" courtesy. Actually, its mission was to protect American lives and property following a serious local riot. The Spanish officials in Havana treated the captain and crew of the vessel courteously, though the visit naturally aroused some suspicion. Then, on February 15, a tremendous explosion rocked the vessel, sending it to the bottom of the harbor with the loss of over 250 lives.

Although some Americans urged withholding blame until the facts were fully known, most leaped to the conclusion that the sinking had been the work of the Spaniards. Spanish authorities extended condolences and proposed an investigation jointly with the Americans to determine who was responsible. But many Americans demanded immediate retaliation. Theodore Roosevelt, always quick to take a belligerent stand, wrote that he "would give anything if President McKinley would order the fleet to Havana tomorrow. . . ." "The *Maine*," he insisted, "was sunk by an act of dirty treachery on the part of the Spaniards. . . ."

To this day no one knows for sure who or what caused the explosion. The

Spanish authorities claimed that it was either the result of an internal explosion of faulty boilers or faulty ammunition or the act of Cuban rebels, who had the most to gain by involving the United States in a war with Spain. When American experts were able to examine the hull of the ship, they discovered that the explosion came from outside the vessel, but they were never able to determine who had done the deed.

Regardless of who was actually responsible for sinking the warship, most Americans were now eager to fight. Mass rallies erupted all over the nation at news of the disaster. Excited crowds paraded through the streets chanting, "REMEMBER THE MAINE. TO HELL WITH SPAIN!" in their clamor for American intervention. The yellow press demanded Spain be punished with all the force of America's might. Pulitzer's *World* shrieked: ". . . THE DESTRUCTION OF THE MAINE BY FOUL PLAY should be the occasion of ordering our fleet to Havana and *demanding proper amends within forty-eight hours under threat of bombardment.* If Spain will not punish her miscreants, we must punish Spain."

For months McKinley had been under great pressure from pro-Cuba politicians and the press to intervene. But he had refused to be stampeded. He had already warned the Spanish government that the United States could not remain indifferent to what was going on so close to its shores and had offered America's good offices to mediate the conflict but had refused to deliver anything that smacked of an ultimatum. The Maine's sinking now forced his hand. In March he instructed the American minister to Spain to demand that the Spanish government grant an armistice to the rebels and end the cruel concentration camp policy. If Spain did not accept these terms by October, the United States would step in and impose a settlement.

The Spanish government, weak and vacillating, was caught in a dilemma. If it yielded to the Americans, it would antagonize many of its own people and might be overthrown; if it refused to budge, it would precipitate war with the United States. At first the Spanish government chose to concede very little, but then, responding to the advice of the Pope, it reconsidered its position. In April 1898 Madrid accepted the armistice and abandoned the concentration camp policy. Apparently the United States got virtually everything it wanted.

But it was too late. By now the American people would accept nothing less than "Cuba Libre." The president was still reluctant to approve outright armed intervention but feared the force of public opinion. Besides, if he ignored it, the Democrats would make political capital of his reluctance. And within his own party, a damaging split over Cuba might emerge. In Congress the pressure to declare war was becoming irresistible. Although the Spanish governmen had accepted American terms, on April 11 McKinley yielded and sent his war message to Congress. This body, surprisingly, acted rather slowly. On April 19 it passed several resolutions defining America's war aims, declaring: (1) Cuba must be free; (2) Spain must withdraw from the island; and (3) the United States would not annex Cuba. This last clause—the Teller Amendment—was approved without any dissenting vote. Shortly after, on April 25, Congress formally declared war on Spain.

VI

The brief conflict with Spain, in John Hay's estimation, was a "splendid little war." In some ways he was right. The war was certainly little. More American soldiers were killed at "Custer's Last Stand" than died in combat in the entire Spanish-American conflict. The whole war, moreover, was over in a few months, and peace was concluded by December 1898. The war was also a financial bargain, as wars go, costing the United States only $250 million.

The "splendid" part was also true, at least from the point of view of most Americans. The success of the American army, and especially the compact but up-to-date American navy, was astounding. The navy's first victory occurred at Manila Bay in the Philippines. On May 1, 1898, Commodore George Dewey, commanding a squadron of six modern ships, sank or captured the entire Spanish fleet in a seven-hour battle, while suffering almost no American casualties. In July the main United States fleet in Cuban waters defeated the Spanish Atlantic squadron in another brief battle off Santiago. Again American losses were virtually nil: one killed, one wounded.

The army's record was less impressive. For years its major task had been to control the Indians in the West, and it was small and not trained to fight a civilized power. When war came it was expanded quickly by volunteer regiments, one of which was Roosevelt's Rough Riders. But Secretary of War Russell Alger botched the job of mobilizing and deploying the army. Amid much confusion, some seventeen thousand ill-equipped men embarked from Tampa, Florida, and landed near Santiago in southeastern Cuba. Fortunately, the Spanish force in Cuba proved weak. After several sharp skirmishes, including Roosevelt's famous charge up San Juan Hill, the Americans captured the heights overlooking the city. On July 17, following the Spanish naval defeat, the Spanish military commander surrendered his troops. Soon after, the American army occupied Puerto Rico without opposition.

On July 26 the Spanish government asked the United States to name its peace terms. The formal peace conference met in Paris in October to work out final details. Spain already had agreed to give Cuba its independence and to cede Puerto Rico and the Pacific island of Guam to the United States. The only serious disagreement concerned the fate of the Philippines. Many Americans wanted the United States to keep the islands. Although Dewey had sunk the Spanish Asiatic fleet and destroyed Spanish power in the islands, he had not yet occupied the port of Manila but waited offshore for American troops to arrive before taking possession of the archipelago. Meanwhile, a German naval squadron was cruising nearby, acting as if the Reich would be happy to pick up some loose islands if the Americans were unwilling to take over.

The fate of the Philippines troubled Americans. Before the war American interest in the Philippines had been minimal. Few Americans even knew where the islands were. Dewey's glorious victory abruptly converted indifference to deep concern. As they considered the fate of the islands, Americans were barraged with conflicting emotions. Could they be allowed to fall into German hands? Since its unification twenty years before, Germany had become an aggressive colonial power and would surely seize the islands if they were left unattended. To most citizens it seemed far better for the United States to take them than to allow the Germans, who had expended nothing to acquire them, to gain control. Second thoughts were more self-serving. Now that the islands were ours for the asking, would they not be a useful base for establishing close trade relations with China? By this time Congress had finally voted to annex Hawaii (July 1898), and with the Philippines, the United States would have a series of commercial stepping-stones across the Pacific to the Asiatic mainland.

Moral considerations also contended in the nation's collective mind. Once the surprise of Dewey's victory had dissipated and Americans confronted the issue of how to dispose of the islands, many of them began to detect a parallel with Cuba. Hadn't Spanish misrule been as deplorable in the Philippines as in Cuba? To return the islands to Spanish tyranny after going to war to free the Cubans was inconsistent and irresponsible. Besides, the Philippines had to be uplifted and enlightened. The United States, many Americans concluded, had a responsibility toward the Filipinos and must not let them sink back into the stagnation, benightedness, and misrule that had characterized them under Spanish dominion.

At first McKinley himself did not know what to do about the Philippines, and as befitted a good Methodist, he prayed for divine guidance. The guidance came unexpectedly:

> And one night late it came to me this way [the President later explained to a group of churchmen]—I don't know how it was, but it came: (1) that we could not give them back to Spain—that would be cowardly and dishonorable; (2) that we could not turn them over to France or Germany—our commercial rivals in the Orient— that would be bad business and discreditable; (3) that we could not leave them to themselves—they were unfit for self-government—and they would soon have anarchy and misrule over there worse than Spain's was; and (4) that there was nothing left for us to do but to take them all, and to educate the Filipinos, and uplift and civilize and Christianize them, and by God's grace do the very best we could by them, as our fellow men for whom Christ also died. And then I went to bed, and went to sleep and slept soundly....

After reaching this inspired and useful conclusion, McKinley told the American negotiators at Paris to insist that the whole of the Philippines be given to the United States. Spain resisted at first but in exchange for $20 million surrendered the archipelago along with the other territories the Americans demanded.

Unfortunately for the imperialists, the United States soon learned that acquiring colonies was not as easy as all that. American forces had now landed in the islands, but they were not greeted with open arms by the inhabitants. Early in 1899, soon after the occupation began, the Filipinos, led by Emilio Aguinaldo, attacked the American garrison in Manila. Like the Cubans, the Filipinos had hoped to gain their independence from Spain and had established a provisional republic the previous June. When they learned that the treaty made them into an American colony, they were appalled and turned against the American occupiers. Eventually the United States was forced to fight a full-scale colonial war to take and keep possession of the islands. Not until mid-1902 were the seventy thousand troops that were sent from America able to put down the insurgents. This was our first war in Asia, and it produced many of the same barbaric atrocities on both sides that disgraced the Vietnam conflict during the 1960s.

The unexpected Filipino enmity confirmed an influential group of Americans in their conviction that colonies were both immoral and expensive. To the vocal coterie of patrician anti-imperialists, world power was all very well, but colonies were a drastic departure from American ideals and traditions. In the words of Professor Charles Eliot Norton of Harvard, a leading anti-imperialist: "America had something better to offer mankind than those aims she is now pursuing. . . ." Norton mourned "her desertion of ideals which were not selfish or limited in their application, but which are of universal worth and validity." By grabbing colonies, America had "lost her unique position as a potential leader in the progress of civilization" and had "taken her place simply as one of the grasping and selfish nations of the present day."

Norton's admonition was more in sorrow than in anger. Other anti-imperialists, however, were furious at their own country for betraying its best impulses. "God damn the United States for its vile conduct in the Philippine Isles," wrote philosopher William James. If we made the islands into a colony, we would leave the Filipinos with nothing; we can "destroy their own ideals," he noted, "but we can't give them ours."

Norton and James expressed the more altruistic and generous side of anti-imperialism. But there was a self-centered and racist side as well, represented by Carl Schurz, the German-American maverick Republican who had served as Hayes's secretary of the interior in the 1870s. Though foreign born, unlike most of the leading anti-imperialists, Schurz was fearful of the racial problems that would ensue if the United States incorporated the Philippines and parts of the Caribbean into its domain:

Imagine [he wrote] . . . the United States to cover . . . [Cuba and Puerto Rico] and, in addition, Hawaii, the Philippines, and perhaps the Carolines and the Ladrones, and what not—immense territories inhabited by white people of Spanish descent, by Indians, by negroes, mixed Spanish and Indians, mixed Spanish and negroes, Hawaiians, Hawaiian mixed blood, Spanish Philippinos, Malays, Tagals, various kinds of savages and half-savages, not to mention the Chinese and Japanese—at least twenty-five millions in all, and all of them animated with the instincts, impulses and passions bred by the tropical sun; and all these people to become Americans! . . . What will become of American labor and the standards of American citizenship?

Even before Spain formally surrendered, the dissenters had organized the Anti-Imperialist League, headed by Edward Atkinson, a public-spirited New England businessman. Composed of forthright, conservative Brahmins, the league failed to stop the treaty signing by American and Spanish negotiators in Paris. But all was not lost. The treaty still had to be confirmed by the Senate, and the fight for ratification promised to be long and bitter.

Most Americans probably favored the Treaty of Paris and what it implied. But many also continued to have deep misgivings about overseas colonies. To defeat the treaty, its opponents had to muster only one vote more than one-third of the upper chamber, and for a while it appeared that they would get it. McKinley and other administration leaders cajoled, persuaded, threatened, promised, and virtually compelled almost all the Republican senators to pledge their support. But Democratic support was needed, too. Bryan, the titular head of the Democratic party, was the key figure on the Democratic side. Despite his defeat in 1896, he still wielded great influence with his fellow Democrats. The problem for the president was that Bryan was not an imperialist. He had supported the war with Spain and even had served in it as a colonel of Nebraska volunteers, but he was not happy at the prospect of the United States becoming a colonial power. If he were to oppose the treaty, it would probably be defeated.

Fortunately for the administration, at this point Bryan chose not to challenge the Republicans or imperialism. Believing that it was important to conclude the war in any way possible, and naively assuming that once we had the Philippines we would free the islands, he refused to help the Senate antiimperialists. When the vote was taken on February 6, 1899, enough Democrats supported it to assure passage. Several pro-Bryan scholars have sought to absolve their hero of any responsibility for the treaty's passage, but whether through ineptness or naiveté, Bryan's tactics helped push the treaty over the line. When the votes were counted, it carried by fifty-seven to twenty-seven, just one vote more than needed.

VII

The struggle over expansion was far from ended, however. Though Bryan had urged Democrats to endorse the peace agreement with Spain, he remained hostile to colonies and believed that the election of 1900 could be turned into a referendum against acquiring them. This, too, was naive. American presidential elections are generally confused affairs where many issues, rather than one, are placed before the public and where personalities as much as issues influence the voters' decisions.

Nevertheless, in his rematch with McKinley in 1900, Bryan tried to push colonialism to the fore. The strategy was not very effective. In the end, the election turned on the issues of silver, reform, prosperity, and the success of the first McKinley administration. Even the antiimperialist leaders failed to regard the contest as a referendum for or against imperialism and consequently split their votes. The results were never in doubt, and Bryan's emphatic defeat revealed little of what the American public felt about overseas expansion.

In the next few years, Americans continued to be ambivalent about the country's newly won empire. Congress authorized limited self-government for Puerto Rico under the Foraker Act in 1900. The Platt Amendment of 1901 directed the president to withdraw American forces from Cuba. While it acknowledged the island's formal independence, it limited its sovereignty in foreign and fiscal affairs and authorized the United States to intervene to maintain law and order. The Philippines were granted limited self-government by the Philippine Government Act of 1902.

These measures were not the acts of a nation totally uninterested in imperial responsibility, but neither did they proclaim the sort of enthusiastic colonial commitment that the European powers had made. For the next decade and a half, the United States pursued a wavering course, first aggressively seeking overseas advantages, then seeming to be indifferent to overseas affairs, and at times reasserting its support of weak nations against the European powers.

Generally in Latin America, we continued to act like an overbearing older brother. Ever since the 1820s, we had considered the lands south of us part of the American sphere of influence. The attitude was an understandable one. The United States was the only great power in the western hemisphere. We had grown up with that situation, and however uneasy it made Latin Americans feel, Yankees found it necessary to their comfort and peace of mind to orchestrate affairs between their southern neighbors and Europe. Any hint that some European country was trying to extend its influence in the Americas immediately set off alarm bells in Washington.

Sometimes our proprietary attitude operated to the advantage of our smaller neighbors. Without United States protection, several of the Latin American states almost certainly would have become colonies once more of one or another of the great European powers. Yet Latin America undoubtedly paid a high price for this protection. The United States insisted that its own strategic, political, and economic interests came first. Frequently it demonstrated this attitude in a way that left a legacy of resentment.

A flagrant instance of American arrogance occurred in 1903 in Panama. After the Spanish-American War, the United States interest in an isthmian canal reawakened. During the recent conflict with Spain the U.S.S. *Oregon* spent many anxious weeks sailing from Puget Sound around Cape Horn in order to defend the exposed East Coast. The ship's snail-like progress underscored the naval advantages of an isthmian canal through Central America. With the war over and American connections with the Pacific more vital than ever, a canal seemed even more urgent.

Two obstacles stood in the way. One was diplomatic, involving the Clayton-Bulwer Treaty, an earlier agreement with Great Britain which denied the United States exclusive control over an isthmian waterway. The second was geographic, hinging on whether the canal should be built through Panama or Nicaragua. The diplomatic obstacle was overcome with the second Hay-Pauncefote Treaty signed in November 1901. (The first Hay-Pauncefote Treaty was discarded because it contained a provision that prohibited the United States from fortifying the canal and was therefore unacceptable to the American people.) Under the terms of the second agreement, the United States could now build, control, and fortify a Central American canal.

There still remained the problem of location. Concerned primarily with costs, Congress vacillated back and forth between Niacaragua and Panama. The issue reached a dramatic conclusion in favor of Panama when a hitherto dormant Nicaraguan volcano suddenly became active. Following as it did a volcanic eruption in Martinique that had just killed forty thousand people, this act of God convinced many Americans that the Niacaraguan route was unsafe. Then politics intervened. Panama was owned by Colombia. At first the Colombians were receptive to an American canal, but deciding that the United States's terms were unfavorable, they demanded a better offer. The Panamanians themselves, once independent, favored the canal and were terrified that they would lose the anticipated economic benefits if Colombia proved intractable and delayed the project. Panamanian patriots had revolted against Colombia in the past, but they had never succeeded in achieving independence. Now, encouraged by the arrival of the U.S.S. *Nashville* at the isthmian city of Colon, the Panamanians rose again. The *Nashville* kept the Colombian troops from landing in the isthmus, and this time the revolution succeeded.

The situation resembled the events in Hawaii a decade earlier and had Cleveland been president, the American government might have refused to accept the results of the coup. But times had changed. Roosevelt, an overt expansionist and an enthusiastic supporter of the canal, now occupied the White House. He immediately recognized the new Panamanian government, and three months later the Senate signed the Hay-Bunau-Varilla Treaty. For a nominal sum, Panama gave the United States the right to construct an interocean canal through a "zone" that would be controlled by

American authorities. Although many Americans objected to the arrogant way this treaty was obtained, most seemed to favor the outcome. The journal *Public Opinion* reported that "the majority opinion of the country approves ... little as this course can be justified on moral grounds. ... The sum of public opinion in this matter being simply that we want an isthmian canal above all things, and that the government has taken the surest means of attaining this object."

Roosevelt also acted aggressively elsewhere in Latin America. TR deplored what he considered the fiscal irresponsibility of the smaller Latin American states. In 1904, when several European nations threatened to blockade the Dominican Republic for failure to pay its debts, Roosevelt announced his "Corollary" to the Monroe Doctrine. The Roosevelt Corollary initiated a new and more overt interventionist policy. The United States would no longer adopt a hands-off policy towards Latin American misdeeds. "Chronic wrong-doing, or an impotence which results in a general loosening of the ties of civilized society," Roosevelt proclaimed, "may ... force the United States, however reluctantly ... to the exercise of an international police power, and compel it to intervene in the offending nation's internal affairs."

This statement would make most Americans wince today. Yet undeniably the financial unreliability of the Latin American republics created a serious problem for the United States. The instability of the smaller republics was a standing invitation to European intervention. If the United States were to protect them against the consequences of their folly, as they in fact wished it to do, did it not also have the responsibility to insure their good behavior? Surely a reasonable argument could be made for this position. But the Roosevelt Corollary opened the door still wider to American intrusion into Latin American affairs and proved galling to the republics south of us.

China and the Far East, too, caught America's attention in the years after 1898. Though businessmen had resisted the Cuban intervention fever before April 1898, after the outbreak of the war they quickly acquired a more positive view of overseas colonies. As we have seen, they were particularly attracted to the possibilities of the China market opened by control of the Philippines.

China in the closing years of the nineteenth century was like some stranded, expiring whale, disintegrating internally while being simultaneously torn apart by scavengers. In the years following 1858, major European powers had secured special "extraterritorial" rights in China for their citizens and envoys. Among other things, these granted foreigners the right to be tried by their own consular courts and to use their own postal services. They had seriously eroded China's sovereignty. Then, bit by bit, the Celestial Empire's outlying provinces were wrenched off and absorbed by France, Russia, and Japan. Within the decaying empire itself, a Western-educated elite intent on modernizing the country vied for power against a conservative ruling group and a tradition-bound antiforeign peasantry.

Americans generally were ambivalent about China. On the one hand, they were fascinated by its ancient glories and civilization, but they were also repelled by its "heathenism" and its political and economic backwardness. For years the gentler side of our response had been expressed by missionary efforts and programs to bring Chinese students to the United States for education in American universities. But there was a harsher side as well. In 1900 we cooperated with the other great powers to put down the antiforeign Boxer Rebellion and accepted the indemnity imposed by the foreign powers, forcing the Chinese to pay for the loss of Western lives and property.

For many years our course toward China was marked by this combination of self-interest and compassion. This ambivalence emerges most clearly in the Open Door policy of Secretary of State John Hay. After China's defeat by Japan during the Sino-Japanese War (1894–95), the great powers renewed their demands for favors and concessions from the Chinese. It soon began to look as if China would be completely carved up by the powers, either into actual colonies or spheres of exclusive commercial and political influence. The British, who already had more colonies than they could manage, were worried about this. So was the United States, which had no designs on Chinese territory, but did want to prevent the other powers from excluding it from the China market.

Encouraged by the British, Secretary of State John Hay in 1899 sent notes to the major colonial nations asking for assurances that none of them would insist on further special privileges for their businessmen in the Celestial Empire. Most nations gave Hay evasive replies, but the secretary chose to read these as acceptance of the Open Door principle. During the Boxer Rebellion in 1900, we expanded the Open Door policy to include, more explicitly, Chinese territorial integrity. In a circular letter on July 3, Hay announced that it was the purpose of the United States not only to protect American life and property in China but simultaneously to "preserve Chinese territorial and administrative entity" and safeguard "for the world the principle of equal and impartial trade with all parts of the Chinese empire. . . ." In a word, we would join together in a characteristically American way a noble defense of Chinese independence and a scarcely veiled defense of American national interests.

Back and forth America's China policy swung between these two principles of self-interest and altruism. Like the other powers, the United States accepted an indemnity from the Chinese for the American lives and property destroyed by the Boxers, but after legitimate claims were satisfied, we returned to China more than half of the sum awarded us. A decade later President Taft used his influence to help American business groups gain a share in Chinese railroad construction, but in 1913 Wilson, fearing that the arrangement might jeopardize China's "administrative independence," withdrew the government's support.

In the end America's foreign adventuring after 1890 amounted to less than many contemporaries feared. Today much is made of the outward thrust of the 1890–1913 period. This is a natural consequence of our recent disenchantment with America's post–World War II role in international affairs and especially with the Vietnam entanglement of the recent past. These events have fostered a skepticism of American diplomatic professions and goals that spills over all of American foreign policy, both past and present. Certainly it would be a mistake to assume that self-interest and even direct economic self-interest were not important concerns of the United States in its relations with other nations. On the other hand, self-interest was not the only consideration. As we have seen, Americans often were influenced by sentiment and idealism, if at times both were naive or misguided.

Finally, one more observation is in order regarding American foreign policy during the vulnerable years. At no time did the United States have truly vital interests in distant parts of the world. With domestic markets unequaled anywhere else, with two broad oceans to insulate us from any hostile power, we could easily afford to relegate foreign concerns to a secondary place through most of our history. Even in the western hemisphere, where we claimed a special strategic and economic interest, we avoided the worst excesses of other great powers. Unhappily, we have left behind a record of Latin American bullying that is not attractive. But what would have been the fate of Latin America had a powerful nation with Teutonic, Gallic, or even British colonial values and attitudes sat north of the Rio Grande, looking south at the ineffectual states below its borders? Viewed this way, we might conclude that the United States exercised considerable restraint in its policies toward its weaker neighbors.

VIII

The 1900 presidential election, whatever it signified for American foreign policy, was a vote of confidence in the McKinley administration. The ticket of McKinley and Theodore Roosevelt won 292 electoral votes to 155 for Bryan and Adlai Stevenson, Sr., with the Democratic vote declining proportionately compared to 1896. Bryan carried only four Northern states and even lost his home state, Nebraska.

Soon after his second inauguration, McKinley set off on a tour that was to take him to the South, the Southwest, and the Pacific Coast, winding up at the Pan American Exposition at Buffalo, New York. The president left Washington in late April and moved in a stately procession through the

South. Wherever he went he was cheered by large crowds, a response that put him in an unusually jovial mood. Early in May the presidential party traveled on through Arizona and New Mexico to Los Angeles and San Francisco. In California the always delicate Mrs. McKinley became seriously ill, and the president canceled the rest of the trip.

McKinley returned to Washington late in the month, but having promised the Exposition managers that he would come to Buffalo, he agreed to make a major address there in late summer. The president arrived in Buffalo on September 4, and spoke the next day on trade reciprocity to a large audience which listened to his words extolling expanded world commerce and responded with enthusiastic applause. The next morning the presidential party visited Niagara Falls. Back at the Exposition grounds that afternoon, as McKinley shook hands with well-wishers at a reception, a deranged anarchist, Leon Czolgosz, shot him in the stomach. McKinley was hurried off to the emergency hospital at the exposition grounds, where the doctors operated to remove the bullet. Soon after, he was carried to the home of John G. Milburn, president of the Exposition. McKinley lingered on for a week, and then on Friday afternoon, September 13, he whispered the words of the hymn "Nearer My God to Thee" and died. With him expired a century and an age.

Chapter Three

Urban Manners, Morals, and Mind

Strictly speaking, not until the census of 1920, when the tabulators for the first time reported that over 50 percent of the American people lived in communities of over twenty-five hundred or more, did the United States become a predominantly urban nation. In 1910 the census-takers had found only 46 percent of the population living in cities and towns. Yet in many ways, the balance of the nation had already tipped in an urban direction. By 1900 there were only 11 million farm workers—laborers and owners combined—only a third of the 29 million people gainfully employed. Most Americans, that is, were no longer tied to the soil by occupation. And even many rural folk were not as rural as they had formerly been. The city had penetrated the countryside and undermined rural values. This trend worried many old-stock Americans; and to help abort the process and preserve rural life, Theodore Roosevelt would appoint the Country Life Commission in 1902 with Liberty Hyde Bailey, a Cornell University professor, as chairman.

Certainly the cities were the most dynamic part of the nation by the turn of the century. In the years 1896–1917, individual American cities grew at a tremendous pace. Between the 1890 and 1920 censuses, New York–Brooklyn, for example, grew from 2.5 million to 5.6 million; Chicago from 1 million to 2.7 million; Philadelphia from 1 million to 1.8 million; Detroit from 205,000 to 994,000; and Los Angeles from 50,000 to 577,000. Only in the South was urban growth sluggish, and even there the smaller cities, especially the new textile towns of the Virginia-Carolina-Georgia Piedmont area, expanded rapidly.

These trends are impressive, but actually they are somewhat misleading. Cities grew not only because they attracted newcomers but also because they enlarged their boundaries. In 1889 Chicago almost tripled its area by annexing bordering communities. Baltimore and Seattle also expanded dramatically by geographical accretion. The most spectacular annexation of all, however, came in 1898 when New York absorbed Brooklyn, Staten

Island, the southern part of Westchester County (the Bronx), and Queens on Long Island to form Greater New York.

Nevertheless, the cities grew mainly because they attracted and held people. There were three major sources of urban population growth. One was the hordes of European immigrants who arrived on American shores—over 14 million between 1896 and 1917. Some of these newcomers went to rural areas and small communities, of course, but the overwhelming majority moved to the cities. In 1910 almost 80 percent of New York's population consisted of the foreign born and their children. The proportions in other large towns and cities were almost as great, at least outside the South and Far West. In some smaller factory and mining communities, where particular industries depended almost totally on foreign labor, figures for "foreign stock" approached the 100 percent mark.

A second important source of urban growth was migration from the farms and villages of America. During these years birthrates among rural Americans were high, yet rural opportunity did not grow commensurately. Though farm incomes rose, and new areas were brought into cultivation, especially in the Plains and Far West, the new areas were not extensive enough to provide farms for every rural boy and his future wife and family. Existing farms, of course, might have been subdivided among farmers' sons, but smaller farms were becoming less economical in an era of growing agricultural mechanization and scientific husbandry, and the trend was toward larger, rather than smaller, agricultural units.

The economic—and demographic—problems of the rural South, as we have seen, were especially acute. Worn out land, falling cotton and tobacco prices, and especially a vicious sharecrop, crop-lien system created a dead end for thousands of tenant farmers and farm workers. In addition, a racial system that was brutal, degrading, and repressive, most dramatically expressed by the rising number of lynchings, created a tremendous incentive for young black men and women to leave their native region. For a while, some black leaders hoped that black workers might be absorbed into Southern industry. Booker T. Washington, the influential black educator who established the famous manual training institute at Tuskegee, Alabama, believed that blacks would find their salvation as skilled workers in the South and advised them to "cast down their buckets" in their home region. But Washington was self-deceived. Most blacks did not find expanded opportunities in the South. The color line proved far too strong, and well into the early twentieth century, racial segregation, both economic and social, grew ever more complete and pervasive. Characteristically, when the cotton mills moved out of New England into the southern Piedmont area, they turned for their labor supply almost entirely to rural whites. As the new century began, thousands of young blacks, confronted by the limited economic opportunity of their home section and bitter at the discrimination they encountered, yearned for the freer life of the Northern cities and the greater, though still limited, opportunities of Northern factories, mines, and workshops. The tidal wave of rural blacks cityward did not begin until World War I curtailed European immigration, but by 1900 a substantial flow had already begun.

Besides the farms, the small towns and villages were another source of urban growth. Time, distance, and perhaps guilt would cover Americans' memory of their village origins with a golden haze. And small town life at the end of the nineteenth century did have virtues. Living costs in the smaller communities were lower than in the cities; fewer extremes of wealth and poverty existed; people were friendlier. But the villages were also isolated and dull, and life in them often seemed narrow and bigoted. They promised enough of a broader, wider, more exciting and intelligent world to whet the appetites of the bright and perceptive young, but they could not satisfy it. Village life weighed down many talented and restless young men and women, and each year thousands of them packed their possessions into carpetbags and cheap suitcases, kissed their families good-bye, and took the train for Chicago, Omaha, Atlanta, New York, Cleveland, or San Francisco. The total of this domestic migration from farm and small town to city was enormous. The urban historian Blake McKelvey has estimated that 11 million city dwellers in 1910 were transplanted native rural and village folk.

A final source of urban growth was the natural increase in the size and number of urban families. City birthrates were high. So were infant mortality rates. In 1900 in the country as a whole, 162 infants out of each 1,000 born died before their first year. The death rates for children under five was 1 out of 20. City rates were even higher than these, for American cities were not healthy places. Knowledge of the bacterial origins of disease was beginning to revolutionize the treatment of infectious illnesses, but the everyday practices of most citizens, including many doctors, lagged behind the most advanced medical thinking. City milk was still not pasteurized in many places as the century opened, and drinking water often was contaminated by sewage. In many cities at the turn of the century, "earth closets" unconnected to sewer outlets served for the disposal of human waste. Among the great health triumphs of the first two decades of the century were the introduction of pasteurized milk and filtered water, the improvement in sewage disposal, and the extension of new medical discoveries to the protection of the young. By 1900, city families were more than merely reproducing themselves—the middle-class woman's new interest in birth control notwithstanding—and this surplus was also added to the swelling city populations.

Obviously the city was a powerful magnet for Americans. Urban life offered many attractions to men and women in these years. Above all, it offered jobs at every level, from unskilled ditch-digging and domestic service to the highest reaches of the learned professions and corporate management. As the economy shifted from its agricultural base to one that rested on manufacturing, commerce, finance, services, and communication, its focus inevitably became more urban. This process, of course, did not begin in 1896; it had been going on for several generations, but it accelerated markedly in the years following the 1890s.

Much of the economic pull of the city was no longer purely industrial. Of course, industries continued to expand, and cities continued to draw people to newly opened factories. The heaviest industry, like iron and steel, often created new population centers. Homestead, Pennsylvania; Birmingham, Alabama; Gary, Indiana; and Pueblo, Colorado, were new communities that grew up around the steel mills that were erected in the last years of the nineteenth century or the first years of the twentieth. Older communities continued to add light industry—textiles, clothing, drugs, notions, hardware—to their economic bases.

But increasingly the jobs that the cities had to offer the newcomers were in the so-called tertiary occupations, those that involved neither the production of "primary" goods from the fields, streams, mountains or oceans nor the "secondary" function of converting these into finished products. As the economy became more sophisticated, cities came to serve more and more as the service and communications centers for the nation. Banking, insurance, advertising, publishing, administration, accounting, education, retailing, entertainment, fashion, and government expanded more quickly than manufacturing. City streets soon came to be as crowded with shopgirls, messenger boys, clerks, typists, accountants, journalists, lawyers, school teachers, and "ad" men as they had ever been with factory operatives, day laborers, and construction workers.

II

Many of these new service occupations required literacy, conscientiousness, and punctuality more than physical strength. This opened the economic door to women in great numbers. Hitherto limited to working as seamstresses, laundresses, and domestic servants or confined to hard, low-paying factory or home work making cheap garments (the so-called sweated trades), women now had better opportunities working in stores and offices. These jobs still did not pay well when compared with skilled men's work, but they were clean, respectable, and light, and the hours of work were relatively short. Accordingly, they attracted crowds of lower middle-class young women, many of them single girls or younger married women who had not yet begun their families.

New work opportunities for women had wide ramifications socially. For one thing they altered standards of female dress and appearance. Until the 1890s women commonly wore long skirts, bustles, layers of petticoats, and stiff corsets. The bicycle craze of the 1890s put an end to the bustle and replaced it with a flatter skirt. But the multiple petticoats still remained, as did the tight corsets and floor-length hemlines. The new need for shopgirls and typists to get around in busy, dirty city sreets gradually raised the hemlines until they reached the mid-calf by World War I. Along with the shorter skirt lengths came the shirtwaist, a more versatile garment for working girls, fewer and lighter undergarments, and silk stockings, a total luxury when skirts trailed the ground but a more sensible investment now when legs could be seen and admired. Cosmetics, too, became an acceptable part of the female toilette when women started to work in offices. Until the twentieth century, only actresses and women of ill repute used cosmetics openly. "Painted women," in fact, had been a common euphemism for harlot. But now girls of good family began to use powder, rouge, and lipstick without fear of being mistaken for prostitutes. By the eve of World War I, then, young city women with their paint, powder, and shorter skirts were beginning to look more like the flappers of the 1920s than like their over-stuffed, overcorseted, and excessively demure mothers.

But the effects of city life on women went deeper than dress and appearance. With jobs, which brought them into daily contact with the hurly-burly of city offices, and with money in their pockets, young city women after 1900 already were beginning to exhibit the pertness, the freer relationships, and the sense of equality with men that we associate with the years after 1920. Nor was the change all on the surface. Carl Degler has suggested recently that as early as the 1890s, well-educated women had begun to consider sex an interesting and enjoyable experience, not merely a procreative duty.[1]

Not every social critic liked what was happening to young urban women, however. Novelist Margaret Deland, writing in 1910, presented a rather acerbic and exaggerated portrait of the emerging flapper:

> This young person ... with surprisingly bad manners—has gone to college and when she graduates she is going to earn her own living. . . . She won't go to church; she has views upon marriage and the birth rate, and she utters them calmly, while her mother blushes with embarrassment; she occupies herself, passionately, with everything except the things that used to occupy the minds of girls.

Deland's barbed estimate marks her no doubt as something of an old fogey. And yet to people of conservative temper, the changes taking place in the behavior and deportment of young women promised to have serious repercussions. Anything that affected women inevitably affected the family as well. For millions of immigrants, the combination of new work situations and city life made an enormous difference in the way the family functioned. Most immigrants to the United States from the 1890s onward were people from the rural peasant cultures of Eastern and Southern Europe. In the

---

[1]See Carl Degler, "What Ought to Be and What Was: Women's Sexuality in the Nineteenth Century," *American Historical Review* (December 1974).

European villages of their origin, families were father-dominated and large, often housing under one roof unmarried adult children, grandparents, and other relatives, as well as parents and children. The move to urban America broke down most of these extended families and left them as the nuclear family of father, mother, and children that we have come to accept as typical of American life. At the same time, it reduced the authority of the father and parents in general. Second-generation young men and, especially, second-generation young women, both more adept at getting along in the new environment than their elders, often won for themselves a degree of freedom from parental control that would have been unthinkable in Europe.

Among native American urbanites, too, working wives and daughters, as well as the general impact of the city, had important consequences for family life. As Margaret Deland's attack suggests, the new young woman had strong views on the birthrate, or to put it in franker terms, she practiced birth control. Voluntary family limitation did not begin abruptly in 1900, of course. Even the ancients apparently knew how to avoid conception. In America birthrates had been falling all through the nineteenth century. In 1890 they leveled off, but then, between 1910 and 1920, they dropped once again, this time rather sharply. By present-day standards, they were still high—over 27.7 per 1,000 population as compared with 15.0 in 1973—but the change between the end of the nineteenth century and the twenties was substantial, especially among white, native-born women.

This decline was probably connected with the new lifestyles of urban women that made family postponement and smaller families more attractive and encouraged wider dissemination of birth control information. But the advocates of family limitation, despite the social changes that made contraception information more eagerly sought after, had to fight an uphill battle. Birth control during the first two decades of the twentieth century was still considered an immoral practice, roughly on a par with abortion until very recently. It was condemned by churchmen, particularly the Catholic clergy. It was also deplored by civic leaders, most notably Theodore Roosevelt, as a form of "race suicide" that would reduce the predominance of the educated middle class and surrender the nation to "lesser breeds." Whether for religious or social reasons or for both, its public advocates were treated as dissolute and dangerous people. In 1912, when Margaret Sanger, who had seen the effects of excessive childbearing on New York slum women, first began to publish birth control information, she collided head-on with the authorities. Mrs. Sanger was indicted by the federal government for sending her pamphlet *Family Limitation* through the mails and had to flee the country. In 1915, when she returned, she helped organize the National Birth Control League. Three years later, Mrs. Mary Dennett's Voluntary Parenthood League joined the older organization in the battle for smaller families.

Sanger's original purpose was to ease the childbearing burden of slum women. Actually, she was more successful with middle-class women, most of whom were native-born and quicker to accept new lifestyles and adopt new ways than their poorer immigrant sisters. Birth control, reflecting the new independence of single women before their marriage, in turn freed married women from long years of child raising that had kept them tied down at home. For women born between 1880 and 1889 (those who married between about 1900 and 1910), the period spent in taking care of children until maturity declined more than five years on the average when compared to a century before. This longer, childless life span liberated married women from family obligations, enabling many to turn to jobs, self-cultivation, or civic work as outlets for their energies.

At first glance we might suppose that this progressive liberation of women would weaken the family, and in some ways it did. It certainly reduced the authority of fathers. Wives who worked were not as dependent as their nonworking sisters on their husband's largesse and could assert a voice in family affairs that they did not have before. In effect, female employment helped improve the relative position of women in the family at the cost of traditional male authority.

More effective in eroding paternal power, however, was the ever-growing physical separation between job and home that characterized the urban environment. Where mothers were not absent from the home, fathers were. In the new urban world, more than in the old, factory and office workers lived far from where they worked. With the rapid spatial extension of cities, the distances traveled by men between their homes and their offices lengthened. By the opening years of the twentieth century, rapid transit had reduced the time it took to travel about the city, but many urban men spent an hour or more on the streetcar or subway traveling to and from their jobs. Fathers, accordingly, were apt to be away from their families for longer periods than ever before. The role of fathers in middle-class households altered considerably, and for the worse. Sociologist Arthur Calhoun, writing in 1919, revealed the ambivalence that many men felt toward the new situation:

> Under the new order, the homes come to be run for the women and children rather than for the man; husband and father is more rarely abusive; he adopts what an English writer represents as the "tame cat" attitude and becomes an earning mechanism whereby the other members of the family attain to vacations, dress and "society."

This shift of status and authority within the family might have contributed to weakening family ties if it had not been offset by other developments. The smaller size of families and the greater freedom of women and children was accompanied by a lower death rate. Not only did more children survive, but adults lived longer. In an earlier era, the early death of parents had been an important factor in family instability. Before the twentieth century, many women died from the complications of pregnancy and childbirth. Men lost their lives in home, farm, or industrial accidents. Both men and women often succumbed to disease, dying before reaching their expected life span. New advances in the health sciences not only reduced the high death rates of children under five but also lengthened the lives of adults. By the twentieth century, orphanhood, which had so often deprived children of their homes, economic support, and secure futures, was less common than formerly. And where parents did die young, fewer children were around to suffer from the effects.

Smaller families were also more cohesive. This posed both advantages and disadvantages. The new, smaller families provided better nurturing for children. In the large families of the past, children were forced to be more independent, and older children frequently carried much of the burden of raising the younger ones. Now parents could give their children more attention than formerly. If we assume that adult guidance was superior to that of children, then this was an advance. But there is reason to believe that the smaller family also had its drawbacks. Social historian Richard Sennett concluded in a study of late nineteenth-century urban families that the intensive family of the nuclear sort failed to prepare most young men for the highly competitive worlds of shop, office, and workbench facing them when they left home. Families that were looser in structure—as were the larger ones—did not provide the closeness of the smaller families, but their male members were better-prepared for the abrasive job world of laissez-faire America.[2]

Smaller families also tended to place excessive emotional demands on adults and children alike. This was less true of the older extended family structure of earlier times, where children were relatively unimportant and all family ties were looser. In the case of children, escape from these ties was possible either by apprenticeship or leaving home early; adults could form easy, illicit relationships. The small, strict, tight-knit, highly moral family of the late ninteenth century, the family that we label "Victorian," did not allow these safety valves, and they could be oppressive institutions. Since it had to provide so much of its members' satisfactions, the small family was often unendurable when it failed.

The advent of smaller, tighter, and more oppressive families, says William O'Neill, explains the great growth of divorce in the period. Divorce afforded an emotional escape that could not be achieved in the older ways. When the strains of the family became too great for adults, divorce intervened to save everyone's sanity. Instead of reflecting a loosening of family ties, easier

---

[2]See Sennett, "Middle-Class Families and Urban Violence: The Experience of a Chicago Community in the Nineteenth Century," in Michael Gordon, ed., *The American Family in Social-Historical Perspective* (New York: St. Martin's Press, 1973).

and more frequent divorce, he concludes, grew out of an actual tightening of these ties.[3]

Whatever the reason, whether it was O'Neill's emotional safety valve, the strains of the new urban environment, or the greater ability of women to support themselves, the divorce rate skyrocketed in this period. In 1890 there were some 33,000 divorces in the United States, or 3 per 1,000 existing marriages. By 1910 there were 83,000 divorces, 4.5 per 1,000 existing marriages. By 1920 the number had reached 167,000, or 7.7 for each 1,000 marriages.

Since women and the family were affected by the urban environment, so too were children. In middle-class families, as we have seen, they were more closely attended and more carefully nurtured than ever before. But by no means were all American families middle class. Among working-class folk, families continued to have many children, and in the new urban environment these children got less attention than they formerly did in rural settings. The city, along with the industrial system that was so essential to urban life, reduced the effective control of working-class parents over their offspring. Many immigrant families and many transplanted farm families, for example, had to accept the necessity of child labor. Children had worked on farms in the past and had continued to do so into the twentieth century, but farm labor had been open-air work that was closely supervised by adult relatives and seldom taxed the strength or impaired the health of young boys and girls.

Factory work was something else. Some 16 percent of the 1.6 million children under sixteen gainfully employed in 1900—or about 300,000— labored in canneries, cotton mills, and coal mines away from parental supervision to help eke out meager family incomes. This was not body-building, character-strengthening work. It was long, hard, dirty, and dangerous toil that destroyed the health, stunted the growth, damaged the morals, and blighted the lives of thousands of children. John Spargo, a socialist critic of American industrial society writing in 1906, described the appalling condition of the "breaker-boys" in the Pennsylvania coal fields:

> Work in the coal breakers is exceedingly hard and dangerous. Crouched over the chutes, the boys sit hour after hour, picking out pieces of slate and other refuse from the coal as it rushes past to the washers. From the cramped position they have to assume, most of them become more or less deformed and bent-backed like old men. . . . The coal is hard, and accidents to the hands, such as cut, broken, or crushed fingers, are common among the boys. Sometimes there is a worse accident: a terrified shriek is heard, and a boy is mangled and torn in the machinery, or disappears in the chute to be picked out later smothered and dead. Clouds of dust fill the breakers and are inhaled by the boys, laying the foundation for asthma and miners' consumption. I once stood in a breaker for half an hour and tried to do the work a twelve-year-old boy was doing day after day, for ten hours

[3]O'Neill, *Divorce in the Progressive Era* (New Haven, Conn.: Yale University Press, 1967).

a day. The gloom of the breaker appalled me. Outside
air was pellucid, and the birds sang in chorus with the
he breaker there was blackness, clouds of deadly dust
harsh grinding roar of the machinery and the ceaseless
air. . . .

was not averse to exaggerating the failings of
is unquestionably true that children were at times
ly twentieth-century industrial society, and the
many contemporaries had real ills to feed on.
ss father, of course, sent his son or daughter out
ildren attended school at least until the age of
ey nor their parents wished it, for school systems,
re rapidly lengthening the years of formal educa-
n. Whether or not children always saw this as a
is doubtful. The schools of the early twentieth
xed, permissive places that we aim for today. At
kindergarten, introduced from Europe about 1860,
ated to arousing interest, encouraging individual
and creating delight through a playful, warm at-
e kindergarten, schools tended to be grim, rigid,
where children were taught rote lessons by strict
the right to inflict corporal punishment on high-
edient pupils. John Dewey, one of the pioneers of
on his early experience in Chicago to illustrate
l meant in day-to-day classroom terms in a simple
go," he wrote:

chool supply stores in the city, trying to find desks and
ughly suitable from all points of view—artistic, hygien-
needs of children. We had a great deal of difficulty in
and finally one dealer, more intelligent than the rest,
afraid that we have not what you want. You want
ren may work; these are all for listening."
traditional education. It is all made "for listening"—
lessons out of a book is only another kind of listening;
of one mind upon another.

Dewey, Ella Flagg Young, Felix Adler, and other
hat we call progressive education had begun to
uthoritarian school into the more flexible, activist
rs. But the process still had a long way to go, and
suffered in silence, both literally and figuratively

er deficiencies, too. Besides the mechanical and
uction, there was apt to be a sharp cultural gap
her. Many of the children in the city schools of

1900—1917 literally did not speak the language
them. The foreign-born children of the urban slu
born women, often spinsters, who frequently fou
with children in general and Italian-speaking, (
speaking or Yiddish-speaking children in particul
dren became bored and unruly, and teachers bec:
ed. Despite these difficulties, the schools manag
skills and some knowledge of geography and Ame
ed in inculcating a few middle-class habits of deco
that traditional educators considered important, '
at the expense of childish creativity, curiosity, a

One improvement in education that was to ma
the new century was the enormous expansion of
society became more complex, it needed a mo
"Three R's" no longer sufficed for an urban eco
sands of teachers, accountants, lawyers, business
and other professionals and semiprofessionals. U
ing job opportunities in the middle and upper ra
demand for high school education swelled. Sta
sponded to the economic pressures by increasing a
ary education. School budgets grew enormously
outlay for education was $146 million. By 190
million, and by 1913, $525 million. Much of thi
ondary schooling. In 1870 only 2 percent of Ame
or older were high school graduates; by 1914 o
school diplomas.

The young city people of the years before Wor
or prepared for work; they also played. Recreatio
society of early America had been primarily a s
activity. In the summer boys and girls enjoyed p
ties. They played sandlot baseball or went fishin
ice skating and sleigh riding. These were simple
that for many years continued to awaken the nost
But cities presented greater obstacles to youthfu
and girls took to the streets and empty lots of
proved inventive in adapting traditional games, b
pean, to urban settings. Unfortunately, few Am
teenth century had the foresight to preserve op
populated centers, and hopscotch, handball, tou
and roller skating were played or performed und
amid the legs of horses and busy adults.

Luckily for everyone's safety, health, and pe
began to devote attention and money to playgro
1898 the mayor of Boston opened up city schoo
grounds, and he was followed soon after by the

Education. In short order these small beginnings swelled into a full-scale movement. In 1906 the Playground and Recreation Association was formed to advance the cause of improved play facilities for city children. Soon scores of communities had created playgrounds and parks, some of them carved out of valuable and expensive commercial property, and had provided trained staffs and caretakers to supervise and maintain them.

III

Play is not just a child's occupation or a family concern. It is a vital ingredient of life in general, and as the lives of most Americans became associated increasingly with cities, the urban centers had to provide all their citizens with ever-expanding opportunities for play, recreation, and entertainment.

To a large extent, these opportunities were not ones that grown men and women could participate in actively. Municipal golf courses and tennis courts were mostly innovations of the future. In the 1890s the bicycle craze that swept over the country for a time gave adults an outlet for surplus energies and allowed men and women to get out of the cities for picnics and sightseeing. The paid summer vacation, still a rarity for all but the rich, provided a few city dwellers with the chance to get some needed pleasurable exercise. But increasingly, city amusements, like city life in general, became sedentary and passive.

The process of tailoring recreation to fit the new urban mold took many forms. In the generation preceding 1920, large-scale spectator sports first emerged as an element of city life. Baseball, the first of the nineteenth-century games to be commercialized, had developed out of a number of primitive childrens' amusements popular for centuries. By the 1850s, baseball clubs composed of amateur players were common in the country's cities and towns. Their matches soon attracted enthusiastic spectators and reports of their encounters began to appear in the newspapers. Before long the teams were charging admission to defray the costs of equipment, uniforms, and traveling expenses.

The next steps in commercializing the sport quickly followed. In 1858 the National Association of Baseball Players was organized, and in 1869 the Cincinnati Red Stockings began to hire professional players. Seven years later the older league of amateurs was superseded by the National League of Professional Baseball Clubs with teams initially in New York, Philadelphia, Hartford, Boston, Chicago, Louisville, Cincinnati, and St. Louis. In the next few years, the National League expanded, and in 1899 it was joined by the American League. These two groups struggled for supremacy for a while and then amicably divided up the audience. In 1903 the first World Series game between the champions of each of the leagues was held with the American League's Boston Red Socks beating the National League's Pittsburgh Pirates.

By this time thousands of spectators turned out each week to watch the home team battle the visitors for nine exciting innings or, hopefully, more. The fans enjoyed the strategy and elegance of the game and the relaxed, unbuttoned atmosphere of the ball park in summer. Baseball also provided an outlet for hero worship, apparently a persistent American character trait. The stars of this period included the famous Chicago Cubs' infield of J. J. Evers, Joseph Tinker, and F. L. Chance ("Tinker to Evers to Chance" became the formula for a razzle-dazzle double play), pitcher Christy Mathewson of the New York Giants, shortstop John ("Honus") Wagner of the Pirates, and the slugger Ty Cobb of the Detroit Tigers. Attendance, while small by the standards of later decades, grew rapidly, and in the 1913 World Series, gate receipts reached $326,000 for the five games. In 1908 the popular song "Take Me Out to the Ball Game" captured the enthusiasm of thousands of fans for what unchallengeably had become America's national sport.

Compared to baseball, other spectator sports had minor followings. Boxing was just emerging from the brutal bare-knuckle phase when the new century began. In 1892, "Gentleman Jim" Corbett defeated John Sullivan, the "Strong Boy of Boston," using padded gloves and following the Marquis of Queensberry rules. In 1897 Corbett defeated Bob Fitzsimmons to become world champion. Though more humane than before, prizefighting still carried the stigma of a blood sport and in many places was forbidden. It remained a peculiarly masculine sport and one associated with working-class men and with gamblers and the underworld.

At the opposite end of the social scale was football. Still an amateur sport confined to the colleges, its largest following was among upper middle-class people who had college connections. By the turn of the century, however, commercialism was intruding rapidly into football as the audiences grew larger and the profits to the colleges swelled. By 1917, charges of subsidized plays, exaggerated attention to stadiums, extravagant hoopla, and excessive violence and brutality were leveled at the game, and reformers attacked the colleges that sponsored it.

The urban throngs of the early twentieth century craved other amusements besides sports, and resourceful entrepreneurs were happy to meet the demand. Streetcar companies in these years erected amusement parks with merry-go-rounds, funhouses, freak shows, food stands, and ferris wheels at the outskirts of large cities to provide weekend business for themselves. Larger seaboard cities often developed whole districts at the beach, like Coney Island (Brooklyn–New York), Revere Beach (Boston), and Kennywood Park (Pittsburgh) devoted to a combination of bathing, amusement park rides, and various kinds of shows, both vulgar and edifying.

The circus also provided an enthralling spectacle to thousands of city people. Earlier traveling circuses had played mostly in the smaller towns. By the last years of the nineteenth century, many of the companies had been merged, and with their large menageries, immense tents, heavy equipment, and scores of performers all traveling by train, they were forced to seek out the larger audiences of the cities to pay for their increased expenses.

The theater was scarcely an urban novelty in this period. Even before the American Revolution, English acting companies had toured American cities. After 1783 this cultural dependence on Great Britain continued, though American actors and even a few minor American playwrights joined the British. Not until the very end of the nineteenth century did the American theater shake off this subordination. Among the first serious American playwrights were Bronson Howard and David Belasco, two men talented enough to create plausible characters and place them in believable situations.

Yet the commercial stage remained at a modest artistic level in the United States. The public wanted melodramas and spectacles rather than serious dramatic works or sharp satire. The vaudeville show, the musical comedies of George M. Cohan, burlesque performances of low comedians and scantily clad chorus girls, and the flamboyant reviews of Florenz Ziegfeld, "glorifying the American girl," pleased city audiences more than Shakespeare, Sheridan, or Shaw. Even the advent of the little theater movement in the second decade of the new century, which was dedicated to performing serious plays on a repertory basis, did little to improve mass theatrical taste.

A new form that catered to the large, unsophisticated urban audience was the motion picture. The motion picture was made possible by the development of a flexible base for photographic emulsions, a camera that could take a fast series of still frames, and a projector that could run these through and project them at the correct speed on a screen. Some of the important technical work for the movies was done in the 1890s by that "inspired tinkerer," Thomas A. Edison. Edison had little faith at first in the new toy. But he initiated the first commercial showing of projected moving pictures at Koster and Bial's Music Hall in New York City in 1896. The performance produced a sensation. Soon vaudeville hall managers, always seeking new ways to attract the public, were buying Edison company "vitascope" projectors to show five- to eight-minute films of a girl dancing, prizefighters in the ring, or a rushing railroad locomotive.

The audience for motion pictures proved to be enormous. The live theater was expensive, and its appeal even at the popular level relied on too many conventions to suit simple audiences. The early film, with its giant images and its elementary story line, reached the lowest common denominator and became phenomenally popular. Even its silence was advantageous for city audiences, many of whom were foreign born. Although Edison and his associates attempted to monopolize the production of films for the new runaway entertainment medium, they did not succeed. Despite their efforts, dozens of small picture makers using equipment of their own make or imported from Europe were soon grinding out motion pictures.

At the distribution end, hundreds of exhibitors were in business by 1900 showing films in empty stores, lodge rooms, town halls, and almost any place where they could assemble some chairs in a darkened room. These early movie houses generally charged no more than a nickle for their eight-minute shows, which consisted of sketches that depicted some humorous or exciting incident. (An employer flirts with his stenographer; and just as he kisses her his wife enters the office and protests loudly; a dignified man strolling in a garden with a pretty girl steps on a hose and is squirted in the face, ruining the budding romance—and so forth.) Most of these primitive sketches were created on the spur of the moment by directors, camera men, or other employees of the small firms formed to provide material for the nickelodeons.

This impromptu approach to film making rapidly gave way to more deliberate creative efforts. In 1903 Edwin Porter of the Edison Company produced "The Great Train Robbery," telling a story of some complexity in almost a full reel of film. Soon two other companies, Vitagraph and Biograph, were creating one-reel films with complete stories. Equipment became better, theaters more permanent and comfortable, and the artistic quality of films more impressive. By 1905, many of the classic film genres already had become established—the western, the comedy romance, the crime film, the chase, and the travelogue.

At first, most of the film studios were located in eastern cities. Vitagraph was located in Brooklyn, Biograph in Manhattan, Edison across the river from New York City in New Jersey. Other important studios were located in Philadelphia and Chicago. Each of these cranked out films as fast as they could for what seemed to be an insatiable market. In 1908 the *New York Herald* reported that two hundred thousand people daily were attending film shows in New York City alone.

Edison contended that many of the film-producing companies were using equipment that violated the Edison patents. To avoid expensive patent infringement suits, eight of the largest firms joined with the Edison people and agreed to pool their patents. The new film trust planned to charge high fees to other producers to continue in business and was prepared to extract good rental rates from the thousands of exhibitors who showed their films.

Between 1909 and 1914, the new movie trust and the surviving independent producers fought constant legal battles in court and even physical battles within the studio walls. To escape the reach of the trust, and also to take advantage of good weather for outdoor shooting, William Selig, a Chicago producer, moved his operation to Los Angeles. Here in the brilliant southern California sun, where it was possible to dispense with expensive sets for westerns and other outdoor pictures, it was also possible to jump across the border to Mexico to avoid process-servers if the long arm of the trust reached to the Pacific Coast. Soon Selig was joined by other independents. By the time the Edison patents were modified by the courts in 1912, the Los Angeles suburb of Hollywood had become a major center for film production.

By this time, too, the audience for films had grown to between 10 and 20 million people annually. Also by this time, the star system, which relied on particular performers to attract customers and accordingly rewarded them with fantastic salaries, was fully developed. Among the earliest stars were Tom Mix, Mary Pickford, Charlie Chaplin, Bronco Billy, G. M. Anderson, and Theda Bara.

The star system created a whole new breed of popular heroes and heroines to satisfy the urban public's deeply felt need for vicarious adventures and glamor. So long as the movie industry lasts, uncomplicated escapism will continue to be its major commodity. But as with all new art forms, its devotees came to expect more of the medium with passing time, and directors and producers proved capable of meeting the more demanding standards.

In the years after 1910, D. W. Griffith began to work with Biograph and helped to make its pictures unusually successful. Griffith was the first producer-director who truly understood the medium of the film and attempted to exploit the potential of its unique qualities, in the process abandoning both the practices of the legitimate theater and the confining, short format of the one-reel film. In 1914 Griffith produced for a startlingly high $100,000 "The Birth of a Nation," based on the novel *The Clansman.* Concerned with the tribulations of Reconstruction, the movie was blatantly racist and aroused fierce opposition among blacks and white liberals wherever it was shown. Nevertheless, it was a milestone in movie making. Twelve reels long, it employed the fade-out, the dissolve, symbolism, and at the special theaters where it was shown, live orchestral music with great effect. However deplorable the "Birth of a Nation's" political or racial message, it brought the movies to the point where they did not merely pander to the public's unformed taste but actually helped to elevate it.

Music was another important form of recreation for the urban masses in the opening decades of the twentieth century, and city dwellers heard their music in many forms. The musical stage was a traditional display case for musical entertainment, as were concerts and recitals. These performances were available at many different levels of sophistication, from vaudeville and musical comedy to opera, from band concerts in city parks to the major symphony orchestras and classical musical societies of New York, Boston, Philadelphia, Chicago, and Cincinnati. At an intermediate level, the operettas of Victor Herbert—"Babes in Toyland" (1903), "The Red Mill" (1906) —placed a serious, if highly romantic, story in a moderately sophisticated musical setting.

A form of entertainment that particularly delighted the urban masses was vaudeville, a pastiche of songs, skits, dancing, acrobatics, and trick "acts" that flourished most exuberantly from 1890 to 1920. The Palace Theater in New York, which opened in 1913, was the capital of vaudeville, but vaudeville's popularity was nearly universal among city dwellers. New York in this period had some thirty-five vaudeville houses; Philadelphia, thirty; and Chicago, twenty-two; while there were two thousand other theaters that booked vaudeville acts in smaller cities. One contemporary estimated that between 14 and 16 percent of the country's urban population attended vaudeville shows at least once a week.

Although serious music attracted growing numbers, few Americans as yet wrote or performed it. Most of the composers whose works filled the opera houses and concert halls of the cities were Europeans, and most of the performers—whether singers, instrumentalists, or conductors—were European artists on tour or in permanent residence in the United States.

In the popular music field, on the other hand, "Tin Pan Alley," the region around Twenty-eighth Street in Manhattan, was the source of most of the music Americans sang, whistled, hummed, or played on the parlor piano. Much of this music was tuneful but vapid. The themes of most popular songs of the period expressed either nostalgia for the countryside that many Americans had by now abandoned ("Down By the Old Mill Stream," "When You and I Were Young, Maggie") or saccharine boy-girl romantic attachments of the June, moon, spoon variety ("Sweet Adeline," "By the Light of the Silvery Moon").

But something better was just over the horizon. In the 1890s a little-known type of black secular music (as opposed to the already popular Negro spirituals) pierced the national consciousness and, in the form of ragtime, won a large audience. Especially popular were the instrumentals of Scott Joplin, who improved on the simple marchlike syncopation of early ragtime and converted it into music that was remarkably subtle. By 1900 the special combination of African, American, and Creole musical elements present in New Orleans had been merged into "Jass" by a talented group of black musicians, which included Buddy Bolden, King Oliver, and Jelly Roll Morton. Jazz, to use its later spelling, combined the instrumentation of the wind band, traditional march tunes, African rhythms, and the improvisation universal to fine musicians everywhere into a new form that was exuberant, expressive, and exciting. In New Orleans Negro jazz bands played at funerals, public celebrations, and in the Storyville houses of ill-fame. Local white musicians found the new style fascinating and quickly learned to imitate it. In 1911 Irving Berlin capitalized on the new musical vogue with his hit "Alexander's Ragtime Band." But not until 1917 when one of the white groups from New Orleans, the Dixie Jass Band, opened at Reisenweber's Cafe in Chicago did a northern white audience actually hear something close to real jazz.

Until 1877 to experience music one had to attend live concerts or play or sing oneself. In that year the fertile brain of Edison created the phono-graph. The original Edison instrument was too crude for commercial use, but it was improved slowly by Edison, Emile Berliner, and others. Gradually the hand-cranked instrument using a tinfoil cylinder record was replaced by one with an electric or mechanical spring motor, a better acoustical system, and flat wax or hard rubber discs that could be stamped out in limitless numbers from a master recording.

For a number of years, phonographs were found mostly in restaurants, saloons, and drug stores, where for a nickel or a dime they were played by patrons like a modern jukebox. Only slowly did they become home enter-tainment instruments. Although electronic recording and reproduction were unavailable until the 1920s, the quality of the sound was much im-proved by the "Gramophones" manufactured by the Columbia Company and the new "victrolas" produced by the Victor Talking Machine Company. Serious musical artists like Enrico Caruso, Antonio Scotti, Nellie Melba, and Adelina Patti were induced to perform for the record companies, but popular music was better-suited to the three- or four-minute running time of the standard phonograph record, and consequently most record sales were of monologues, dance music, popular hit songs, marching bands, and the like. By 1919 the country spent $339 million on records and phono-graphs.

By 1917, urban needs and urban opportunities had made commercial entertainment into an important cultural phenomenon. The city dweller, already accustomed to working away from home without the close family bonds or the ties of community or friends that had characterized rural areas and small towns, sought out the music hall, the nickelodeon, and the profes-sional baseball game. In the new urban setting, even the home relied on commercial entertainment as never before. By 1917 the family victrola— and the mechanical player piano—had displaced the family musicale in many city homes.

IV

As commercial entertainment expanded to meet the demands of the growing city masses, the nation's cities continued to serve their venerable role as centers of new ideas and traditional high culture.

America's big cities produced many of the country's most creative people. One contemporary expert analyzing the names in *Who's Who in America* for 1908–09 discovered that towns of eight thousand and more were the birthplaces proportionately of more than twice as many distin-guished men and women as smaller communities. A contemporary inves-tigator of the sources of scientific talent concluded that a major factor "in reproducing scientific and other forms of intellectual performance" was "density of population." Big cities were also magnets for the inventive, the talented, and the creative from the small towns and the farms.[4] At a time when the country and the village still contained a majority of the nation's population, they inevitably produced many of the nation's most able people. But these people flocked to the city, or to certain large cities—New York, Chicago, Boston, and San Francisco, particularly—to find the training, the appreciative audiences, and the colleagues they required.

The big city environment, in turn, shaped young talent into specific forms. In literature the city's impact spawned realism, the most extreme expression of which was naturalism. Realism-naturalism expressed a new mood of impatience with the hypocrisy of the genteel, romantic novelists of the past who ignored the shocks and jars of life as it was and buried real experience under the conventions of sentimentality and melodrama. To the genteel-romantic novelists, life was sunny, maidens pure, heroes noble, and virtue always triumphant over vice. Evil existed, of course, but it was somehow without cause, personified by evil men, and always defeated. Sex, poverty, and crime were sordid, vulgar, and seldom acknowledged as a part of everyday life. Since the audience for novels presumably consisted of sheltered young ladies, nothing could be included by the novelist in his work that would offend the young middle-class woman's tender sensibilities.

The genteel-romantic tradition flourished best in an America composed of small cities, villages, and farms. It continued into the later age of factories and metropolises as the genre of the second-rate popular novelists who made the best-seller lists with their costume romances, their historical epics, and their family or "women's" novels, but by the 1880s, the genre began to repel the most talented writers. How could the serious artist continue to insist that life was pretty and unambiguous in the age of the Haymarket riot, the Homestead Strike, the tenements of the lower East Side and the buccaneering of the robber barons? Particularly to the bright young men and women from the farms and the villages, the city seemed a brutal and jarring, if exciting, place, one that demanded an approach and style suited to its raw power and abrasiveness.

Among the first of the realists was William Dean Howells, a transplanted Ohioan who came east in 1866. First in Boston and then in crude, creative New York, he earned a reputation as an editor and a novelist. In a sense Howells always had been a realist. From the start of his writing career, he sought to depict the commonplace and the ordinary, but as time passed, his writing became franker in depicting the squalid realities of urban-industrial America. In his best works, *A Modern Instance* (1882), *The Rise of Silas Lapham* (1885), and *A Hazard of New Fortunes* (1890), Howells dealt with

---

[4]See Robert Higgs, *The Transformation of the American Economy, 1865–1914* (New York: John Wiley and Sons, 1971), pp. 73–76.

such diverse subjects as modern marriage, the nouveaux riches, and class struggle. A number of his later novels, *A Traveller From Altruria* (1894) and its sequel, *Through the Eye of the Needle* (1907), belong to that quasi-Socialist genre of works best exemplified by Edward Bellamy's enormously successful *Looking Backward*. Almost as important as Howells's own contributions to realism was the encouragement he gave to the work of younger realist writers, whom he advertised and generously praised through his position as editor of *The Atlantic Monthly* and *Harper's*, two prestigious journals of the day.

Howells served as a bridge between the older gentility of the antebellum years and the full-blown naturalism of the twentieth century represented by Theodore Dreiser. Also a midwesterner, Dreiser was made of coarser clay than Howells and lacked his refining experience of literary Boston. Son of a poor immigrant German workingman, Dreiser grew up in Indiana and never acquired much formal education, a deficiency that shows up in his rough, sometimes half-literate, though powerful style. Moving about constantly, first with his family and then by himself, he got to know the American city as only a new arrival from the country or village could. Cities were exciting; cities were tempting; cities were corrupting. This urban experience, whether that of a poor country girl (*Sister Carrie*, 1900, and *Jennie Gerhardt,* 1911) or a poor country boy (*The Financier,* 1912, and *An American Tragedy*, 1925), aroused the cupidity, the lust, the ambition, and the ruthlessness of his characters and led either to their ultimate ruin or to their transformation into powerful but pitiless human beings.

In Dreiser's works a cruel and indifferent social system is populated by individuals who are swept along by forces they cannot control easily—sex, ambition, greed, or some other elemental urge. Dreiser's reality was harsher and more repellent than Howells's. Dreiser himself was driven by an insatiable need for sex and lived a highly irregular and even bizarre personal life.

The city was the primary setting for the work of both Howells and Dreiser. Other realists and naturalists alternated between the city and the country, but in the latter case, they focused on farms and farmers confronted by the changes imposed by industrialism. Frank Norris's *McTeague* (1899) deals with the deterioration of a San Francisco dentist who succumbs to the temptations of material success and animal passion, much like many of Dreiser's heroes. In *The Octopus* (1901), the first volume of a projected trilogy that was never completed, Norris examines the effects that the great changes taking place in grain production have on a group of California wheat farmers. *The Octopus* depicts the first stage of the process, the growing of grain and the ranchers' victimization by the railroads. In its sequel, *The Pit* (1903), the marketing stage is viewed through the career of a grain speculator who, like so many of the naturalists' characters, is brought to ruin by temptation and greed.

Hamlin Garland, unlike Norris, Dreiser, and Howells, devoted himself almost entirely to the rural scene. But early in his career, he was hardly a sentimentalizer of rural America. Having grown up on farms in Wisconsin and Iowa during the harsh years of the 1870s, Garland was impressed more by the hardships and privations than the bucolic charms of rural life. In *Main Travelled Roads* (1891), *Prairie Folks* (1893), and *Rose of Dutcher's Coolly* (1895) he depicts people who experienced nothing of what rural life supposedly promised in the way of independence, communion with nature, and personal satisfaction. Instead his characters found farm life dreary, isolated, and cruel. In his later years, Garland returned to his own past with a series of biographical memoirs that dripped with cosy nostalgia, but the work of his youth was an important stone in the edifice of realism that was rising in the generation before 1917.

Architecture and painting among the high arts also reflected the influence of the urban-industrial environment. Until the end of the nineteenth century, there was no truly indigenous American architecture. From the colonial period to the Civil War, American builders had adapted European styles, whether Georgian, classical, or Gothic, to American circumstances and at times had done so with considerable finesse. During the Gilded Age their tastes worsened. Until late in the nineteenth century, domestic and commercial architecture in the United States aped—and bastardized—one European style or another. The mansions of the rich on Fifth Avenue, Nob Hill, and Newport copied French chateaux or English country houses. The office buildings of Manhattan or the Chicago Loop were great Victorian Gothic piles. These styles were seldom pure; rather they were eclectic jumbles of elements that created an impression of clutter and confusion.

The first small step out of this aesthetic morass was the work of Henry Hobson Richardson, Charles F. McKim, and Daniel H. Burnham in their purer, more graceful adaptations of traditional styles. Richardson's Trinity Church in Boston, McKim's Boston Public Library, and the buildings at the 1893 World Columbian Exposition at Chicago, inspired by Burnham, represented a return to the successful adaptation of the best European design to the American environment that had characterized the years before the Civil War. The Chicago Fair deeply impressed the thousands of visitors and set off the "city beautiful" movement that in the next decade would produce a rash of monumental neoclassical civic centers all over the country.

But the real breakthrough in creating an architectural style that fully expressed the mood and capacities of the new era awaited the work of Louis Sullivan and his student Frank Lloyd Wright. Of the two, Sullivan found the city the more congenial environment. Taking advantage of cheap steel, which allowed the economical construction of a steel cage framework covered by a thin outer skin, and of the elevator, which permitted the ready vertical movement of passengers and freight, Sullivan promoted the development of the skyscraper. Skyscraper construction was not, of course, the creation of one man. It was encouraged by the high price of land in the

made possible by the new technology of steel and
on became both a necessity and a status symbol
city. But in Sullivan's hands, they also became an
ng on an idea that had been followed implicitly by
nerations, Sullivan announced that "over all the
follows function, and this is the law." In sum,
st be built for commerce and their appearance
se proudly, honestly, and firmly. Other architects
buildings, department stores, and warehouses with
their windows into Gothic arches, or distort their
owers, but Sullivan worked with simple, unclut-
ons, and plain but handsome textures. Wright, on
the urban setting and designed few large, commer-
ities, but his domestic buildings in suburbs, with
s, their simple and natural materials, and their
lowed the whole school of modern home architec-

ects were creating an indigenous American style
and expensive private homes, they did little to
the urban poor. Particularly in New York, the most
the country, the poor were housed in solid blocks
th rudimentary plumbing, crowded rooms, and
heir aesthetic failings, these structures were often
ught fire because of their narrow wooden stair-
d shoddy construction.
e authorities sought ways to improve the distress-
the big cities. In 1879 a state law limited the
New York City tenement could occupy to 65
required that every bedroom have a window with
square feet. In 1887 another measure mandated
or bathroom for every fifteen inhabitants in each
building. In 1898 and again in 1902, Chicago
o impose higher standards on builders. In 1901
rbade the further construction of the "dumbbell"
a narrow airshaft along the building side was the
adjacent structures and the only source of air and
But by that time, more than two-thirds of New
ly lived in these dreary, inconvenient "old law"
y were first built, had been hailed by humanitari-
oon to poor city dwellers.
ew York and other communities attempted to
that would humanely meet the housing needs of
an adequate profit to landlords and builders. In
Brooklyn philanthropist and engineer, completed

the "Home Buildings" near the Brooklyn waterfro... combine successfully "philanthropy and 5 percen... benefactors also tried to mobilize the profit motiv... central city wage earners. Unfortunately, cheap a... well over 5 percent on investment, and in the end... able to induce more than a handful of private buil... new housing at reasonable rents for the urban w...

Like architecture, American painting respond... emerging urban environment. The work of the n... ployed the themes of the cities with their turbul... They depicted prizefights, people waiting for ta... flying over tenement roofs, children playing in c... El at rush hour. Called vulgar or brutal by the cus... realists gloried in the charge and denounced the ... day as anemic, "merely an adjunct of plush and ...

The core of realist painters consisted of Everett ... Sloan, and William Glackens, all of whom had be... in Philadelphia during the 1880s. Trained to do th... pher does for newspapers today, they developed ... and city types. About 1891, they came under the ... a teacher at the Pennsylvania Academy of Fin... Europe where he had been strongly influenced b... ists. Toward the end of the decade, Henri and his ... moved to New York. There they were joined b... Arthur B. Davies, and Ernest Lawson.

In 1904, six of the group held an exhibition at th... was described by one conservative critic as "an ou... under her most lugubrious mood, where joyousn... where unhealthiness prevails to an alarming exten... Henri were being referred to derisively by the tra... can School."

Offended by the tight rein on the world of ... conservative National Academy of Design, whic... prestigious exhibits, a group of the young realists... MacBeth Gallery in New York in 1908. This ... crowds but did not result in many sales to the pu... were called, did not stay together as a group for ... ence was important in inspiring such young A... George Bellows, Jerome Myers, Edward Hopper... tant, they helped break down the wall of gentil... America generally and enabled the still more radi... were revolutionizing painting and sculpture in E... America.

In 1913 the Henri group and the more radica...

major exhibition of the best European work at the Sixty-Ninth Regiment Armory in New York. They shocked, amused, or delighted the public and had a powerful impact on all subsequent American painting and sculpture. The exhibition consisted of two parts. One displayed the painting of the young American realists. The other, more important segment, exhibited the work of Cezanne, Van Gogh, Gauguin, and the still more radical canvasses of the cubists, who had all but abandoned any attempt at a traditional representational approach. The sensation of the show was Marcel Duchamp's *Nude Descending a Staircase*, a cubist painting that suggested the motion of a woman walking from the top to the bottom of a flight of stairs through a succession of closely overlapping images. The Duchamp painting, like much of the radical work, excited an immense amount of ridicule. Conventional critics reviled the modernists as pandering to "cheap notoriety," and exhibiting "incomprehensibility combined with symptoms of paresis."

Both in New York and in the other cities where it was exhibited, the Armory show attracted immense crowds of people, most of whom came to smirk but many of whom stayed to marvel and appreciate. Some 235 of the paintings were sold eventually, and American tastes were given a tremendous push in the direction of modernism.

V

The intellectual changes of this period, as much as the artistic ones, reflected the powerful forces of technology, science, and urbanism. During the nineteenth century, much of the God-centered world view that had survived the breakdown of the medieval synthesis came under a renewed attack, especially from science. The development in the laboratory of organic compounds, such as urea, hitherto only found in natural substances, helped destroy the sharp distinction between the biological and the physical world. The work of Sir Charles Lyell in geology disclosed that inanimate forces operating over immense periods of time, rather than God in the six days of the bible, created the mountains, plains, oceans, and continents.

But it was the work of Charles Darwin, above all, that shattered the nineteenth-century God-centered view of the world. Elaboration on Darwin's scientific contributions is unnecessary. His two major works, *On the Origin of Species* and *The Descent of Man*, replaced God's act of creation posited by the Judeo-Christian tradition with the gradual process of "natural selection" as creatures competed for scarce food. Under Darwin's scheme of evolution, all living species were descendants of those individual plants or animals that had survived in the competition for a particular environmental niche owing to some useful characteristic, and had passed along that characteristic to their offspring. Man was not exempt from this process of struggle, adaptation, and evolution. He was merely the most successful example of it, and all the talk about humankind being made uniquely in God's image and belonging as much to the spiritual realm as to brute creation was mere superstition.

Darwinian ideas traveled quickly to America, where they produced both enthusiasm and dismay. The dismayed included the multitude of orthodox believers who considered evolution a direct assault on the bible, already under severe attack by the skeptical scholars of the "higher criticism," who insisted that men rather than God had composed the Holy Scriptures.

Actually, Christians reacted in one of two ways to the new assault. Some, especially in rural areas and in the South, rejected entirely the tide of modernism that the new science encouraged. Calling themselves fundamentalists,[5] they labeled evolution the work of the Devil, refused to consider it seriously, and denounced every effort to teach it in the schools. At the other end were those Christians who were able to come to terms with the new ideas. Evolution, the modernists noted, did not abolish God; rather, God must be regarded in new ways. He could not be considered a bearded patriarch who constantly intervened in the affairs of men. He was a being who operated entirely through natural laws, and His glory and mystery lay in the ultimate origins and meanings of things.

Modernism affected the ethical content of Christianity. With God removed from immediate day-to-day existence, much of the old concern with personal salvation and personal sin subsided. Modernist Christians repudiated the fundamentalist focus on the individual act of faith that led to eternal bliss in Heaven and rejected such old, conservative doctrines as infant damnation. Instead they embraced a new gospel—the social gospel— that was man-centered and secular rather than God-centered and spiritual.

The social gospel defined sin in a new way. It was an affront primarily against man, not God. This redefinition reflected the change of emphasis from the Deity to mankind. Furthermore, the social gospel view considered sin not so much a matter of violating the moral law individually as violating it collectively. To social gospelers, in the complex, interconnected society of the modern industrial and urban world, sin was often the consequence of acts performed by individuals in good faith that in their cumulative effect caused harm and suffering to others. Conventional piety and good works were not enough to avoid sinful behavior, noted the Revered Washington

---

[5]At least after the first appearance in 1910 of the *Fundamentals*, a set of pamphlets condemning the higher criticism and Darwinism and reiterating biblical infallibility, Christ's Virgin Birth, His atonement for mankind, Resurrection, and the Second Coming. These "Five Points" became the basis for the fundamentalist creed which thereafter had a quasi-official core. In a less precise way, however, fundamentalist ideas had flourished long before 1910.

Gladden in 1902. Many of those who had been converted and lived exemplary personal lives were, nevertheless, sinners:

> The trouble with them is that they have been converted as individuals; religion is with them too much an individual matter between themselves and God. The fact that one man can no more be a Christian alone than one man can sing an oratorio alone is the fact that they have not clearly comprehended. The failure to realize this truth results in highly unsocial conduct on the part of many whose piety is unquestioned. I could easily multiply instances which have come under my observation of men and women who were humble, trustful, prayerful; who obeyed, also, all the ordinary duties of morality,—being chaste, truthful, honest, and bountiful in their gifts,—and yet were deeply distrusted and even cordially hated by those who knew them best. . . . Their defective conduct arose from their failure to comprehend their fellow men. . . .

The social gospel churches and ministers were responding in part to the larger questions raised by a complex urban society where the relations among men often were obscured or attenuated by many intermediary institutions and obstructions. But they were responding also in a practical way to the loss of central city communicants. Protestantism was dying in the cities. Many central city dwellers were no longer churchgoers. The new urban immigrants were mainly Jewish or Catholic. Protestant immigrants, as well as Protestant newcomers from the farms and small towns, had lost touch with the urban churches which increasingly seemed to be middle-class institutions. Reflecting this unfortunate fact and also exacerbating it, many of the older Protestant congregations simply abandoned the areas where many of them had been located for decades and moved out to the suburbs to join their middle class worshipers. In New York alone, between 1868 and 1888, seventeen Protestant churches abandoned the city below Fourteenth Street and moved elsewhere. Meanwhile, the area, which included the immigrant portal of the lower East Side, increased its population by two hundred thousand souls.

The social gospel leaders hoped not merely to develop a philosophy appropriate to new urban relationships but also to stem this loss of contact with the day-to-day problems of city dwellers. They labeled their effort the "institutional church" and included under it a broad array of new church activities. In the 1890s the churches established athletic clubs and social halls and hired welfare workers to minister to the urban poor. Often they cooperated with the settlement houses that were springing up in the slum neighborhoods of the large cities. They also concerned themselves with the labor movement. In 1903 the Presbyterians established a department of church and labor, placing at its head a clergyman who had been a machinist. In 1908 the Methodists officially endorsed the right of labor to organize into trade unions. The Federal Council of the Churches of Christ in America, a social gospel–oriented body composed of thirty-three Protestant groups founded in 1908, favored the abolition of child labor, the six-day work week, workmen's compensation, old age insurance, a living wage, and other labor reforms. At the far left end of the social gospel spectrum was a small but vocal group of Christian Socialists who advocated replacing capitalism by the cooperative commonwealth.

The modernist and social gospel movements within the churches represented the liberal response to modern science's impact on morals and social attitudes. But another response, social Darwinism, buttressed conservative, laissez-faire doctrines and traditional American "rugged individualism." Social Darwinism was an attempt to extend the idea of biological competition to the social realm and make it the primary cause of human progress. Modern scientists know more about the complex interactions of living creatures than their predecessors and realize that cooperation and mutuality are as important to evolution as are conflict and struggle. But during the 1870s, men like Professor William Graham Sumner of Yale, historian John Fiske, and scientist and lecturer Edward Youmans—drawing on the English philosopher Herbert Spencer as much as on Darwin himself—attempted to convince their fellow Americans that a competitive model of society, politics, and the economy was validated by the fundamental dictates of nature.

Social Darwinists adamantly rejected the humanitarian impulses of their day. According to Spencer, laws to aid the poor, to provide publicly supported education, to regulate housing, to provide cheap mail service, even to protect citizens against medical quackery were all misguided. Every effort by the state to eliminate inequality in social and economic life was certain to lead to disaster. "Let it be understood," wrote William Graham Sumner, "that we cannot go outside this alternative: liberty, inequality, survival of the fittest; not liberty, equality, survival of the unfittest. The former carries society forward and favors all its best members; the latter carries society downwards and favors all its worst members."

Sumner at least was consistent in his position. He opposed protective tariffs that benefited large manufacturers as well as welfare legislation that benefited the poor. But most social Darwinists were not so rigorous in applying their principles. Conveniently forgetting that government in the late nineteenth century did more to help the rich and the powerful than the poor and the weak, they wielded the new ideas primarily against those reformers like the Populists and Socialists who sought to use the government to equalize the benefits of the burgeoning economy.

Scholars have probably exaggerated the impact of the social Darwinists. No doubt they provided a rationale for the social and economic inequalities that existed. At times businessmen echoed their views. Oil tycoon John D. Rockefeller supposedly told a Sunday school audience that "the growth of a large business is merely a survival of the fittest. . . . The American Beauty rose can be produced in the splendor and fragrance which brings cheer to its beholder only by sacrificing the early buds which grow up around it." But Rockefeller's remark was unusual. Few businessmen liked Darwinian competition. The influential trade journal *Iron Age* attacked those who "glibly" referred "to the destructive competition in the industrial world as a 'struggle for the survival of the fittest.' "

They were "cynical" men who forgot that "survivors" also suffered losses. In 1886 *Bankers' Magazine* asked rhetorically whether "a portion of mankind must be slaughtered that the rest may live." If conflict seemed less than perfect as a prescription for business relations, it was still worse as applied to labor relations. The business press sought to establish the principle that business and labor had identical interests. Whatever injured "business inflicts loss upon both" labor and capital, *Iron Age* proclaimed shortly before the Bryan-McKinley election.[6]

Although social Darwinism failed to convince businessmen, it was embraced by influential educators, publicists, and politicians, and helped to mold the way Americans perceived the world. Its impact on contemporary thinking was particularly profound in matters having to do with race and overseas expansion. If some individuals were superior to others, some races and nations were also superior to others. (We have already seen how such a concept affected the mood of Americans when they confronted the option of overseas colonies.) America, as a superior society, was entitled to impose its will on inferior peoples both for their benefit and ours. As Richard Hofstadter has pointed out, colonialism and conquest did not have to await on the *Origin of Species* to find justification, but social Darwinist ideas were enlisted quickly in the service of the expansionist impulse that emerged toward the end of the nineteenth century.

The most pernicious product of misapplied evolutionary thought was the pseudoscience of eugenics. If mankind consisted merely of higher apes, then men, like animals, might be improved by selective breeding. Not until the Nazis was this view carried to its logical conclusion, but well before the 1930s, various social thinkers and scientists endorsed biological selection as a method to improve the human race. Inferior stock, they urged, should be dissuaded from reproducing themselves and people with congenital defects should be sterilized, while superior stock should be encouraged to have large families.

If only by implication, eugenicists endorsed the biological basis of human personality and human capacity and denied the social element in both. In the classic and persistent argument between the proponents of heredity and those of environment as the fundamental source of human differences, the eugenicists took the thoroughly conservative hereditarian position. At no time in the United States did eugenicists, of course, have the latitude of later Nazi ideologues to experiment with human breeding and eliminate "inferior strains." Their contribution to our understanding of human differences was hardly a useful or constructive one, however.

---

[6] I am indebted to the unpublished master's essay of my former student, Laird Klingler, for these insights and these quotations. See Klingler, "Business Thought in the Gilded Age ... ," New York University, 1968.

But, social Darwinism cut two ways. If it served to rationalize privilege and inequality, it also could be used to defend change and progress. Evolution represented a new way of looking at the world that emphasized its impermanent, changing nature. In place of fixity of forms and relationships, the Darwinians offered a model where both were constantly evolving and altering. If the universe and all that was in it seemed to earlier thinkers to resemble a giant clock or some other piece of machinery, the thinkers after Darwin tended to see it as an analog of a living organism. This change in perspective, as applied to social thought, Morton White calls the "revolt against formalism," defining formalism as ideas and concepts that were rigid, abstract, formally logical, and mechanistic.

The revolt against formalism was an effort to assimilate evolutionary ideas to law, philosophy, economics, history, and education. In line with this, it introduced the notions of change and movement and the necessity of referring to the past to explain the present. Just as the present species of animals and plants were derived from earlier forms, so current human ideas, practices, and institutions were derived from past ones and would inevitably change into new ones. Antiformalism was also a response to the complexity, the variety, the turbulence, and the conflict of modern urban-industrial society. As a result of these beliefs, the antiformalists insisted on taking seriously the experience that men underwent in this new, abrasive, jarring, and down-to-earth environment and in bringing to social thought the insights growing out of the reality of everyday life in the modern, city-centered world.

The revolt against formalism took a distinct form in each area of social thought. In jurisprudence, where it first appeared, it was an attack on the concept that the law was a static set of principles struck off by some great mind or minds in the past and transmitted to the present in toto like the Ten Commandments or, as some believed, the federal Constitution. The law was not a fixed system of propositions from which lawyers, judges, or legal scholars might deduce rules to suit particular cases; it was, said Oliver Wendell Holmes, Jr., one of the great legal minds of his generation, a dynamic entity that grew gradually in response to the needs of particular periods. "The felt necessities of the time, the prevalent moral and political theories, institutions of public policy, avowed or unconscious, even the prejudices which judges share with their fellow men," Holmes wrote, "have a good deal more to do than the syllogism in determining the rules by which men should be governed."

If the law responded to existing circumstances effectively, there would be no need to quarrel with it. Unfortunately it often lagged behind the actual needs of the day or merely expressed the prejudices of particular judges in particular eras or communities. Naturally the law was frequently out of touch with modern conditions. Judges pronouncing on modern events claimed that they were speaking with the collective wisdom of the ages, but often they were expressing merely the biases of past ages or particular classes, when they were not indeed merely reflecting their own social and philosophical limitations.

In practical terms, antiformalism in law, as Holmes was to act upon it himself as an associate justice of the United States Supreme Court, meant that the law must be made flexible enough to suit the times and the felt needs of the community. It would adjust eventually, in any case, but it would do so slowly, inefficiently, and ineffectively unless judges recognized the bases for their decisions and sought to bring those decisions in line with the spirit of the community's needs and wishes.

Holmes's attack on the deductive concept of law and his insistence that to understand the law one must look at its history and development found a parallel in Thorstein Veblen's work in economics. A second-generation American of Norwegian origins, Veblen was an eccentric whose life was marked by erratic personal and social behavior. At each of the universities where he taught—Chicago, Stanford, the University of Missouri, and the New School for Social Research—Veblen offended colleagues and administrators by his acid tongue and his irregular marital relationships. His frequent employment moves and his isolation in turn left him a shy, bitter, and despairing man.

Yet he was a highly original thinker. In the spirit of the antiformalists, he brought to economics the insights of other disciplines. He rejected the simplistic, logical propositions of the prevailing economic orthodoxy. In books such as *The Theory of the Leisure Class* (1899), *The Theory of Business Enterprise* (1904), and *The Instinct of Workmanship* (1914) Veblen ridiculed the notion, fundamental to the classical economists, that men made rational economic decisions based on self-interest. The economic man posited by the classical thinkers existed only in their minds. In reality men often behaved as illogically and nonrationally in the economic realm as in others. Rich men, for example, were not driven to increase their wealth by simple considerations of gain for its own sake. Rather, they were often influenced by yearnings for prestige and status that derived from earlier times when "conspicuous consumption," the ability to waste goods in colorful, extravagant ways, separated the powerful from the weak. Even the more constructive classes in society—the "engineers" as distinguished from the leisure class—were moved more by inherited drives and values—in this case the instinct of workmanship—than they were by a purely rational interest in material gain and comfort.

Veblen drew his insights from anthropology, sociology, psychology, and the other social sciences. But above all he relied on history. Economic behavior could not be reduced to logical propositions. It could be understood only by examining its development over time. The history of economic institutions, not theoretical models based on and deduced from first principles, was the key to understanding economic behavior. This institutional approach, focusing on economic history, was to become an important, if secondary, school of academic economics during the first half of the twentieth century.

In the discipline of history itself this same antiformalistic spirit pervaded the years following 1890. Needless to say, historians did not have to be convinced that present institutions evolved from past ones. In that sense they always had been evolutionists. What distinguished the "New History" of Charles Beard and James Harvey Robinson from traditional history was its extensive use of the other social sciences and its overt present-mindedness.

The concept of present-mindedness requires little explanation. Beard, Robinson, and their disciples informed their work with sociology, economics, anthropology, and the other new fields that were being carved as separate academic disciplines out of the late nineteenth-century's composite social science. Present-mindedness was a quality of focusing on those parts of the past that were interesting because they concerned modern men. This meant, in effect, an expansion of social, intellectual, and economic history, and the downgrading of conventional political history. The word *conventional* here is important. Beard in particular respected political institutions and believed it was important to study their evolution, but the concern for reigns, wars, and dynasties that made up the stuff of traditional political history was dismissed as arid, uninteresting data not worth the scholar's attention.

Not all political institutions equally concerned the New Historians. Those that figured in the news, those that were stirring current controversy, those that were under attack—these were the institutions to which the historian should devote his attention. Thus Beard's 1913 study, *An Economic Interpretation of the Constitution*, grew out of the Progressive concern for the way the federal Constitution was being used particularly by the courts to frustrate the desires of the public for significant social and economic reforms. Beard saw the great fundamental document of American government as a conservative instrument designed by the founding fathers to protect property, especially mercantile and financial property, against attack by the propertyless masses and their patrician agrarian champions. The Constitution was not an eternal monument to disinterested wisdom; it was a class document, constructed by a coalition of merchants, speculators, and assorted businessmen, designed to defend their interests against attack. That it had served the ends of capitalism ever since 1787 was, accordingly, no surprise.

Philosophy was still another area where the antiformalistic approach produced new insights. Until the last years of the nineteenth century, American philosophers had been disciples of one or another of the great schools of European thought. Whether idealists or materialists, rationalists or empiricists, American thinkers had argued endlessly, as had their European counterparts, over issues that seemed to have no solutions. Especially moot were questions of experience and knowledge. Philosophers had wrangled about how men perceived and how they distinguished what was true from what was false for centuries without coming to agreement.

Beginning in the late 1870s with Charles Peirce's "How to Make Our Ideas Clear," a group of American philosophers including Peirce, William James, and John Dewey sought to develop a new theory of knowledge, or a new theory of truth, that avoided the abstractions of traditional approaches. Truth, they said in varying ways, was not the correspondence of a statement with some sort of abstract fixed reality. Even if such a reality existed, it would be unknowable, particularly in the realms of values, ethics, social thought, and religion. Ideas or propositions were those that experience demonstrated worked to produce results we wanted to achieve. The test of the truth of any concept was whether it led to consequences or goals that had practical significance. One could, of course, ask other questions or posit other sorts of concepts, but if these had no practical consequences, they were meaningless.

This philosophy, which James called pragmatism, seemed at times to be saying that only questions that led to results that were profitable in a day-to-day way had any meaning. James, by speaking of the "cash value" of an idea seemed in fact to be expressing a peculiarly vulgar concept of truth, and Europeans sometimes attacked pragmatism as nothing more than a rationalization of American materialistic values. But this was unfair. Both James and Dewey, the first by his use of vigorous everyday American expressions and the latter by his turgid style, often misled and confused their readers. What they both meant was that experience was the guide to truth whether we acknowledged it or not. In most matters of daily life, we were content to ask only those questions that had practical significance. In this respect we were all informal pragmatists. But in other, more fundamental areas as well, the pragmatic approach was implicit in what people did. Science especially employed it by requiring a true statement to have predictive value. In "instrumentalism" in fact—Dewey's version of pragmatism—the prototype of all truth seeking was the experimental method of the natural sciences.

In thinking about society too, said James and Dewey, the valid method of approach was experimental rather than deductive. The solutions to social problems would come not by seeking to apply rote moral or ethical principles but by experimenting and testing various hypotheses and judging the validity of the conclusions by their concrete results.

On a higher, more abstract level, James and Dewey believed that the world was open rather than closed and that religion, morality, social institutions, and bodies of knowledge were all evolving. The final returns for the universe, both in its human and in its natural aspects, would not all be in until the last stroke of recorded time. This was an explicit blow against closed systems of thought that declared that the world was either all matter and motion, all spirit, or all thought or that it was moving inexorably to a single, final end, whether perfection, the Second Coming, chaos, heaven, death, or whatever.

The pragmatic vision of the world and society was, then, optimistic, relativistic, experimental, and practical, and wherever pragmatic approaches were applied, they led to changes that were designed to accord with the disorderly world as it actually was rather than to an ideal world that perhaps ought to be but was not. To the pragmatic thinkers, this world was that of volatile, turbulent, diverse, urban-industrial America, not some abstract and timeless human society that had never existed except in some old-fashioned philosopher's mind.

Dewey in particular had little patience with the abstract, the timeless, the perfect, and the ideal. Generally philosophers had elevated these qualities above those of a workaday sort. This sort of dualism, he felt, was arid and pointless, but so were all dualisms. Especially unfortunate was the split between knowledge and practice that had led thinkers to reject experience as a moral and ethical guide and exalt deduction from fundamental principles. What did these traditional modes of thought have to do with twentieth-century America? Very little, he decided, and it is not accident that he spent his entire adult life in the country's two greatest cities, New York and Chicago, involving himself in their scruffy day-to-day problems.

The pragmatic mood was expressed most effectively in the area of education. Dewey was intensely interested in educational reform to replace the passive receipt of knowledge by an active involvement in learning, something that the Progressive educators who were his disciples often characterized as "learning by doing." Educators, he also believed, should be democratic and cooperative rather than authoritarian and coercive, as befitted a society that was democratic and that increasingly was interconnected. The classroom should become not merely a place where knowledge or skill was received but rather a training ground for a more egalitarian and less competitive society.

Apart from a new way of teaching, the pragmatic version of education also demanded new content. Subject matter had to be suited to the new age. The traditional curriculum had emphasized the dead languages, polite literature, ancient history, and formal mathematics as training for the mind. These subjects had to be replaced by matter that was geared to modern needs. Vocational training, both in the narrow sense of skills that suited men and women who had to deal with the jobs and personal problems of the industrial world, and in the broader sense that as citizens in that world they had to understand how it worked, was to replace the "liberal" subjects inherited from the Renaissance. These traditional disciplines were appropriate only for an elite who would enter the learned professions. Most boys and girls had greater need for draftsmanship and woodworking, nutrition, and home economics than for Latin or trigonometry. History, Dewey believed, should be the history of a student's own society; geography should be that of his own city and neighborhood. Out of the new school would come the new citizen, suited to the new democratic age.

The pragmatists, whether they expressed themselves in philosophy or in education, both reflected and molded the changes that were taking place in American life. Another group of thinkers who overlapped the pragmatists also both expressed and affected the emerging urban civilization of twentieth-century America. These men and women, called communitarians by Jean Quandt,[7] were defined by their relationship with the city. All were born in small towns, but all cast their lot with the growing metropolises. Dewey, the most famous communitarian, was a Vermonter who became a Chicagoan and then a New Yorker. Frederick Howe came from Meadville, Pennsylvania, to Cleveland and then New York; Josiah Royce moved from a small mining town in the Sierra Nevada to San Francisco and then to Boston-Cambridge; Jane Addams came from Cedarville, Illinois, to Chicago. Almost all the men and women of this group made the journey from small towns to great cities.

They were, however, ambivalent about life in both cities and small towns. They revered the neighborliness and community spirit that had flourished in their early environment, but they deplored village narrowness, cultural aridity, and intolerance. The city offered freedom, opportunity, widened cultural and intellectual horizons; but it also brought loneliness, social disintegration, and moral chaos. In an analysis of the collapse of social norms within cities, foreshadowing such modern urbanologists as Jane Jacobs, Jane Addams remarked:

> We have all seen the breakdown of village standards of morality when the conditions of a great city are encountered. . . . The spirit of village gossip . . . may be depended upon to bring to the notice of the kindhearted villager all cases of suffering . . . but in a city divided so curiously into the regions of the well-to-do and the congested quarters of the immigrant, the conscientious person can no longer rely upon gossip.

Addams, as we shall see, sought to restore the lost sense of community throuugh the neighborhood settlement house. Mary Parker Follett, who believed that evil consisted of "non-relation," devoted her life to creating community centers to focus the common civic efforts of neighbors. Dewey, of course, placed his faith in the school as an engine for creating an organic society. All these transplanted village intellectuals, each in his or her own way, experienced some of the penalties that urban-industrial society exacted from the American people in the early twentieth century. To use a recently popular formula, their experience made them part of the problem; their work would also make them part of the solution.

---

[7]See Jean B. Quandt, *From the Small Town to the Great Community: The Social Thought of Progressive Intellectuals* (New Brunswick, N.J.: Rutgers University Press, 1970), p. 37.

Chapter Four

The Progressive Persuasion

It is unusual when the opening of a new political era coincides with a major calendar change. Sometimes, however, the end of one century and the beginning of another do conveniently coincide with a shift in some important historical dimension. Most historians of America believe that the date 1900 (or 1901) represents one of these instances. The historians' focus in this case is political, and the event they point to is the advent of the progressive movement.

At one time no one would have challenged the view that an important political movement was launched in the first years of the twentieth century. Men who lived through the period 1900–1917 believed that it represented a distinct political era, and when journalists, politicians, reformers, and thoughtful public men later wrote about their experiences during these years, they had little doubt that something called progressivism had existed and that it had enrolled millions of citizens in a movement to safeguard and improve the quality of American life.

And yet if we look closely at the history of the country during these years, the concept of progressivism turns out to be curiously elusive. Contemporaries differed among themselves about what it was and who or what was behind it. William Allen White, America's quintessential small-town editor, distinguished the reform mood after 1900 from the populism that had preceded it by emphasizing the urban, middle-class quality of progressivism. As the brash, young editor of *The Emporia Gazette*, his vitriolic editorial attacking populism ("What's the Matter with Kansas?") became a McKinley campaign document in 1896. After 1900 White turned to reform and became one of the most articulate Midwestern spokesmen for progressivism. White believed that the new political urge was a middle-class movement "to the core." It was composed of "the successful middle-class country town citizens, the farmer whose barn was painted, the well-paid railroad engineer and the country editor." The people at the Chicago Progressive party convention of 1912, he noted, consisted of men and women like himself, neither rich nor poor. "It was a well-dressed crowd," that unlike the Populists was also well educated and well informed about the complex world of the day.

White emphasized the middle groups in society, but big business also supplied part of the impetus behind the progressive movement, or so a number of contemporary businessmen believed. Members of the prestigious National Civic Federation, an organization formed in 1900 to foster better relations between capital and labor, reflected the views of enlightened top-level businessmen who believed that labor-business cooperation would safeguard the American business system as well as guarantee "the very foundations of prosperity" for both businessmen and wage earners. George W. Perkins, one of the NCF's strongest supporters and a director of both United States Steel and the International Harvester corporations, noted in 1910 that the big businessman as represented in the NCF was "no longer controlled by the mere business view" but increasingly was playing "the part of the statesman." Individual businessmen like New York banker Joseph Schiff, Boston department store magnate Edward Filene, and newspaper publisher Edward Scripps never doubted that they and their peers had made important contributions to progressive reform.

Contemporaries also traced progressivism to—or blamed it on—labor or labor agitators. Samuel Gompers, president of the American Federation of Labor, was suspicious of such advanced progressive measures as health insurance and unemployment insurance. Nevertheless, he was happy to claim credit for helping the progressives enact such political reforms as the initiative, referendum and recall, and for the passage of the anti-injunction clause of the 1914 Clayton Antitrust Act.

Each of these contemporary views has its modern scholarly equivalent. Borrowing from editor White, and from historians George Mowry and Alfred Chandler, Jr.,[1] Richard Hofstadter has located the source of progressivism in the status anxieties of men and women who belonged to "the old-family, college-educated class that had deep ancestral roots in local communities and often owned family businesses, that had traditions of leadership, belonged to the patriotic societies and the best clubs, staffed the governing boards of philanthropic and cultural institutions, and led the movements for civic betterment. . . ."[2] These worthy folk, Hofstadter believed, were being shouldered aside by crude, aggressive captains of

---

[1] For Mowry, see the following works: George Mowry, *The California Progressives* (Berkeley: University of California Press, 1951) and *The Era of Theodore Roosevelt, 1900–1912* (New York: Harper & Bros., 1958), Chapter V. For Chandler, see Alfred D. Chandler, Jr., "The Origins of Progressive Leadership," in Elting Morison, ed., *The Letters of Theodore Roosevelt* (Cambridge, Mass.: Harvard University Press, 1954), Volume VIII, pp. 1462–65.

[2] Richard Hofstadter, *The Age of Reform: From Bryan to FDR* (New York: Alfred A. Knopf, 1956), p. 137.

industry and simultaneously threatened by the potentially restless laboring masses of the factories, mills, and mines. The first had seized both the power to influence and the prestige that the older elite had enjoyed in an earlier, simpler age. The second seemingly had developed the ability to create social turmoil and endanger the traditional prerogatives of private property. Caught between the two millstones of big business and big labor, the middle-class, old-family progressives sought a way to frustrate plutocracy on the one side and radical anarchy on the other.

The Hofstadter-Mowry-Chandler emphasis on the white, Anglo-Saxon Protestant, middle-class origins of progressivism has been challenged by a number of scholars. J. Joseph Huthmacher and John Buenker believe that wage earners, immigrants, and their champions helped put much progressive legislation on state and city statute books. State legislatures representing working-class urban constituencies, they say, voted consistently for child labor laws, stricter housing standards, and workmen's compensation measures and supported the progressive Sixteenth (income tax) and Seventeenth (direct election of United States senators) Amendments to the federal Constitution.[3]

The Hofstadter-Mowry-Chandler thesis has also been challenged by a group of scholars who conclude that the leaders of the conservative, old-guard factions within both major parties cannot be distinguished from either the leaders of Theodore Roosevelt's Progressive party of 1912 (the Bull Moosers) or from the progressive elements within the Democratic and Republican parties in matters of ethnicity, occupation, class, or education. The leadership of both progressives and standpatters, they say, was middle class, old stock, college educated, and Protestant, though generally more of the conservatives were businessmen, and progressives tended to be a little younger. Clearly, if middling status characterized both conservatives and reformers, it cannot be considered a distinguishing feature of progressives.

Still another challenge to the Hofstadter school comes from a number of scholars who believe early twentieth-century reform the work of a business elite. The hypothesis comes in several versions. According to Gabriel Kolko, big businessmen feared the anarchic, cutthroat competition that emerged toward the end of the nineteenth century. They tried to counteract this trend by mergers. But mergers and other devices to restrict competition proved inadequate, and they eventually turned to government regulation as the answer. In cooperation with the politicians, they designed measures that appeared to subordinate business to the public interest but actually enabled it to avoid competition. The new laws forbade competitive practices that businessmen disliked while preserving those they favored. Meanwhile the

---

[3]See J. Joseph Huthmacher, "Urban Liberalism and the Age of Reform," *Mississippi Valley Historical Review*, September 1962; and John Buenker, *Urban Liberalism and Progressive Reform* (New York: Charles Scribner's Sons, 1973).

consumer was served poorly, if at all. In the end, says Kolko, progressivism must be considered a conservative attempt to rescue American capitalism from the chaotic laissez faire that threatened the political and economic power of the great tycoons.[4]

James Weinstein concedes that early twentieth-century reform sprang initially from working-class or middle-class grievances. But it was quickly annexed by the more enlightened big business leaders. Fearing that the alternative to the reform of capitalism was its replacement by socialism, the big business–dominated National Civic Federation supported a wide variety of federal regulatory legislation. Although reluctant to go along with big business leadership in the domain of federal regulation, writes Weinstein, the more intelligent small businessmen, organized into the National Association of Manufacturers, also cooperated with reformers by helping to improve the quality of municipal government and services.[5]

Samuel Hays's influential study of municipal reform also emphasizes the role of the elite in the advent of progressivism. "The leading business groups in each city and professional men closely allied with them," he states, "initiated and dominated municipal [reform] movements." These businessmen, lawyers, educators, and doctors despised the city machines and worked for city manager plans and other municipal governmental reforms, not because the machines and the bosses were dishonest or antisocial, but because they were inefficient and expensive, and because they were overly responsive to the needs of the wage earner and lower middle classes. Ultimately, the successes of the municipal reformers shifted political power from working-class and middle-class voters to urban business interests.[6]

To varying degrees, Kolko, Weinstein, and Hays are quite skeptical of claims that progressivism was an honest effort to offset the excesses and abuses of capitalism. Each tends to reduce progressivism to one ingredient, either its business regulatory component or its urban reform element, and each implies that progressivism was a defensive movement, primarily negative in nature, intended to protect the interests of a big business elite under the guise of public-spirited reform. Kolko and Hays also imply that progressives were hypocritical in claiming democratic and egalitarian ends.

A more balanced treatment of the role of business in early twentieth-century reform is that of Robert Wiebe, who quite rightly sees progressivism as more than a one-dimensional effort to regulate business practices or encourage efficiency. It was also, he says, an attempt to increase the respon-

---

[4]See Gabriel Kolko, *The Triumph of Conservatism: A Reinterpretation of American History, 1900–1916* (Chicago: Quadrangle Books, 1967).

[5]James Weinstein, *The Corporate Ideal in the Liberal State, 1900–1918* (Boston: Beacon Press, 1968).

[6]Samuel P. Hays, "The Politics of Reform in Municipal Government in the Progressive Era," *Pacific Northwest Quarterly* (October 1964).

siveness of government to the needs of unorganized citizens' groups and to provide the "dispossessed" with a more fulfilling life in America. Some business elements—shippers, country bankers, businessmen from the South and West—favored certain economic reforms, but others fought reform vigorously. And in any case, little if any of the reform legislation of the progressive era, even measures most closely connected with the business-man's practical concerns, was the product of business pressures alone. Reform measures were usually initiated by consumer groups, politicians, or professional reformers, and businessmen generally could expect merely to modify or to influence the final outcome. Where their interests coincided with an aroused public opinion, they were effective; where they conflicted, they often suffered defeat. Moreover, businessmen were strongly suspicious of politicians and were often ludicrously inept and amateurish in their efforts to manipulate Congress, legislatures, and public officials. Generally they did more harm than good to the causes and positions they supported.

The confusion of voices that characterizes the recent discussion of progressivism has convinced at least one historian, Peter Filene, that there simply was no progressive movement! Filene notes the seemingly endless number of aims and views ascribed to progressives, many of them mutually incompatible, and concludes that the concept of a progressive movement, in the sense of a coherent, self-consistent, collective effort to effect liberal change, "seems very much like a mirage." Filene points to the diversity and irritating inconsistency of the various currents that made up progressivism. He is careful to preserve room for a progressive "era" and acknowledges that certain people could be identified as progressives, but the thrust of his argument rejects progressivism as a valid category of historical discourse.[7]

II

This historiographic babel suggests the complexity of the phenomenon we are dealing with. Filene and the others demonstrate the real difficulty of extracting a simple principle that defined the whole of progressivism, one that created a common bond uniting all those who called themselves progressives.

Part of the difficulty in defining progressivism is its evolving nature. Although it had a central core, it was not a static entity. It appeared first on the state and local level during the 1890s, where it fused ideological, pragmatic, and political elements, most of which dated to the earliest days of the republic. It became a national movement somewhere in the first years

---

[7]Peter Filene, "An Obituary for 'The Progressive Movement,' " *American Quarterly* (Spring 1970).

of the twentieth century when it pulled into its orbit all manner of reformers, mavericks, opportunists, idealists, and malcontents. As time passed, its mass grew and its qualities altered in response to new groups of adherents and to new ideas, goals, and programs that emerged to meet new circumstances. What was true of progressivism in 1900 was no longer entirely true in, say, 1916. Progressivism was a growing movement that was as inconsistent in its "behavior" as any living organism that advances from infancy to maturity to senility. Walter Lippmann recognized this fact in *Drift and Mastery* (1914) when he noted how the focus of exposé journalism that was so vital a part of progressivism had shifted over time from one aspect of corruption and wrongdoing to others.

In part, it is the failure to note this evolutionary process that makes progressivism seem so inchoate and shapeless. Scholars have foreshortened a complex phenomenon and by so doing have distorted it. Their disregard of change over time does much to account for the recent difficulty they have had in explaining the progressive movement.

In spite of its evolutionary pattern, progressivism did maintain a center. At its core it was the early twentieth-century version of a common feeling or mood that had stoked American political movements since the earliest days of the United States. This attitude is best described as a sense of vulnerability—vulnerability to the "vested interests," the power without outside check or responsibility, that seemingly had gained control of the government, the economy, and virtually all public institutions, and had subordinated them to its own selfish needs and advantage.

As a political force among particular groups of people, the sense of vulnerability had roots deep in the American past. Public uneasiness over the power of vested interests can be traced at least as far back as the antimonopoly sentiments of the Jackson era and probably extends even further to the agrarian Antifederalists of the 1790s period who feared and fought the Hamiltonian program. In the 1890s these fears were a prominent feature of the Populist uprising. At that time Populist strength was confined to the hard-rock miners of the Mountain states and the staple crop farmers of the Plains and the deep South. It had been feeble in the East, the older Midwest, the Pacific Coast, and the upper South, as well as in the cities and the towns where both the middle class and the working class rejected its excessive emphasis on monetary nostrums, and educated men were disturbed by its irrational and paranoid side.

Yet if Populism failed to win a following among a majority of Americans, it nevertheless gave eloquent voice to the anger and disquiet of some of them at the loss of self-determination that accompanied the new America emerging at the turn of the century. The United States was a nation increasingly dominated by large economic units. The first big businesses in the nation, as Alfred Chandler has shown, were the railroads, and accordingly, the earliest groups to attack the arbitrary power of vested interests were the farmers and merchants whose dealings with the railroads forced them to confront the dangers of unregulated economic might.

By the 1890s, other businesses had advanced to a stage where, like the railroads, their decisions inevitably affected the lives of millions of ordinary folk. The last decade of the century represents the culmination of a process of national economic consolidation that had been under way since the canal-steamboat era of the 1830–50 period. As the cost of shipping goods declined, local markets evolved into regional markets and then into national markets. For a while this development produced sharper business competition. Companies that formerly enjoyed local monopolies found that they had to compete with other firms that could now penetrate their marketing areas with their goods. Consumers at times benefited from this intensified competition at first. But frequently competition declined. As the more efficient businesses undercut their adversaries, they absorbed their markets and their customers. When the contest among firms in the same line was not settled by the overt victory of one over another, it often led to some sort of merger of interests, whether through such casual arrangements as gentlemen's agreements and pools or by the more formal devices of the trust and the holding company.

Mergers were of two kinds. Vertical mergers united under one management all the sequential operations needed to produce and market a given commodity. The Carnegie Steel Company, which owned iron and coal mines, ore-carrying vessels, a railroad, iron mills, and open-hearth steel furnaces, as well as plants to produce rails, structural steel, and bridges, typified this sort of integration. Horizontal mergers joined many different firms in the same field and the same stage of economic activity. Typical of these was the Distillers Company, formed in 1889 out of eighty competing Midwestern whiskey producers.

The two types of combinations were derived from different impulses. Vertical integration was designed to reduce costs and increase efficiency. Horizontal integration was more frankly an effort to control prices and reduce competition. Yet both had the same effect as far as the consumer was concerned. Both wielded a decisive power over the market that left the public at the mercy of a few giant firms run by aggressive promoters responsible solely to themselves and their stockholders.

Public awareness of the business integration process probably began with Henry D. Lloyd's book *Wealth Against Commonwealth* (1894), which revealed the unscrupulous efforts of John D. Rockefeller's Standard Oil Company to eliminate competition and gain absolute control of American petroleum refining. Five or six years later, the newspapers and the business press carried almost daily reports of new mergers, most of them under the aegis of such large investment banks as J. P. Morgan and Company, Kuhn-Loeb, Kidder-Peabody, or Lee-Higginson.

How effective these combinations actually were in reducing competition in price and quality is not entirely clear. After 1900, as we have seen, consumer prices rose, but this rise applied to all prices, agricultural as well as industrial, and there is no way of knowing whether the business consolidation movement of the period contributed substantially to the result. In fact, some scholars are not certain that a measurable concentration of industry control even took place in this era. But as a historically significant force, the reality here is less important than the belief. By 1900, many Americans were certain that the "high cost of living" was the result of collusion and feared the monopolistic power of the "trusts," as the new combinations were loosely called.[8]

These trusts were now found not only in banking and railroads—combinations that the Populists had earlier attacked—but in almost every area of economic life. By the opening of the new century, the list of supposedly "trustified" businesses had grown to include steel, farm machinery, sugar refining, petroleum, barbed wire, cans, tobacco, copper, and many others. Writing in 1904, the financial expert John Moody enumerated some 318 trusts with an aggregate capital of over $7.2 billion, "covering every line of productive industry in the United States." Whether myth or reality, by the opening years of the new century, few alert Americans doubted that they were at the mercy of giant monopolies as never before.

Business consolidation, or the fear of it, would have created strong anxiety among ordinary Americans under any circumstances. But the public's feeling of vulnerability was enormously enhanced by urbanization. When most Americans lived on farms, their dependence on the goods and services supplied by others was far less than it became when they moved to the towns and cities. Never have American farmers been as isolated and self-sufficient as the old myths would have us believe. Indeed, it was their market orientation that made them so dependent on railroads and banks. But even through the Granger and Populist eras, American farmers generally slaughtered their own hogs and cattle, raised their own fruits and vegetables, and produced their own eggs and milk. In the simpler days of the early nineteenth century, villagers and small town dwellers bought what they consumed from local farmers and butchers, who were usually people they knew and trusted.

In other areas of consumption, too, the average rural or village citizen could either provide for his own needs or purchase commodities and services from suppliers whom he met personally. In the age of the farm and the village, the average American burned wood in his stove, read by candle-

---

[8]Actually a trust was a specific business device whereby stockholders agreed to deposit a controlling portion of their stock with trustees in exchange for trust certificates. The board of trustees then controlled and managed the firm. The trust form was dropped by the 1890s after it came under attack by the courts as violating the rights granted to stockholders under corporation charters.

light or firelight, communicated with friends and associates either by mail or by direct personal contact, traveled to work on foot, and doctored himself with nostrums supplied by his own garden patch or by the village medical practitioner. In each of these cases, he relied on himself or on someone he knew personally.

How different were the circumstances by 1900! By then many Americans were city dwellers, and their relations with the economy at large was as consumers as much as producers. And as consumers they were exposed and unprotected. Much of what urbanites consumed was supplied by some anonymous corporation and came to them in the form of boxed, packaged, and canned products. The change was particularly dramatic in the meat industry. Until the 1890s the meat-packing industry concentrated almost entirely on pickled provisions put up in barrels in such centers as Cincinnati and sold to the poor, to the merchant marine, or—before 1861—to Southern planters to feed their slaves. With the development of the refrigerator car in the late 1870s, the fresh-meat industry began to coalesce in a few key Midwestern cities, especially Chicago, which became the headquarters of giant packing establishments controlled by Gustavus Swift, Nelson Morris, Philip Armour, and others. These firms could supply fresh, chilled beef in vast quantities at moderate cost to thousands of retail butchers in the towns and cities of the nation. The public undoubtedly benefited ultimately from the efficient operations of the great meat-packers, but it also became more dependent on others. Could the packers be trusted? They might set prices where they wished. Controlling the price of meat, the "beef trust" had a stranglehold on the public. They were also in a position to deceive and cheat their customers. Located hundreds of miles from the consumers of their products, armed with all the power and influence of giant corporations, they were not accountable in any serious way to those who consumed what they sold. The old legal principle "let the buyer beware" had protected consumers in the past against the fraudulent practices of producers and sellers, but it no longer made any sense when the offender was located hundreds of miles away and when the only alternative was merely another distant, depersonalized firm that engaged in equally irresponsible practices.

The new marvels of modern science made the city consumer doubly vulnerable to deception. Already modern chemistry was increasing industrial and agricultural output, but it also was being used to defraud: spoiled beef could now be doctored to appear fresh; lard and suet could be turned into imitation butter; cheap vegetables like turnips could be processed and canned as peaches or pears. Most deplorable of all, useless medical concoctions, or harmful ones, were fortified with alcohol or even opium and advertised and sold to the public as remedies for every disease known to man. Harmful or worthless patent medicines were not new in 1900, but never before had they been so widely advertised and dispensed.

Modern technology made urban people vulnerable in other ways, too. By

1900 most American city dwellers used electricity for lighting and gas for cooking. They were also dependent on streetcars, or the "El," to get them to their jobs and enable them to do their errands. Many of them now relied on the telephone for business and social contacts. In a word they were in the same dependent position regarding urban public utilities as farmers had been in relation to the railroads for over a generation. Dependence is an uncomfortable condition that invariably encourages suspicion and hostility. Urban Americans often perceived the power and light companies and the "traction" (streetcar) corporations as arrogant, arbitrary, and corrupt, much as farmers had viewed the railroads in the period 1870–90. Promoters of public utilities and street railways, they believed, extracted generous franchises from city councils and state legislatures by bribery without being required to protect the consumer. The firms they established were poorly run and often set rates that blackmailed the public for an indispensable service.

As the urban proportion of the population grew, more and more Americans came to feel that they were at the mercy of the arbitrary decisions and the antisocial tendencies of men who wielded vast power over their daily lives. This concern affected all classes, except the truly rich, who were always able to protect themselves, and who in many cases were the direct beneficiaries of monopoly power, since they owned the stock, managed the firms, or in other ways were identified with the new business trends. Virtually all other urban citizens—immigrants and the native born, skilled and unskilled labor, the growing white-collar and sales groups, professional people and small businessmen alike—now found themselves, as consumers, in the same predicament as farmers a generation earlier: potential victims of unrestrained private power.

Most exposed of all perhaps were the white-collar people, those whom sociologists have called the new middle class: the salespeople, the junior executives, the engineers and technicians, the bookkeepers, and the schoolteachers who swelled the population of the cities. Their numbers were increasing at a much greater rate than the population as a whole between 1870 and 1910,[9] and they were fast becoming an important element in the population.

---

[9]Hofstadter, borrowing from Lewis Corey, notes that whereas the total population of the United States increased by two and a third times between 1870 and 1910, that of the new middle class expanded by eight times, from about 750,000 to over 8.6 million. By 1910 they formed 63 percent of the whole middle class. See Richard Hofstadter, *The Age of Reform*, pp. 215–16. Stephen Thernstrom's study of Boston between 1880 and 1970 does not confirm this trend for the early twentieth century, but Thernstrom ignores women in his sampling. See Stephen Thernstrom, *The Other Bostonians: Poverty and Progress in the American Metropolis, 1880–1970* (Cambridge, Mass.: Harvard University Press, 1973), table 4.1, p. 50.

These people were urban and therefore vulnerable to the typical urban uncertainties, but in addition, they constantly hovered on the edge of disaster, unlike the older urban middle class of small businessmen and independent professionals. Stephen Thernstrom's study of social mobility in Boston between 1880 and 1970 concludes that "men in the low white-collar jobs [clerks, salesmen, and small proprietors] were in a more vulnerable position than those in the upper stratum and were far more likely to skid."[10] And psychological insecurity reinforced economic insecurity. Recruits largely from blue-collar ranks, these clerks, bookkeepers, and salesmen often suffered the anxieties of the easily declassed. For such people, the power of the trusts seemed especially awe inspiring and frightening, and they would prove particularly susceptible to the progressive appeal.

The city dweller's feeling of vulnerability, in part then, was a response to impersonal forces from outside the urban environment. But the cities produced their own distinct brand of insecurity. Cities were alien places where transplanted rural folk felt lost. Hamlin Garland wrote of Chicago at first sight as "august as well as terrible" and noted how, after his initial glimpse of the metropolis from a train window, he would have returned to his country home if not "for the fear of ridicule." Persons born in the city were seldom so easily intimidated, and with time and experience, the newcomer generally lost some of his anxiety, but even seasoned city dwellers frequently remarked on the frightening vastness of the city and the loneliness and sense of isolation it produced. This condition, for which the French sociologist Emile Durkheim coined the phrase *anomie* in these years, was another powerful force in creating a receptive public for progressive ideas.

Anomie generated grave social pathologies among urbanites. Crime, high suicide rates, broken homes, prostitution, and alcoholism had always been city problems. Now that many more people lived in cities, and these were becoming ever larger, more impersonal places, the difficulties were exacerbated. Whole districts of the bigger cities were occupied by flophouses and sleazy hotels inhabited by single men cut off from family and supportive friends and living mean, squalid lives.

To offset their isolation, urban men and women joined churches, clubs, ethnic societies, political parties, and fraternal orders. For many men the local saloon was not so much a place to get drunk, as temperance reformers believed, as a convivial environment where good fellowship could be found for the price of a glass of beer.

But not all the problems of the city could be solved by voluntary associations and informal social arrangements, and to relieve these difficulties an

---

[10]Thernstrom, *The Other Bostonians*, p. 58.

expanded government role alone would suffice. Well before the twentieth century, urban reformers had turned to the state and local governments for laws against cruelty to animals and children, ordinances to prevent milk adulteration, laws to prevent spitting in public conveyances, and the like. Several of these, most notably those having to do with children and the family, reflected the breakdown in social institutions under the corrosive influence of the big city. All of them reflected the growing recognition by city people that the state had to take on new functions if the cities were to be made into humane and livable places. In effect, the lessons of the urban environment had made many thoughtful city people into pragmatic progressives well before Herbert Croly and the other New Nationalists emerged.

Progressivism, then, cut across class lines and across the ethnic, cultural, and national divisions that had separated the two major parties during the Gilded Age. The Progressive (Bull Moose) party of 1912 was probably more attractive to old-stock, middle-class voters than to working-class, foreign-born or second-generation voters; but the progressive *program*, as opposed to the Progressive *party*, won a sympathetic response from almost all segments of the American population. Irish-American progressives, Polish-American progressives, Jewish-American progressives, or blue-collar progressives may not have supported Theodore Roosevelt on the third party ticket in 1912, but many of them apparently supported Democratic candidate Woodrow Wilson and merely registered their progressivism under a different party label.

Inevitably, then, progressivism not only transcended class and ethnic lines but also muted and blurred the cultural battles that had divided the parties in the past. For over a decade, it replaced "social" politics with "interest" politics and aligned nine-tenths of the American people against the privileged and the powerful. One corner of progressivism, temperance reform (see pp. 122-23), undoubtedly served to maintain the gap between pietists and liturgicals. But temperance reform remained a secondary movement confined, until World War I, largely to the most traditional rural areas and the deep South. Not until the 1920s, with the decline of the feeling of vulnerability that united most Americans before 1916, did it become an important divisive force in American political life.

Meanwhile, in the first years of the twentieth century, the cultural conflicts of the past that had helped define the voting patterns of Americans receded. The American Protective Association reached its crest in 1895 and was dead in all but name by 1900. Until World War I changed the terms of political discourse, most Americans found common ground in a political persuasion that went beyond mere party designations, and those who held back from the new crusade did so, it would seem, for reasons of temperament, traditional party loyalty, or because they feared the dangers of rapid social and political change.

III

One of the puzzles of progressivism is its timing. Ordinarily it is a depression that triggers a reform movement. But the progressive era was a period of prosperity. With only a few brief and shallow dips, times were good after 1900. The first decade of the century saw one of the lowest average unemployment rates since the Civil War, under 4 percent for each of the ten years. The period 1910–17 was not as exemplary, but it was still quite good. Long-term trends were also favorable. Average American incomes were increasing. Real wages rose more than a third from 1890 to 1914, an annual compound rate of 1.3 percent.

But however auspicious the economic balance sheet appears to us, many contemporary Americans, especially those who saw themselves primarily as consumers, were uneasy. Business was good—yes. But prices were high and climbing higher every year. Today we would consider the price advances of the 1900–17 period trivial, but to people of the day, used to the long price slide of the preceding generation, they seemed a serious matter.

But whether the economy was actually flourishing or limping was less important than how it was perceived by Americans. Perception of events in a complex society is seldom based on direct personal observation. A modern nation is too heterogeneous and technically complex in its arrangements and processes to be understood easily by ordinary men and women. Very few citizens see more than their small segment of reality, and even fewer can comprehend the causes for what they perceive or can fathom how to change it. For large masses of people to share a common understanding of the facts of their times, and for them to agree on what must be done to alter these facts, requires that the data be identified, and furthermore, interpreted.

In the progressive period, this function was performed by several different agents. Most influential perhaps was the group of editors, journalists, novelists, and essayists now known as the muckrakers. They were perceptive, educated, literate men and women who carried forward the great American tradition of exposure journalism. Whether motivated by displaced aggression, a desire for notoriety, or an irresistible urge to right wrongs, the muckrakers aimed a dazzling spotlight into every dark corner of American political and social life and revealed much that could not bear close scrutiny.

Today, exposé journalism can use several media outlets. In the early twentieth century, its medium was print. Muckraking books and novels proliferated, and a number of daily newspapers regularly featured exposé articles; but the weekly or monthly magazine provided the major showcase for the muckraking essay.

This situation was made possible by a technical revolution that sharply reduced printing costs to the point where mass circulation magazines could sell for ten or fifteen cents a copy and reach an audience of as many as a million weekly. Exposure journalism already had become an important feature of the urban press toward the end of the nineteenth century as newspapers sought to interpret the big city to the urban newcomers. But most magazines in the 1880s and 1890s remained bland entertainments for the prosperous upper middle class, scarcely penetrating the surface of the readers' minds or emotions. According to the incomparable Mr. Dooley, these genteel publications contained stories of "Angabel an' Alfonso dashin' f'r a marriage license. Prom'nent lady authoresses makin' poems at the moon. Now an' thin a scrap over whether Shakespeare was enthered in his own name or was a ringer, with the long shot players. But no wan hurt. . . ." After 1900 a new print medium appeared based on the city and appealing to a new high school–educated clientele. With larger audiences and larger revenue, the successful magazine publishers were willing to pay good prices for well-written, well-researched articles on controversial, disturbing, or sensational subjects that could capture the interest of the urban reading public.

Beginning with *McClure's* January 1903 issue, a tidal wave of exposure journalism rolled over the nation and helped to transform its self-perception. In that issue three young writers tackled three of the major themes of progressives during the next decade and a half.[11] The lead article, "The Shame of Minneapolis," by Lincoln Steffens, a young, intellectual Californian, probed municipal corruption in the largest Minnesota city. Ida Tarbell's article on the Standard Oil Company examined John D. Rockefeller's efforts to evade the laws against monopoly and to crush business competition. Ray Stannard Baker's contribution dealt with the misdeeds of organized labor and the exploitation of industrial workers by ruthless employers.

S. S. McClure's instinct for profitable journalism was sound if at times disconcerting. He would have paid well, one wag observed, for "a snappy life of Christ." However irreverent, his success with the exposé formula soon encouraged other publishers to copy it. William Randolph Hearst, Frank Munsey, and John Brisben Walker, among others, hired talented writers to investigate and expose wrongdoing in every aspect of American life. What followed was the greatest outpouring of exposé journalism that the country had ever experienced. Besides the work of Steffens, Tarbell, and Baker, there were Samuel Hopkins Adams's articles on the patent medicine business, Thomas Lawson's revelations about the shady doings of the stock

---

[11] Actually, the first muckraking article, "Tweed Days in St. Louis," by Lincoln Steffens and Claude H. Wetmore, was published in the October 1902 *McClure's*. The following month, Ida Tarbell's first installment of "The History of the Standard Oil Company" appeared. But not until January 1903 was the muckraking trend identified by the editors, who suddenly realized that three major articles dealt with the same motif.

market manipulators and the financial tycoons, David Graham Phillips's exposé of the venality of the United States Senate, Upton Sinclair's attacks upon the cruel exploitation of labor and the disgusting and unsanitary conditions in the meat-packing industry, Charles Edward Russell's indictment of the profiteering practices of the beef trust, and scores of others.

Few of the muckraking articles have stood the test of time. Most were ephemeral, as we must expect of journalistic pieces written for popular periodicals. But a more substantial genre of progressive analysis made a permanent contribution to America's stock of ideas. Among the progressive journalists of this era, three—Walter Lippmann, Herbert Croly, and Walter Weyl—made a lasting impression on the American mind. In 1914 all three joined the new liberal journal *The New Republic* as an editorial triumvirate.

By this date, all three were already established as important progressive thinkers. Though their ideas differed in detail, they all emphasized the failure of the older liberalism. Each in his own way rejected the view that the ideal society was one composed of small men and that the proper role of government was primarily to prevent private power from oppressing the individual. Perhaps this Jeffersonian creed had served the nation well when it had been rural and agricultural, but it was of little use when the country became urban and industrial. Americans, unfortunately, had failed to see this fact and through such measures as the 1890 Sherman Antitrust Act had sought unrealistically to break up monopolies and restore an outdated regime of competition and small-scale economic units.

Against the older, outdated liberalism, Croly, Weyl, and Lippmann posed a new liberalism based on strong government. Both Weyl and Croly advocated a philosophy later called New Nationalism in which government would be controlled and restrained by well-defined goals directed toward the general well-being. Government would not merely provide guidelines but also would initiate programs to improve the quality of national life. It would not seek to break up the trusts—that would only restore the inefficiency of the small businesses of the past. It would, instead, guide and direct the big combinations and, if all else failed, take over, manage, and run them. Lippmann, strongly influenced by Freud and by the French philosopher Henri Bergson, seemed at first less concerned with defining the role of government than with power and action for their own sakes. But all three wished to see a powerful state capable of social and economic engineering able to restrain the antisocial forces at large in the nation and also to guide actively the course of national development. Hamiltonian means were to be used for the Jeffersonian ends of a just society that benefited the great mass of the American people.

Undoubtedly the three young critics had identified an important truth. The Jeffersonian ideal of the small producer remained a potent image in the American mind but was fast becoming unrealistic and dated. True, the New Nationalists exaggerated its failings. At the very least, old-fashioned Jeffersonian liberals retained a respect for individual judgment and autonomy and a healthy skepticism of big government. The new critics also overstated the case against their competitors within the progressive fold. The New Freedom Jeffersonians like Woodrow Wilson, William Jennings Bryan, and Louis D. Brandeis who favored dispersed power and the restoration of vigorous competition were not so limited as Lippmann, Croly, and Weyl believed. The young men of *The New Republic* were certain that the neo-Jeffersonians could conceive of no role for government beyond that of the public-spirited policeman who would keep the aggressors and bullies in line. In fact, Wilson would prove remarkably flexible when given the opportunity to formulate policies. Yet the fact remains that *The New Republic* group had identified the limitations of Jeffersonian liberalism: in both old and new versions, it was inadequate to deal with many of the problems of the twentieth century. The New Nationalists, rather than the New Freedomites, were the authentic voice of the future.

Estimating the impact of thoughtful men's ideas is always hard. We know that the muckrakers' sensational revelations stirred Americans already made uneasy by events and situations that they could observe in their daily lives. For a decade or more almost every national magazine, and eventually many newspapers as well, opened their pages to the new exposé journalism, making it difficult for any literate American to be unaware of social injustice, economic dangers, and political corruption. Mr. Dooley, never content, was soon lamenting that when he picked his "fav-rite magazine off th' flure," he found that "iverythin has gone wrong," and "th' wurruld" was "little betther thin a convict's camp. . . ."

Books such as Croly's *The Promise of American Life* (1909), Weyl's *The New Democracy* (1911), and Lippmann's *A Preface to Politics* (1912) unfortunately reached comparatively small audiences. Croly's book went through three editions but sold only some 7,500 copies. The other two works had equally modest sales. All three, however, received a great deal of favorable attention from the reviewers. Most important of all, they were noticed by Theodore Roosevelt, who, as we shall see, was looking for a new sense of purpose and direction. Already committed to bold and active leadership, Roosevelt would find in the New Nationalism the intellectual basis for his dynamic bid in 1912 to regain national leadership.

The polemical writing of the period helped rivet the public's attention as never before on the failings of modern American society. And the work of the journalists and the polemicists was reinforced by the efforts of the reform politicians. A few of these were erstwhile Populists. Following the 1893 panic, some Populists in Wisconsin joined the proto-progressive reform groups that arose to tackle the state's severe economic crisis. In Oregon the Lewelling family and William U'Ren had been Populists in the 1890s, and the latter especially was to be the sparkplug of the state's progressive leadership during the following decade. In Alabama, according to Sheldon Hackney, a small number of Populist leaders made the transition to progressivism.[12] Elsewhere in the South, C. Vann Woodward notes, by the early years of the twentieth century a number of Populists had returned to the Democratic party, bringing with them "their ideological baggage, for which room had to be found."[13] In both the South and the Midwest, progressive reform, particularly as expressed within the Democratic party, would be indebted to former Populists or near-Populist Bryan supporters.

The Populist heritage of progressivism must not be exaggerated, however. By and large progressive leaders had been neither Populists nor Bryanites during the nineties. Indeed many later progressives were avowed enemies of populism. We have noted already William Allen White's scathing attack on Kansas populism and its adherents. Most future Republican progressives —Theodore Roosevelt, Robert La Follette, and Lincoln Steffens, for example—voted for McKinley in 1896, while such later progressive Democrats as Woodrow Wilson, John Johnson of Minnesota, and Hoke Smith of Georgia were conservative gold Democrats in the 1890s. If the progressive leaders were reformers of any sort before 1900, it was usually of the genteel, mugwump variety that did not see beyond honest civil service, sound money, and free trade as the limits of reform.

Yet sometime between 1896 and 1905, young men such as these became influential propagandists for the Populist view that the world was out of joint and that the root of the difficulty was the failure to curb irresponsible economic and political power. There can be no doubt that the charisma and eloquence of men such as U'Ren, La Follette, Wilson, and especially Roosevelt reinforced the writings of the muckrakers. Wherever their ideas came from—and they borrowed heavily from populism, the exposé journalists, and the writings of progressive thinkers like Dewey, Holmes, the social gospel ministers, Lippmann, Brandeis, Croly, Weyl, and others—whatever the source of their views, they turned the state houses, the mayors' offices, the United States Senate, and the White House into immensely influential forums for the progressive diagnosis and the progressive remedy for the nation's ills.

No politician was a more effective propagandist for the progressive outlook than Theodore Roosevelt. During his first term as president, Roosevelt was willing to go along with Ohio boss Mark Hanna and the Republican regulars and was often impatient with the exposé journalists. Annoyed at

---

[12]Hackney notes, however, that the Alabama Populists and the Alabama progressives were not related as parent to child. In that Southern state, he shows, the progressives evolved out of the antirailroad, anticorruption wing of the Democrats during the 1890s, the same period when the Populists were flourishing as a parallel group in the state. See Sheldon Hackney, *Populism to Progressivism in Alabama* (Princeton, N.J.: Princeton University Press, 1969), pp. 116, 122 ff.

[13]C. Vann Woodward, *Origins of the New South, 1877–1913* (Baton Rouge: Louisiana State University Press, 1951), p. 372.

what he believed to be their excessive carping and naysaying, it was he who called the new breed of writers muckrakers, after the morose John Bunyan character who "continued to rake to himself the filth of the floor" even when offered a "celestial crown."

Nevertheless, Roosevelt was to become an extraordinary advertisement for progressivism. His dramatic flair, his colorful phrase making, his gusto and sense of fun, his impetuous activism, his kindliness and broad social sympathies, even his remarkable inconsistencies, made him the most delightful and endearing figure to the American people since Lincoln. Disdainful of "malefactors of great wealth," as befitted the scion of a distinguished, old, civic-conscious family, Roosevelt was also a man of emphatic deeds, characterized by William Allen White as "pure act." As president this combination of noblesse oblige and activism pushed him inevitably in the direction of progressivism. Not until 1910 did Roosevelt attempt to define a coherent progressive ideology, but during his years as chief executive, an office he considered a "bully pulpit," he made the national government in general and the presidency in particular into a positive, countervailing force against irresponsible and overweening private power. By the time he left office in 1909, the public had come to associate progressivism with one of the most charismatic political figures of the century.

And Roosevelt was scarcely an isolated case. Political progressivism was generally well served by its leaders. In the Midwest the eloquent, impassioned "Fighting Bob" La Follette came to the United States Senate in 1906 after three terms as Wisconsin governor during which he had enacted a legislative program of progressive tax reform, utility regulation, a direct primary, resource conservation, and banking regulation that became the model for other states. Also from the Midwest was Indiana's handsome, square-jawed Albert J. Beveridge, a young man who combined the progressive animus to vested interests with a rabid expansionism not unique among progressive politicians. In the Far West, Hiram Johnson of California and William U'Ren of Oregon helped to make their states into social laboratories of direct democracy, social reform, and big business regulation. In the East the decade produced progressive governors like Charles Evans Hughes of New York and Woodrow Wilson of New Jersey. Even in Southern state houses in these years men of progressive temperament brought the reform message to the public. In the mayors' offices, Samuel M. ("Golden Rule") Jones and Brand Whitlock of Toledo, Tom Johnson of Cleveland, Seth Low and John P. Mitchell of New York, and Joseph Folk of St. Louis instituted progressive reforms. Since so many of the public's anxieties revolved around consumer and household concerns, the mayors, close to citizens' daily concerns, were unusually successful in dramatizing and popularizing the progressive vision and the progressive program.

IV

Progressivism first emerged as a distinct political mode on the state and local level. In the cities, municipal reform movements go back at least to the 1870s when George Jones of the *New York Times*, corporation attorney Samuel J. Tilden, and cartoonist Thomas Nast together helped to destroy the Tweed Ring and jail its leader, William Marcy Tweed. Other cities also boasted clean government coalitions in the Gilded Age.

These were alliances of what Richard Wade has called "structural reformers." They were concerned predominantly with honesty and economy in administering city finance, and their impetus often came from business and taxpayer groups who were outraged as much by the extravagance as by the knavery of boss-ridden city machines. Generally they were ineffectual in defeating the machines. The bosses usually could count on immigrant and working-class voters to support them because they dispensed jobs, money, and other favors and respected the customs and national sensibilities of these clients. When the machine became too corrupt or so arrogant that it took the voters for granted, the reformers sometimes were carried into office on a tidal wave of public indignation. Typically, however, the reform regime's obsession with economy and the exact enforcement of the local blue law ordinances against Sunday amusements, saloons, and the like soon disillusioned the city electorate. After one term the reform mayor and his friends were usually swept out of office and the machines restored.

This discouraging pattern was broken first by the proto-progressive reformers of the 1890s. In cities as widely diverse as Detroit, Toledo, Milwaukee, and New York, reform movements arose, often under some magnetic leader who offered reform "with a heart." In Detroit Hazen Pingree attacked the street railway monopoly for its high fares and its reactionary labor policies. A rich, self-made shoe manufacturer of Yankee Protestant background, Pingree rode into office as reform mayor of polyglot, predominantly Catholic Detroit in 1890, following the indictment of several Democratic aldermen for taking bribes. At first Pingree differed from the traditional reformers in style more than in program. His first platform was the structural reformers' typical one of strict economy and cutting the "extravagant rate of taxation." But at the same time, he avoided the usual "goo-goo" (good government) attacks on the voters' cultural preferences and launched his first campaign by a round of drinks with the boys at "Baltimore Red's" saloon.

With time, however, Pingree learned that more was required of the job than accommodating the Detroit voters' lifestyles. To retain his political hold, he recognized that he also had to acknowledge their economic needs. During the city's street railway strike of 1891, the mayor sided with the strikers and attacked the traction company's labor policies. During the hard years following 1893, he initiated a much-publicized "potato-patch plan" by which the city donated vacant lots to needy families so that they could help support themselves by raising vegetables. He also tried to shift some of the city's tax burden from consumers to the corporations that did business within the city.

Toledo's equivalent of Pingree was Samuel "Golden Rule" Jones. In Toledo, Jones began a program of municipal utility ownership, initiated popular referendums on the extension of city franchises, and launched a major expansion of the city's system of parks, playgrounds, and municipal baths. Like Pingree, he refused to go along with the conventional middle-class reformer prejudice against working-class customs and amusements or, for that matter, vices. Mayor Jones rejected demands that he close the saloons and refused to put drunks in jail. When local ministers asked him to drive prostitutes out of the city, he asked pointedly, "to where?"

Social justice reform at the municipal level was a catalyst for the progressive movement, particularly during the 1890s when it was joined with the need to relieve the consuming public of the burdens of hard times. In Wisconsin the Milwaukee Municipal League and other reform groups, galvanized by the growing power and arrogance of the street railway and gas and electric companies, began the shift to progressivism when they made municipal control of utilities their major reform issue. Until the panic and depression of the 1890s, municipal reformers in Wisconsin, David Thelen notes, had been of the usual good-government, mugwump type, intent on enforcing virtue not only on the bosses but also on Catholics, working men, foreigners, and the "dangerous classes." Hard times encouraged the utilities to consolidate and led them to defy the demands of mayors and consumers. Outraged by the arrogance of the state's utilities magnates, who raised rates and refused to pay their taxes, the urban reformers abandoned their traditional good-government attitudes, formed alliances with farmers' groups and working-class people, and began a concerted attack on privilege that in the next decade helped make Wisconsin the banner progressive state.[14]

During the progressive period, one aspect of the urban reform movement —the drive for efficiency in municipal government—continued to fit Wade's structural formula more closely than the new pattern of reform with a heart. A number of scholars, in fact, have considered it the characteristic mode of urban progressivism. Hays, for one, reduces early twentieth-century urban reform to a handful of schemes to professionalize and improve the efficiency of urban government and urban services through city-manager and commission systems, the net effect of which was to take power out

---

[14]See David Thelen, *The New Citizenship: Origins of Progressivism in Wisconsin, 1885–1900* (Columbia, Mo.: University of Missouri Press, 1972).

of the hands of wage earners and the lower middle class and give it to the rich and influential.[15]

At the very least, Hays stretches his thesis. Such urban political reforms as proportional representation, for example, often enabled prolabor minority parties like the Socialists to win a place on city councils. But even if Hays is generally right, his hypothesis describes at most only a small part of the urban reform movement. Far more important than urban constitutional change was the liberalizing and humanizing of civic functions.

This side of reform is well illustrated by the case of Cincinnati, a city that in the last years of the nineteenth century experienced all the crime, vice, and social disorder that invariably came with rapid change and physical expansion. Cincinnatians were not willing to suffer these afflictions quietly. They responded in the 1890s by supporting an honest and efficient political machine under the leadership of Boss George B. Cox, a Republican who pleased both the businessmen and the more stable working-class elements by bringing honesty, order, and efficiency to Cincinnati's government. His actions confound both the standard reformer picture of the corrupt city machine and Hays's view that municipal efficiency was provided at the expense of the urban working class.

Developments of the next decade in Cincinnati also refute Hays's thesis, as the "Queen City" witnessed an extraordinary efflorescence of progressive class cooperation. During these years organizations such as the Chamber of Commerce, the Cincinnati Woman's Club, and the Central Labor Council brought together men and women from both the rich "Hilltop," outer city wards and the working-class–lower-class, "Circle-Zone," inner city districts for various causes ranging from sewer extension to new parks and playgrounds, civil service reform, better housing and improved schooling for the poor, pure food legislation, and the initiative, referendum and recall.

Especially effective among the new civic forces in Cincinnati were women. No longer typified by the "ringleted damsel of wasp-like waist, simpering voice and satin slippered feet, . . ." the new Cincinnati woman belonged to a "noble army of broad-minded women [who realized] that they too, are responsible for gang rule, graft, greed, child labor, pauperism and prostitution."[16] The women reformers of Cincinnati were mostly Protestant middle-class ladies, but they also included Catholic and Jewish women and representatives from the working-class zone. Joined together, they became the formidable political force that served as the city's conscience, pushing the politicians further than they might otherwise have gone. Frequently ahead of the men, the women, it was said, gave their laggard husbands no

---

[15]Hays, "The Politics of Reform," p. 162.
[16]The words were those of Mary C. Gallagher of the Cincinnati Woman's Club.

respite in their homes and contributed disproportionately to the reforms undertaken by Cincinnati's civic and political leaders.

V

The reform with a heart that emerged during the 1890s on the level of state and municipal government was supported by a profuse undergrowth of voluntary organizations led by compassionate and dedicated men and women. Reformers during the progressive era were a very mixed group with very mixed motives and goals. One common type consisted of well-educated young men and women who were dissatisfied with the social and moral limitations of their middle-class lives and sought to find meaning in serving the urban poor. Hundreds of such idealistic young people became volunteer charity workers or took up the new professional calling of social worker.

Many of these young people came to live and work in the new settlement houses in the slum districts. The settlement house movement in the United States was inspired by Toynbee Hall and similar English ventures initiated in the nineteenth century by such English Christian Socialists as John Ruskin and Charles Kingsley. Beginning with the Neighborhood Guild on New York's lower East Side and Hull House in Chicago in the late 1880s, settlements established by young college-trained women just out of school began to spring up in the major cities. These were places where slum children could go for recreation and entertainment; where slum mothers could learn about nutrition, child care, and household management; where slum fathers could learn skills, improve their English, or meet with other men to discuss city politics and neighborhood problems. The settlement was also a place where middle-class reformers could learn what bothered the poor and what could be done to improve their lot. Unlike the earlier charity workers who were generally distant, olympian figures who dispensed money to the "deserving poor," the settlement workers believed in a reciprocal relationship between the poor and the middle class and used their knowledge of slum conditions to formulate reform legislation and policies that would produce concrete benefits for the underprivileged.

Such settlement workers as Jane Addams of Hull House, Lillian Wald of New York's Henry Street Settlement, Vida Scudder of Boston's Denison House, Robert Woods, Mary Simkhovitch, Robert Hunter, Florence Kelley, and William English Walling fought for workmen's compensation, consumer protection, child labor laws, clean government, tenement regulation, equal opportunity for blacks and immigrants, and improved recreational and educational opportunities for the urban poor. A few settlement workers became active Socialists who tried to alter fundamentally the relations between capital and labor.

The views of the settlement leaders epitomizes the "advanced" progressivism, or "social justice" progressivism, that belies the skepticism of Kolko,

Hays, and Weinstein. The advanced progressives essentially believed in what we today would call the welfare state. The government at every level, they contended, must step in to protect the weak against the strong and must seek to reduce the hazards and uncertainties of life for the average citizen. This required a wide spectrum of protective legislation. Progressives like Lawrence Veiler, Jane Addams, and Jacob Riis sponsored city and state laws to set minimum housing standards for the city's working class. Progressives believed that better housing was not only a humane reform in itself but that it penetrated to the root of the poverty problem in America. As Florence Kelley regretfully observed, "instead of assenting to the belief that people who are poor must be crowded, why did we not see years ago that people who are crowded must remain poor?" Although they did not succeed in tearing down and rebuilding the existing decrepit city neighborhoods, the progressives bequeathed to twentieth-century liberalism a yen for slum clearance and tenement reform that would profoundly affect the city environment a generation later.

Advanced progressives were also effective in publicizing the evils of child labor and the wretched conditions under which many women worked in factories and tenements and in getting the state to intervene to protect these vulnerable groups. Florence Kelley was a whirlwind here, too, and it was she more than any other progressive reformer who mobilized and organized sentiment against child labor. As Illinois factory inspector under Governor John Altgeld, Kelley tried to enforce an imperfect pioneer child labor measure and then, in cooperation with the Hull House social workers, got the Illinois legislature to pass a better bill in 1903. Progressives actively supported the Women's Trade Union League, a group dedicated to improving working conditions for female wage earners, and lobbied in state legislatures and Congress for laws to set maximum working hours for women, end night work, and forbid work under dangerous or unhealthy conditions. Between 1909 and 1917, some nineteen states and the District of Columbia enacted measures of this sort.

The progressives concentrated on protecting working women and children because they seemed the most exploited and the most defenseless, but they also tried to help male wage earners. Unfortunately this proved more difficult. Part of the problem was the skeptical attitude of that portion of organized labor, influenced by Gompers, who emphasized "voluntarism," or the reliance on the standard trade union weapons of strikes, boycotts, and collective bargaining to improve labor's lot. Contributing to the problem was the attitude of conservative Americans who were sympathetic to efforts to protect working women and children, traditionally deserving of public solicitude, but who held that for adult male workers the laws of supply and demand must prevail. This conservative attitude not only hampered social legislation in the state capitals but also was used by the state and federal courts to strike down a number of laws protecting male workers. The most notable instance of the reactionary role of the judicial branch was the decision of the federal Supreme Court in *Lochner v. New York* (1905) declaring unconstitutional a New York law to limit the working hours of bakers on the grounds that the law exceeded New York's police powers.

Nevertheless, the progressives did succeed, primarily under the police power rubric, in enacting legislation in a number of states to regulate working conditions for male employees. These laws emphasized hours limitations and essentially applied to workers engaged in dangerous trades, such as mining and construction work. A number of states also passed minimum wage laws.

More important were the laws enacted during the progressive era to compensate wage earners for injuries sustained while at work. Until the progressive period, the common law principles applying to injury on the job required that the workman must prove the direct fault of the employer in order for him to collect compensation. This could be done only in a court of law, where the employer could escape liability if he could show that the negligence was that of either the worker himself or his "fellow servant." Given the unequal power of employer and employee, and given the substantial costs of a lawsuit, this meant that few, if any, wage earners or their families could make recovery for death or injury.

A few employers, especially the larger ones, supported changes in the law in order to eliminate the element of risk to themselves in suits for compensation. Most small- and middle-sized businessmen opposed it, however, and fought the reformers and union leaders who favored some system of compulsory insurance to cover employee injury and death regardless of who was to blame. By the end of the progressive era, in spite of the opposition of employers, the concept of workmen's compensation—a form of no-fault insurance—had been accepted widely in the industrial states owing to the effective lobbying of labor leaders and the social justice progressives.

The welfare program of the advanced progressives was designed so that ordinary citizens might recapture some control over their environment and their lives. For obvious reasons it received the support of working-class members of the various social reform organizations. These people hoped to use the state to protect themselves against exploitation and mistreatment by others. For the many middle-class social reformers, however, workmen's compensation, child labor laws, tenement legislation, and the other welfare measures had little direct personal relevance. Yet their motives also can be related to the fear of irresponsible power that was at the heart of progressivism. When middle-class people contemplated the changes that had been taking place in American life during the last years of the nineteenth century, they were as much dismayed and frightened as working-class Americans were. No longer would their modest achievements and successes protect them against the massed power of giant corporations and concentrated wealth.

If middle-class reformers had spent all their time fighting the trusts and demanding pure food and drug regulation, it would be easy enough to understand what they were about. But how do we explain their efforts on behalf of the poor? No doubt the position of the poor was even worse than the situation of the dedicated, young college graduates who came to the settlements. But pure and simple social empathy is a rare commodity, vouchsafed to saints and a few philosophers in each generation. None of the reformers was a saint and few were philosophers. Something else was clearly at work.

Far more common than pure empathy across class lines is a social identification that comes from the sense of a common fate. Such a sense united the middle-class reformers with the urban poor. Many of them, as we have seen, were exiles from the nation's villages and small towns and poignantly experienced a sense of rootlessness and loss in the impersonal urban world. Such men and women found it easy to understand at least a part of what the poor felt when faced with the cruelty and abrasiveness of twentieth-century urban life.

If the identification had not existed, if the middle class had blamed the poor for their unease and disquiet, if socialism or anarchy had seemed to be the greater danger to society than the poor, then perhaps the country might have undergone a wave of reaction. In Germany and Italy in the twentieth century, the middle-class response to these fears resulted politically in fascism. On occasion progressive businessmen raised the specter of socialism as the only alternative to reform, but few middle-class reformers took the threat seriously. Indeed many of them were sympathetic to socialism and a substantial number of the most active advanced progressives were avowed Socialists.

The point here is that the danger was perceived as coming from the plutocrats, not the radicals, a response that foreclosed middle-class reaction. Under the circumstances yet another characteristic of an uneasy or beseiged middle group, especially one imbued with the traditional American ethic of social justice, could come into play: social guilt. The consciences of many middle-class doctors, lawyers, teachers, and small businessmen in this age of giant monopolies troubled them deeply when they contemplated the miners, the factory workers, and the day laborers who bore the brunt of industrialism. Middle-class settlement workers who came to Hull House or the Henry Street Settlement to live among urban slum dwellers were not only re-creating a sense of community, but also, like the Russian *Narodniki* of the nineteenth century who left comfortable homes and careers to live among the peasantry, they were assuaging the persistent pangs of class guilt.

This guilt seems to have been particularly acute among educated middle-class women. If some of the new women of the period 1900–17 seemed frivolous and self-indulgent, others were earnest, public-spirited, and socially sensitive. Blessed with superior educations that seemed to equip them for nothing very useful, many responded to poverty like Jane Addams, who, as a tourist in Britain during her twenties, was shocked by what she encountered in London's East End. The sight of "heavy-laden market women and underpaid street labourers," she later wrote, "tormented" her "with a sense of her uselessness." Jane Addams could do little about the London poor, but she never forgot the experience and spent much of her subsequent life putting her talents and education to good use in the service of her own country's underprivileged.

During these years thousands of middle-class women were brought into the reform movement through various women's clubs. These often started out as purely social or literary organizations that housewives joined to while away time, amuse themselves, or acquire a little culture. By the early part of the new century, however, the clubs began to exhibit a new spirit. As the president-elect of the General Federation of Women's Clubs noted in 1904, the federation's members were abandoning the study of Dante's *Inferno* and the like and were beginning to "proceed in earnest to contemplate our own social order."

By 1914 the General Federation with over a million members was only one of a number of women's organizations dedicated to reform. Another was the National Consumers' League, led by a group of alert, well-educated women, including Josephine Shaw Lowell, Maud Nathan, Josephine Goldmark, Frances Perkins (the future New Deal secretary of labor), and the ubiquitous Florence Kelley. The league initiated a White List campaign and a White Label campaign to improve the labor policies of employers in retail trade and manufacturing, respectively. Employers who adhered to fair labor practices were, in the case of the retail businessmen, advertised by the league in its official list; the manufacturers who were judged generous towards their employees were allowed to affix the league's white label to their products.

One important women's reform organization with somewhat ambiguous progressive credentials was the Women's Christian Temperance Union. The WCTU, founded in 1874, was a late flowering of the antebellum zeal for uplift and public morality. By the progressive era, in alliance with the predominantly male Anti-Saloon League, it not only propagandized actively in the schools and churches against alcohol but also lobbied for statewide and federal laws prohibiting the consumption, production, and sale of alcoholic beverages.

Both the WCTU and the Anti-Saloon League had a generous, reformist side and a puritanical, coercive side. Unquestionably alcohol consumption was a problem in the United States. Alcoholism and drunkenness were common afflictions, especially among the poor. Many men working the long, exhausting hours of the mines and factories of the day sought release in the camaraderie of the saloon and the warm glow produced by alcohol.

Often this got out of hand. Conviviality turned into chronic drunkenness, the inability to hold a job, and sudden rages against family and friends. Temperance advocates were by no means wrong when they depicted alcoholism as a major social problem, especially among the urban working class.

On the other hand, temperance reformers refused to recognize that drinking did not always, or even usually, lead to family disruption, poverty, and crimes of rage and passion. In many of the ethnic enclaves in the cities, wine, beer, and whiskey were a part of ordinary diet and conventional social life and were closely interwoven with the texture and rituals of daily existence. To deprive these people of the right to drink was to impose the values of one community on another. Temperance advocates at times failed to understand the implications of their demands; often they simply did not care. This indifference makes the temperance movement, and still more its prohibitionist wing, seem not so much a generous reform urge as a deliberate cultural assault by old-stock Protestant Americans on the newer, predominantly Catholic population of the cities.

Nevertheless, temperance advocates were frequently active reformers. The WCTU under Frances Willard fought for child labor laws and other progressive legislation. At her death in 1898, Willard's reform work was taken up by Anna Shaw, a formidable woman who was both a doctor and a licensed Methodist preacher. Both Willard and Shaw were effective propagandists for women's suffrage, arguing that giving women the vote would not only give half the American people their just political due but also would strengthen immensely social justice causes. Women, they argued, would not stand for the amoral, pragmatic politics to which men acquiesced. They would favor social legislation, especially as it affected children, the family, and community morals, and in international affairs they would be a strong force for world peace.

Not all suffragists were temperance advocates; nor were all temperance advocates suffragists. In the South especially, the WCTU was conservative politically. Elsewhere many ardent women's rights advocates were indifferent to the liquor question. Generally the suffragists were committed reformers who not only fought for the enfranchisement of their sex but also filled the ranks of organizations fighting for child labor laws, better treatment of working women, and a wide array of general political reforms. The membership and leadership of the National American Woman Suffrage Association largely overlapped the membership and leadership of such groups as the Women's Trade Union League, the National Consumers' League, and other progressive groups where women were the predominant voice. Women suffrage leaders were reluctant to identify themselves too closely with a particular political party. But in 1912 many found the new Progressive party irresistible because it endorsed voting rights for women and reformist goals simultaneously. As Jane Addams told a group of women who questioned the wisdom of suffragists playing party politics: "When a great party pledges itself to the protection of children, to the care of the aged, to the relief of overworked girls, to the safe-guarding of burdened men, it is inevitable that it should appeal to women and seek to draw upon the great reservoir of moral energy so long undesired and unutilized in practical politics."

The claim that women voters would be an effective voice for reform causes was only a part of the battle to induce liberal male Americans to grant women full civil rights. Middle-class women reformers demanded the vote as a valid end in itself. The disfranchisement of women was an injustice that deserved the same treatment as labor exploitation, decrepit housing, inequalities of wealth and power, and municipal corruption. Women, they held, always had been second-class citizens, and yet they were informed, intelligent adults who increasingly performed the work of the nation and were acquiring a vital place in the professions and business. On what grounds except those of gross prejudice and blindness to modern realities could they be deprived of full participation in the country's political life?

The progressives did not invent the women's suffrage movement. By 1900 the demand for full political equality for women was already half a century old. It had begun in 1848 with the "Declaration of Sentiments," drawn up by Elizabeth Cady Stanton, Lucretia Mott, and others, to protest women's inferiority. In 1890 it became a full-fledged crusade when two rival women's organizations merged into the National American Woman Suffrage Association. The merger infused new life into the drive for women's voting rights. Although the association's presidents during its first few years were the veterans Elizabeth Cady Stanton and Susan B. Anthony, a new group of younger women soon took charge of the suffrage fight. Less radical ideologically, they were more militant tactically, and under their direction women all over the country persuaded, paraded, picketed, and protested, some of them adopting the disruption strategy of Alice Paul, a vigorous and often truculent militant who had learned to admire the aggressive tactics of the Pankhurst sisters in England.

In the battle for the vote, women allied themselves with any male who would extend support. After 1900 these were found largely in the progressive ranks. Both Roosevelt and Wilson eventually supported women's suffrage. Earlier and even more sympathetic were Robert La Follette, Louis Brandeis, Gifford Pinchot, William Allen White, and Herbert Croly. In the state capitals, many lesser progressives were willing to cooperate with women's groups to secure suffrage rights. Early suffrage victories on the state level came in Wyoming in 1890, Colorado in 1893, Idaho and Utah in 1896, followed by Washington and California in 1910–11. In the older states of the South and Northeast, there was greater resistance to change. But in 1913 Illinois adopted women's suffrage, and in 1917 the crucial state of New York finally granted the vote to women. By this time the fight to secure federal action was all but won. In 1919 Congress passed an amendment forbidding the denial of suffrage on the grounds of sex, and on August 26, 1920, the Nineteenth Amendment became part of the federal Constitution when Tennessee became the thirty-sixth state to ratify it.

Another reform of the progressive era that involved women both as "part of the problem" and "part of the solution" was the crusade against organized prostitution. Curiously historians have failed to give the early twentieth-century movement to destroy the "white slave traffic" the attention it deserves. One is tempted to blame the reticence on some misplaced academic delicacy. Yet the reformers themselves, many of them middle-class women and Protestant ministers, showed no such prudery. From 1907 onward, Americans were subject to a barrage of exposé articles, some catering to readers' prurient interests, others sincerely concerned, that described how immigrant and farm girls were recruited for big city brothels and how they were mistreated and cruelly exploited by pimps and madams.

The campaign against white slavery managed to combine every element of progressive reform. It provided an opportunity to attack selfish vested interests: the pimps and madams who induced young women into a life of vice were as intent on profit and crass gain as J. P. Morgan or John D. Rockefeller. It provided the reformers with the opportunity to denounce inequalities of wealth: poverty, reformers noted, was "the principal cause, direct and indirect of prostitution. . . ." It gave the reformers the excuse to denounce waste and inefficiency: if men "could compute the human values daily destroyed by this vice," they would "face the greatest of all losses to the sum-total of the world's resources. . . ." Finally, prostitution provided women's rights advocates with still another compelling argument for women's suffrage. As Jane Addams wrote, an "energetic attempt to abolish white slavery will bring many women into the Equal Suffrage movement simply because they too will discover that without the use of the ballot they are unable to work effectively for the eradication of a social wrong."

The attack on the white slave traffic, like most progressive crusades, had mixed results. In February 1907 Congress passed an immigration act forbidding the importation of alien women and girls for immoral purposes and providing for the deportation of foreign women who became prostitutes after they came to this country. But the vice reformers were not only concerned with the vice traffic in foreign women; they also sought to prevent American girls and women from being lured into the cities to be forced into a life of sin. Their efforts culminated in the passage of the Mann Act in 1910, which prohibited the transportation of women into the United States or across state lines for immoral purposes. Neither of these two measures, unfortunately, ended vice traffic, and the Mann Act was used at times to blackmail indiscreet husbands; however, both acts represented a sincere effort by humanitarians to use federal authority to prevent exploitation of the weak and powerless.

The progressives' concern for the downtrodden was feeblest in the area of race and nationality. Progressives like the economist Richard Ely, Albert Beveridge, and Roosevelt were often unselfconscious bigots who accepted explicitly the superiority of the white race and especially its north European branch. Many were frankly skeptical of the new immigrant groups from southern and eastern Europe. Southern progressives were unrelenting on the color line, no matter how strongly they endorsed lower tariffs, presidential primaries, and public utility and railroad regulation. Although lynching was declining in the nation as a whole, in the South, during the progressive years, it remained a brutal weapon wielded to keep blacks in their place.

But not even blacks were deprived entirely of the benefits of progressivism. Many of the urban reformers and the settlement workers were sensitive to the problems of the urban black population. Frances Kellor of New York's College Settlement helped form the National League for the Protection of Negro Women after she discovered how black farm girls, like white rural girls and foreign-born women, often were lured to the cities by promises of good jobs only to be exploited by employers or, worse, forced into prostitution. Another white social worker, Mary White Ovington, attempted to establish a settlement in San Juan Hill, a New York Negro slum, but eventually concluded that what was really needed was a national attack on racial injustice and devoted the rest of her life to helping blacks improve their condition. Blacks even benefited from the exposé journalism of the day. Among the most effective muckraking documents of the progressive era was Ray Stannard Baker's *Following the Color Line,* an incisive and remarkably fair treatment of the race problem in the United States; it appealed to Americans to forget the color of a man's skin and only regard his skills, intelligence, and character.

A more important instrument of racial reform than the solicitude of white progressives for the black man was the work of a new group of militant leaders within the black community itself. Until about 1900 the mantle of black leadership had been worn by Booker T. Washington, the author of the Atlanta Compromise, a pragmatic acquiescence of the black community in social and political inferiority in exchange for economic opportunity. First proposed by Washington at the Atlanta Cotton States and International Exposition in 1895, the compromise promised both the white South and northern industrial leaders that blacks would forego their rights as citizens under the Reconstruction amendments and all expectations of a desegregated social system. They would ask only that they be given an opportunity to employ their skills without discrimination and be allowed to progress as far as these skills permitted. Consistent with this philosophy, Washington promoted vocational training for blacks at Tuskegee and urged them to adopt the middle-class work ethic and the habits of sobriety, cleanliness, and frugality that he and white employers held essential for an obedient and successful work force. He also warned fellow blacks against labor unions and labor agitators, who could only hurt their chances for good jobs and expanded economic opportunity.

Washington's opponents, both then and more recently, have attacked the Atlanta Compromise as a surrender of the basic human rights of blacks for a problematical and dubious advantage that in the end the white community refused to confer. Blacks were never accepted as equals in the economic sphere, Washington's critics have pointed out, no matter what their qualifications; meanwhile, during these years the noose of local segregation and statutory inferiority was rapidly tightened around their necks. As for the vocational training that Washington endorsed, it was meaningless. It prepared blacks to occupy only the lowest rungs of the economic ladder or trained them for trades that were fast being made obsolete by machines.

Actually, some of the criticism of Washington was, and is, unfair. No doubt he was flattered easily by white praise and was too quick to mistake crumbs for the main course. Yet his was a difficult role to play. During the years of his preeminence, racism had become rampant in the country as the idealism of the Reconstruction era receded. In state after state in the South, white supremacists erected walls of legal segregation around successive spheres of daily life. They divided everything from schools to parks, cemeteries, trains, and comfort stations into a superior white and an inferior black facility and closed off trades and occupations formerly open to blacks. Through use of the poll tax and the all-white primary, the white South obliterated the last vestiges of black political influence by 1900. At the same time, it made lynching a weapon of terror to keep blacks frightened and acquiescent. In 1915 Southern white supremacists revived the Ku Klux Klan as an instrument for protecting white Anglo-Saxon America from aliens and blacks.

What could any black leader hope to do against this rising tide of racism and repression? Washington tried to fight the trends of the day. He struggled to contain the white supremacists' campaign to eliminate the last vestiges of the black franchise in the South and contributed money to groups testing state disfranchisement laws in the federal courts. He also fought to prevent the exclusion of racial liberalism from the Republican party in the South. Washington was careful to conceal his efforts for a fairer racial regime. These took place behind the scenes, while in public he sought to calm Southern white fears of black assertiveness. It may well be that his covert efforts helped to prevent an even greater erosion of the black position than actually took place.

But however valid or unavoidable Washington's tactics were, by the beginning of the new century a new generation of black leaders began to challenge his leadership. Unlike Washington they were mostly Northern born and college educated. Men like William Monroe Trotter, J. Milton Waldron, and especially W. E. B. DuBois accused Washington of surrendering fundamental Negro rights and of consenting to permanent second-class citizenship for blacks. In 1905 DuBois convened a meeting of "anti-Booker-ites" at Fort Erie, near Niagara Falls, to raise a radical voice against the Washington acquiescence. The group issued a manifesto that endorsed all types of education for blacks, including college training, and insisted that blacks must fight against every form of discrimination, including the abridgement of their civil and political rights. "The Negro-American," the document stated, must not give the impression that he "assents to inferiori-ty, is submissive under oppression and apologetic before insult."

The Niagara movement attracted the attention of the small group of white progressives who were distressed with the treatment accorded blacks. In 1910 most of the Niagara movement leaders and such white progressives as Mary Ovington, Oswald Garrison Villard, Jane Addams, Lillian Wald, Franz Boas, and Clarence Darrow joined to form the National Association for the Advancement of Colored People (NAACP), with DuBois as editor of its journal, *The Crisis.* By the time Washington died in 1915, the NAACP and its policy of defending the legal and constitutional rights of blacks wherever they were threatened had superseded acquiescence as the predominant tactic of black leadership.

VI

On January 1, 1900, however, much of the progressive mood was still a local phenomenon. In Wisconsin the new governor, Robert La Follette, was just beginning to make his state into a national showplace for progressive ideas. In California Hiram Johnson was still working for the family law firm in Sacramento, though his differences with his conservative father were about to drive him into establishing his own practice in San Francisco. Albert Beveridge, a young man from Indiana, had just taken his seat in the United States Senate, where his second major address was a defense of trusts! Lincoln Steffens was already a member of *McClure's* staff, but he had not yet written his "Tweed Days in St. Louis." Walter Lippmann was twelve years old at the beginning of the new century.

In the city halls and in the state capitals, there was a new awareness of social problems and a new mood of impatience with standpat institutions and standpat leaders. Insurgency was in the air and could be detected by the perceptive. But as yet all was quiet along the Potomac. Progressivism had not yet arrived on the national scene as a self-conscious movement to redress social and economic imbalances and regenerate the country. When it did, it would transform American life.

Chapter Five

The Practice of Progressivism

When Roosevelt heard the news that McKinley had been shot, he was on a mountain-climbing expedition in the Adirondacks. He immediately set out for Buffalo and without knowing it became the twenty-sixth president of the United States in the early morning of September 15, 1901, while hurtling along steep mountain roads on the way to the railroad station. That afternoon TR reached the house where his predecessor's body lay, and after extending his condolences to McKinley's grieving family, he took the presidential oath of office.

The circumstances of Roosevelt's accession to the presidency were characteristic. TR was a man of action who, when he was not challenging nature, was careering constantly from place to place. He had found the few months as vice-president almost intolerable because it allowed no useful outlet for his abounding energies. Now that the combination of "Harvard dude" and "badlands cowboy" was installed in the White House, the American people were to be treated to a rare show of humor, drama, and hectic activity that many of them would come to adore.

Much of TR's presidency could have been extrapolated from what went before. Son of a philanthropic New York businessman of an old, distinguished, "Knickerbocker" family, Roosevelt had received the elite education of the day—Groton, Harvard, and Columbia Law School, all embellished by extensive European travel. TR was a remarkably literate and cultivated young man whose forays into naval and Western history were sound contributions to the historical craft. As a young patrician reaching maturity in the 1880s, he might have chosen a comfortable and undemanding career in law, publishing, or scholarship, or perhaps drifted into the role of gentleman dilettante. But Roosevelt craved excitement and attention, and none of the traditional occupations for upper middle-class young men promised these things. Though "society" in the 1880s considered politics a dirty business better suited to saloon keepers, shyster lawyers, and self-made provincials than to well-bred Eastern gentlemen, Roosevelt got himself elected to the New York legislature in 1881. TR's experience in Albany only confirmed the expectations of his class. New York politicians, he wrote after firsthand contact, were either "vicious, stupid looking scoundrels with apparently not a redeeming trait," or "well-meaning but very weak."

Fortunately the young gentleman was not permanently repelled by the experience. After an intermission of two years on a Dakota cattle ranch, where he actually embraced for a time the strenuous life he so raucously advocated, Roosevelt returned to politics. In 1886 he ran unsuccessfully for mayor of New York. Then successively he served as United States civil service commissioner, police commissioner of New York, and assistant secretary of the navy under McKinley. During the Spanish-American War, the young extrovert and advocate of American expansion could not sit idly in his Washington office while other men enjoyed the fun in Cuba. Roosevelt secured an army commission and, newly outfitted in a lieutenant colonel's uniform from Brooks Brothers, dashed off to the front as second in command of the "Rough Riders," a cavalry regiment composed of Eastern sportsmen and cowboys and ranchers from the Southwest and Rocky Mountain regions.

Roosevelt saw the action and won the glory he craved. Landing in Cuba in June 1898, the colonel and the Rough Riders dismounted, fought a skirmish or two, and then on July 1 Roosevelt led an attack up San Juan Hill that dislodged the Spanish forces. Though weary and even discouraging days in Cuba followed, Roosevelt's charge made him a war hero, a result owing in no small part to his own self-advertisement in the account of the campaign he wrote. After reading *The Rough Riders*, Mr. Dooley suggested changing its name to "Alone in Cubia," or "Th' Darin' Exploits iv a Brave Man be an Actual Eye-witness."

Deserved or not, Roosevelt's fame made him the Republican governor of New York in 1899–1900. Though he had been the candidate of the state's Republican boss, Tom Platt, Roosevelt's administration brought no joy to the state party machine. In the state house, Roosevelt proved to be an enemy of both machine politics and irresponsible business interests. By the end of his two-year term, Platt was anxious to get rid of the bumptious and ungrateful young governor about whom he had always had misgivings and maneuvered him into accepting the Republican vice-presidential nomination in McKinley's second presidential campaign.

Had McKinley not been assassinated, it is entirely possible that Roosevelt's political career might have ended in 1904. Vice-presidents, even ones as irrepressible as Roosevelt, usually disappear into obscurity after their term of office. But Leon Czolgosz spared TR this grim fate, and on September 13, 1901, Roosevelt found himself, at forty-three, the youngest president in the country's history.

The new president was not yet a progressive—and some denied that he ever became one. As governor of New York, his record had been mildly liberal, as befitted a young aristocrat who detested the bosses and the crude new men of wealth but who also feared the uninstructed mob and believed private property sacrosanct. Yet from the outset, TR rejected conservatism. So much could be done to improve the nation! And besides, who ran the country, he or the plutocrats? Clearly whatever specific direction the country was to take, a vigorous hand would control the steering wheel.

Roosevelt had to move slowly at first. The growing reform impulse of the cities and states had not yet affected Congress. The leaders on Capitol Hill of both parties were hidebound, slow-moving men. In the Senate a small group of die-hard Republican conservatives, all rich and all closely connected with corporations, controlled legislative affairs. Four men—Nelson Aldrich of Rhode Island, Orville Platt of Connecticut, William Allison of Iowa, and John Spooner of Wisconsin—were the leaders of the standpat faction, but they were not alone. Other Republican conservatives included Joseph Foraker of Ohio, Matthew Quay of Pennsylvania, and Thomas Platt, the New York Republican boss who earlier, to his regret, had furthered Roosevelt's political career.

Nor were the Democratic leaders any more liberal. Bryan still had his followers, especially among the Southerners and Westerners. But the Southern senatorial managers, Joseph W. Bailey of Texas and Arthur Gorman, a high tariff, business-oriented Marylander, were closer to Aldrich and Allison than to the old Populists or to the putative head of their own party. The major exception to this Democratic conservatism was Benjamin ("Pitchfork") Tillman, an erratic South Carolinian who considered himself the representative of the white farmers and brought both their populistic and their racist values to the upper house of Congress.

Matters were not very different in the House of Representatives. Between 1901 and 1903, the Speaker of the House was Republican David B. Henderson of Iowa, an amiable man who was willing to follow the lead of Aldrich and company. Although the Speaker at this time had immense power through his right to appoint committee members and his position on the all-powerful Rules Committee, Henderson seldom chose to wield it. His successor in 1903, the profane and bibulous "Uncle Joe" Cannon of Illinois, was a far different man. Cannon refused to accept the dictates of anyone and succeeded in establishing himself as an independent power in Congress. Since he too was a staunch conservative, the change did nothing to improve the prospects of reform legislation.

Against this wall of standpat conservatives, Roosevelt launched his first tentative attack with his first annual message to Congress in December 1901. Predictably the president denounced anarchists and assassins. Seeking to establish a continuity with his martyred predecessor, the new chief executive also endorsed the existing high-protection Dingley tariff, asked for an educational test for future immigrants, and, with mild approval, called the great corporations natural phenomena. Few conservatives could object to any of this, and the stodgy New York *Evening Post* was moved to declare approvingly that the message might have been written by a "man of sixty, trained in conservative habits."

But at the same time, the message hinted at future events. Along with the conventional McKinleyesque sentiments and proposals, it noted the need for the country to take stronger measures to conserve its forests and protect its natural resources; called for a new cabinet-level department of commerce and labor that would, among other things, investigate and publicize corporate earnings and protect the rights of working men; and demanded a revision of the Interstate Commerce Act of 1887 to make it a more effective guarantor of equal treatment of shippers by the railroads.

Surprisingly TR succeeded in getting some of his legislative program enacted into law. The 1903 Elkins Act effectively outlawed rebates and other special rates to favored shippers. Supported not only by merchants and farmers but also by the railroads themselves (who were now tired of having their rates beaten down by powerful shipping interests), the Elkins bill comes close to exemplifying what Weinstein and Kolko have said about business support for progressive regulatory legislation.

On the other hand, a bill establishing a Department of Commerce and Labor passed only over the opposition of important business groups. The business objection to the bill was primarily to its provision for a Bureau of Corporations to be included within the new executive department. This bureau, dear to Roosevelt's heart, would have subpoena power to collect information about industry and presumably could use this information for instituting suits against trusts or for recommending new regulatory legislation. Businessmen feared that the measure would give the government another weapon against them, and through Senator Quay and the Pennsylvania House delegation, they fought it vigorously.

Roosevelt for the first time now used his influence against "the interests." If the bill did not pass, he told newspaper reporters, he would call Congress into special session. Rockefeller and the Standard Oil Company, he stormed, were deluging Congress with telegrams opposed to the measure, and the government must not buckle under such pressure. Associating the detested oil tycoon with the bill's opponents did the trick. Public anger at business's effort to influence federal legislation frightened the conservatives in Congress, who yielded and allowed the measure to pass. For the next dozen or so years, until superseded by the Federal Trade Commission, the Bureau of Corporations was useful in stemming the tide of business consolidations by collecting data that the government used for antitrust prosecution.

The Elkins Act, the new Commerce and Labor Department, and the Bureau of Corporations were respectable legislative achievements. But Roosevelt had oversold himself as a man of action, or had been oversold by the media, and the limited results of his first congressional session disappointed many reform-minded observers. Hoping for a more forceful program from the new president, they felt he had let them down. Some critics even charged that Roosevelt was really chummy with the old guard and would never allow his principles to overcome expediency. Obviously the new president was lagging behind the emerging progressive mood.

Then abruptly in March 1902, the government filed suit against the Northern Securities Company under the Sherman Antitrust Act. For some time now the Sherman Act had been virtually a dead letter. In the E. C. Knight case (1895), the Supreme Court had reached the amazing conclusion that the acquisition by the American Sugar Refining Company of additional plants that gave it control of 98 percent of the country's refining capacity did not constitute a violation of the law! Narrowly defining the terms of the act, the justices held that the combine had been organized to manufacture sugar, not distribute it. Since the Sherman Act applied only to commerce, the government's case was invalid. For the next few years, if the emasculated law served any purpose at all, it merely limited the activities of labor unions which, in the case of *The United States* v. *Debs* (1894), had been judged combinations in restraint of trade.

The government's action startled the public. Aside from the rustiness of the Sherman Act, Roosevelt had never been known as a trustbuster. He would never become one. TR always denied that he opposed trusts as such; bigness by itself, he insisted, was not "a sin." On the other hand, he could not condone lawlessness and irresponsibility. When the great business aggregates abused their massive power, they were no better than those other agents of misrule, the Socialists and the Populists, The country, TR proclaimed, could "no more tolerate the wrong committed in the name of property, than wrong committed against property." At times Roosevelt's denunciation of concentrated economic power and those who wielded it seemed indistinguishable from Bryan's, abounding in such terms as "predatory wealth," "stockjobbing," "swindling," "oppression," and the like. Yet TR did not believe it was possible to restore the good old days of free competition by breaking up the giant concerns that had arisen since the Civil War. Antitrust legislation could not be used to reform the economy. Ultimately Roosevelt preferred to use regulatory agencies to control business practices. But in 1902 in the absence of effective federal regulatory powers—or of any better means to bring the masters of irresponsible wealth to heel—he was willing to use the tools available.

The Northern Securities Company seemed a particularly flagrant instance of the consolidating tendencies of the day. A holding company incorporated under the new state laws that allowed a given firm to hold the stock of others,[1] it combined the three giant Northwestern railroads: the

---

[1] A holding company should be distinguished from a trust. In the first the stock of constituent

Great Northern, the Northern Pacific, and the Chicago, Burlington and Quincy. These were controlled by some of the most notorious financial manipulators of the day, including Morgan, Harriman, Rockefeller, and J. J. Hill. The giant combination, Roosevelt feared, would enable these men to put a noose around the neck of one large region of the nation, to be followed perhaps by a move "toward controlling the entire railway system of the country." To destroy the Northern Securities firm would be to strike a blow at some of the most disliked men in the nation's business life, while simultaneously rescuing the whole Northwest and the country from the greedy robber barons.

By and large the public's reaction to Attorney General Philander Knox's suit was favorable, and when the federal court a year later ordered the dissolution of the Northern Securities Company, most Americans approved. Thereafter Roosevelt used the Sherman Act sparingly but well against some forty-four other corporations, including such mammoth concerns as the American Tobacco Company, the Standard Oil Company, the New Haven Railroad, and the Dupont Corporation. Yet all the while TR made the distinction between "good" and "bad" trusts and continued to favor regulation rather than dissolution, constantly renewing his request that Congress grant the government the power to compel the large combinations to engage in fair and socially acceptable practices.

TR's qualified antipathy to big business was matched by his qualified sympathy for organized labor. Roosevelt felt compassion toward working men as a class. He also understood the necessity for labor unions. "One of us," he wrote in his *Autobiography*, "can deal in our private lives with the grocer or the butcher or the carpenter or the chicken raiser, or if we are the grocer or the carpenter or butcher or chicken raiser, we can deal with our customers, because *we are all of about the same size.*" But in a "rich and complex industrial society" individuals were "dwarfed" by the great corporations and could not "deal with them on terms of equality." Individuals had the right, accordingly, "to act . . . in their own self-defense through private combinations, such as farmers' associations and trade unions."

Unfortunately he often forgot this intelligent and perceptive formula. As governor of New York, TR wavered in his position toward labor. At one point he sent state militia to Buffalo to put down the disorder that had followed a labor dispute. At other times he supported labor's demands for tenement regulation and tighter state control of working conditions. As president the test of his attitudes toward unions came in May 1902. After months of struggle with the exceedingly conservative mine owners, the anthracite miners of eastern Pennsylvania called a strike, the culmination

---

firms was actually owned by the holding company. In the second a group of trustees merely retained stockholders' stock in trust and did not claim the benefits of legal ownership, such as the right to dividends, the right of sale, and so forth.

of years of simmering discontent over low wages, long hours, and the low level of mine safety. In 1900 a similar strike had been settled quickly when Mark Hanna, fearing the effects of labor troubles on McKinley's reelection chances, had intervened to force the owners to make concessions. The 1900 settlement did not quiet the basic discontent, however, and early in 1902, John Mitchell, the moderate and skillful leader of the United Mine Workers, called another strike after the miners' new demands had been rejected. By this date organized labor was undergoing a resurgence. Helped along by the prosperity that followed 1897, national trade union membership grew rapidly from the depression low of under half a million. Only some eight thousand of the anthracite miners belonged to the union, but the better organized bituminous miners contributed substantial amounts to the strike fund, enabling the hard-coal miners to hold out against the adamant operators.

The public, confronted by the prospect of a serious winter fuel shortage, might have been expected to support the operators or, at least, to oppose the miners. But it did neither. Of all the major capitalists of the nation, the conservative and arrogant mine owners, mostly officials of the giant railroads that served eastern Pennsylvania, were among the most disliked. Led by George Baer of the Reading and W. H. Truesdale of the Lackawanna, they refused to compromise with what they believed to be their God-given right to run their properties as they wished. When someone suggested at one point submitting the dispute for arbitration to the liberal churchman Archbishop Ireland of St. Paul, Baer replied that "anthracite mining is business and not a religious, sentimental or academic proposition."[2] This haughtiness, contrasted with the moderation and reasonableness of Mitchell, had helped the public overcome a natural tendency to blame strikers for the dislocations and discomforts of strikes and made them unusually sympathetic to the miners' demands.

Roosevelt was sympathetic, too. He believed that the miners' cause was valid; he was offended also by the recalcitrance of the mine operators. As early as June, when the strike was barely a month old, Roosevelt sent his commissioner of labor to Pennsylvania to investigate conditions in the anthracite regions, but then he lost interest. Though the strike dragged on through the summer, Roosevelt did not act, partly because his advisers told him that he did not have the constitutional power to intervene. Finally, on October 1, as bad winter weather grew near, the president sent invitations to both the union leaders and the operators to meet at the White House to discuss ways to settle their differences.

At the all-day conference on October 3, Mitchell agreed to confer direct-

---

[2]A more famous statement ascribed to Baer is the even more outrageous remark that the "rights and interests of the laboring men will be protected and cared for not by labor agitators but by the Christian men to whom God has given control of the property rights of the country."

ly with the operators. If they did not find this acceptable, the United Mine Workers would go along with the decision of a presidential arbitration commission—if the operators also agreed to accept its decision. The owners brusquely rejected this reasonable proposal. Accusing the union of fostering violence in the anthracite district, they demanded that federal troops be sent into the mine fields and that the government initiate an immediate suit against the union under the Sherman Act. When Roosevelt asked the operators point-blank whether they would accept the arbitration proposal, he was met with a direct "No."

The stupid stubbornness of the owners and their contemptuous response both to him and to Mitchell, a man he liked and respected, outraged Roosevelt. In short order TR resolved to send ten thousand federal troops into Pennsylvania to take over the mines, although he could find little constitutional sanction for such a move. Meanwhile, Elihu Root, secretary of war and Roosevelt's close adviser, traveled to New York to confer with J. P. Morgan, the Grand Lama of American business, to see if the government could enlist his good offices to bring the mine owners around. Under pressure from Morgan and faced by what they saw as the prospect of imminent state socialism, the mine owners yielded. On October 13 another White House conference was held at which Morgan's agents arranged for a five-man arbitration commission to consist of an army engineer, a mining engineer, a coal operator, a federal judge, and an "eminent sociologist" to recommend a settlement. None of these was a union man, but Roosevelt got around this inequity by choosing E. E. Clarke, head of the Brotherhood of Railway Conductors, as the eminent sociologist. The miners now went back to work, and in March 1903, the commission announced its decision, which included a wage increase and a reduction in hours, but neither union recognition nor a change in the way that coal was weighed, a procedure that affected total earnings.

Though a mixed award, the settlement satisfied the union. Roosevelt called it a "square deal" for both labor and capital. It seemed to him a balanced arrangement, one that reflected what was due to each in America. Yet it clearly placed the federal government in opposition to the common capitalist assertion of complete laissez-faire in its treatment of its work force. In later years TR's mixed feelings about the relations of labor and capital became more evident. In 1903 he sent troops to Arizona at the request of the territorial governor to prevent violence in a mine strike. The following year he refused to send troops to Cripple Creek, Colorado, though asked to do so by the striking miners, because he believed that in this case both the strikers and the operators were guilty of violence. In 1908 he met the governor of Nevada's appeal for federal troops during a labor dispute and then quickly withdrew them when it became obvious that the trouble they had been sent west to handle was potential rather than actual.

Roosevelt clearly was not an uncritical partisan of labor. He favored uions, though not the closed shop. On the other hand, he did not believe that any labor grievance excused violence or serious interference with the public interest. His view of labor-capital relations was a combination of Christian ethics, paternalism, and political expediency as illustrated in a letter to his attorney general, Philander Knox: "The friends of property must realize that the surest way to provoke an explosion of wrong and injustice is to be shortsighted, narrow-minded, greedy and arrogant ... [and] here in this republic it is peculiarly incumbent upon the man with whom things have prospered to be in a certain sense the keeper of his brother with whom life has gone hard." But beyond this, he told Knox, he hoped the Republicans would avoid identifying themselves too closely with the cause of the employer class. If they did so, the Democrats would be tempted to become the champions of radical measures with consequences that would be disastrous for the country.

II

With the "Square Deal" as his motto, TR campaigned for reelection in 1904. For a while it looked as if he would have to fight to head the ticket. But then death carried off his chief opponent, Mark Hanna. Nominated by acclamation, Roosevelt conducted a leisurely campaign against his conservative and lackluster Democratic rival, Judge Alton B. Parker of New York. The results were never seriously in doubt. Roosevelt easily triumphed with 56 percent of the popular vote and 336 electoral votes to Parker's 37.6 percent and 140 electoral votes. The Republicans had even carried West Virginia and Missouri and many of the trans-Missouri states that had formerly voted for Bryan. In the wake of this victory, the exhilarated president announced that under no circumstances would he be a candidate for, or accept, another nomination. TR would soon learn that politicians are well advised not to make promises about their political futures.

In his second term, Roosevelt moved significantly to the left. No longer faced by the problem—or so he thought—of reelection, TR felt that he could afford to defy the conservatives in his party. In addition, by this time a growing contingent of Republican progressives had arrived in Washington from the states where for years they had been active in local reform movements and had sharpened their skills in the fight with local conservative interests. La Follette of Wisconsin was the most prominent of these, but by 1906 the group also included Senators Albert Cummins of Iowa, Moses Clapp of Minnesota, Joseph Bristow of Kansas, and William E. Borah of Idaho. And several other senators, most notably Beveridge of Indiana and Jonathan Dolliver of Iowa, soon entered the growing progressive camp. These men could and would give both moral and practical support to any progressive proposals that emerged from the White House.

TR's December 1904 message to the nation recommended a child laboi law for the District of Columbia, new railroad legislation, and an employers' accident liability law. Congress did nothing during the short session between December and inauguration day, and Roosevelt could not get lame ducks moving. But after the beginning of his second term, the president launched a strong campaign to strengthen the government's control over railroad rates.

Ever since the Interstate Commerce Act of 1887, the government had possessed some power over the railroads, but this did not extend to setting rates. Roosevelt now proposed to give the Interstate Commerce Commission the power to fix maximum rates, and although he would allow these decisions to be appealed to the courts, the delay in applying the ICC's ruling would be kept to a minimum.

Early in 1906 the House passed a bill incorporating these provisions. When it arrived in the Senate, the House measure came under attack from both ideological extremes. To the right were the railroads, which mounted a major campaign to frustrate any effective new measure of federal control. Although they recognized the inevitability of some additional federal rate-setting power, the railroads wanted to guarantee continued judicial review of government decisions, since review by the courts had been an effective method in the past to delay ICC actions and nullify their effects. To the left were La Follette and other advanced progressives who wanted a stronger bill that would minimize the courts' power to delay or overrule the commission's decisions and would allow the ICC to assess the real physical value of railroad property to determine a fair rate of return on capital for the roads. La Follette, who had spent years fighting the railroads in Wisconsin, tried unsuccessfully to convince the president that the additional power was essential. Roosevelt acknowledged the force of La Follette's argument but felt that the Wisconsin senator was being unrealistic. In the face of the opposition of the railroads and most of the old guard, half a loaf, he believed, was all that could be expected.

In the end the bill that emerged as the Hepburn Act was even less than the president wanted. La Follette's efforts to strengthen the hand of the ICC were unsuccessful. The junior senator from Wisconsin broke with the tradition that senatorial newcomers keep silent, and amid rude inattention, paper shuffling, and loud talking by his tradition-bound colleagues, he delivered a two-day speech on the Senate floor supporting a physical evaluation provision. In this address he warned the conservatives that if the bill passed in its existing form, "the movement will begin anew all over the country for a larger concession to public rights" and would not stop until "control of the public-service corporations *broad enough, strong enough,* and *strict enough* to insure justice and equality to all American citizens" had been established. Although La Follette managed to force a roll call putting his colleagues on record, the physical evaluation clause was beaten decisively, forty to twenty-seven.

Still worse in the view of progressives, the friends of the railroads succeeded in getting the bill modified to allow the courts broad review powers of ICC rate decisions. Unable to defeat the principle of government rate setting by a head-on attack, Aldrich and Lodge were able to change a dangerous bill into a measure that the railroads found acceptable. Regardless of the fact that the Hepburn bill was tolerable to the railroads, it was not their law, introduced by their friends, or designed to effect their purposes. The measure was not so much representative of the progressives' inherent conservatism as it was of their inability as yet to get their own way in the legislative realm.

However disappointing to La Follette, Roosevelt considered the Hepburn Act a partial victory and was pleased with his work. Besides giving the ICC the right to set rates subject to court review, it also placed express and sleeping car companies, oil pipelines, ferry firms, terminal facilities, and interstate bridges under its jurisdiction and restricted the railroads' practice of granting free passes to favored passengers.

More important blows against the abuses of private power soon followed. As we have seen, one of the disturbing qualities of life for most urban Americans was their inability to protect themselves against charlatanism and chicanery in the food processing and drug industries. Queasy stomachs led to queasy minds as the public contemplated what it ate and dosed itself with. For years Dr. Harvey Wiley, the chief of the Department of Agriculture's Bureau of Chemistry, had inveighed against the misrepresentations and deceptions of the canners, meat packers, and patent medicine manufacturers and had demanded that they be forced by law to be honest. In 1902 congressional supporters of Wiley introduced a measure to compel manufacturers to label the ingredients of their products, but this bill was tabled in the Senate.

In the next few years, several events combined to increase the receptivity of Congress to regulatory legislation in the food and drug areas. The enlargement of the progressive contingent in Congress and Roosevelt's liberal shift following his reelection in 1904 helped. So did the growing willingness of the federal courts to allow Congress to regulate all kinds of business activity under the commerce clause of the Constitution. Other positive factors were the rising European resistance to American meat imports on the grounds of health and sanitation and the campaign against dangerous and useless drugs mounted by the American Medical Association's Council on Pharmacy and Chemistry.

Yet without an aroused public, little would have been accomplished. Then, rather abruptly in 1906, the public was seized by a panic over food and drug adulteration. This was set off by the articles of Samuel Hopkins

Adams in *Collier's* on the transgressions of the proprietary drug manufacturers and by Upton Sinclair's sensational novel, *The Jungle*, which described in graphic and explicit detail the disgusting and unsanitary conditions in the meat-packing plants of Chicago.

Of the two, Adams was the more careful reporter. As an undergraduate at Hamilton College, he had prepared for medical school. In researching the *Collier's* series, he spent many hours talking to state agricultural chemists and editors of pharmaceutical journals. He also consulted Wiley, who lent him clippings and read the drafts of his articles. From all this data, Adams wrote a slashing exposé of the patent medicine business that branded it the "nakedest, most cold-hearted" in the world. "Relentless greed sets the trap and death is partner in the enterprise."

Sinclair's novel, however, had the greater immediate impact. A Socialist, concerned primarily with the packing companies' exploitation and brutalization of labor, Sinclair inadvertently became the most effective propagandist for consumer protection until the advent of Ralph Nader. As they read the book, readers invariably ignored the packers' harsh labor policies and only noticed the adulteration of their food. As Sinclair himself remarked, he had intended to touch the public's heart, but he succeeded only in getting to its stomach.

The most important stomach of all was TR's. By this time Roosevelt already had endorsed a pure food bill after consulting with both Wiley and his personal physician, Dr. Samuel Lambert. But TR's recommendations to Congress in his 1905 annual message had been rather bland and had only incited Aldrich's ridicule. After reading Sinclair's descriptions of how men fell into the lard vat and were rendered into cooking fat and how decaying meat was injected with chemicals and then sold to saloon keepers for their free lunch counters, the president decided to act. In March he asked his secretary of agriculture to initiate a department investigation of Sinclair's charges. When the investigators confirmed many of Sinclair's revelations, Roosevelt threatened to publish their full report if the packers and their congressional friends did not yield on a meat inspection bill that Senator Beveridge had introduced. Besides fears of what the American public might do if the department's findings became fully known, what little leaked out was shocking enough to make American meat sales at home and abroad plummet. At this point the packers and their political supporters concluded that they had better get some law on the books to quiet public anger.

Meanwhile, a similar battle was raging on the patent medicine front. By 1905 the pressure to impose federal regulation was so intense that even some members of the Proprietary Association, composed of the patent medicine manufacturers, recommended that preparations containing narcotics or excessive alcohol be phased out. When Congress convened soon after, Weldon Heyburn of Idaho, encouraged by Roosevelt's support for drug labeling legislation, introduced a pure food and drug bill in the Senate.

To everyone's surprise Aldrich did not shoot it down. In the House, however, the bill met stiffer opposition. In addition to the friends of the patent medicine industry, states' righters ridiculed the effort, as one person phrased it, to have the federal government oversee the process of "cutting your toenails or corns." Defenders of the bill countered that even backward Russia had drug regulation laws. Skillfully guided over the hurdles by Doctor Wiley and Representative James Mann of Illinois, the bill passed the House in June. Soon after a joint House-Senate Conference Committee approved the measure.

By this time Congress had also passed the Meat Inspection Act, and on June 20 Roosevelt signed the measures. Both laws were compromises. The Meat Act provided for inspection by government agents whose decisions were subject to court review, but only of a limited kind. The Food and Drug Act required that foods and medicines must carry labels specifying the amount of alcohol, opium, chloral hydrate, acetanilide, and other potentially harmful ingredients they contained or be excluded from interstate commerce. Time would show that both acts were full of loopholes that eventually had to be closed up, but they were honest attempts to protect the public.

Among the contributions the progressives made to the national welfare none was so commendable as their efforts to conserve and intelligently utilize the nation's resources. The need by the opening years of the twentieth century was pressing. Americans had been prodigal with their abundant natural endowment from the outset. Reserves of soil, timber, water, and minerals seemed endless, and it usually was easier to squander than to conserve them. Farmers traditionally exhausted the fertility of the soils by sowing the same crop year after year, knowing that they could always move on to cheaper lands further west. Lumbermen cut down the forests without regard to restoration or to the destruction of watersheds. Hunters and trappers exterminated animals ruthlessly for their skins and fur, not caring whether there would be any left for their successors. Some of this was the result of ignorance; much of it represented shortsighted greed. As late as 1865, vast buffalo herds, numbering millions of animals, grazed the plains. By 1880 the millions had been reduced virtually to zero by hunters interested in their meat for railroad construction crews and their skins for leather or as carriage robes for passengers in the open-top family surrey.

During the 1890s many Americans began to worry about the future of American resources, and in 1891 Congress enacted the Forest Reserve Act, which limited the transfer of federal timber lands to private hands and allowed the president to set aside forested portions of the public domain as reserves closed to entry under the Homestead Act.

Those who were concerned about preserving the nation's natural endowment used two distinct approaches. Conservationists believed that resources should be used, but used carefully and efficiently to ensure abundant supplies of timber and minerals for the future and to protect and enlarge the area of fertile agricultural land. Another group, the preservationists, had more romantic goals. The mountains, lakes, and forests of the nation were aesthetic and spiritual resources that had to be kept as God had created them for the delight and inspiration of present and future generations. Men like John Muir and the members of the Sierra Club of California fought every attempt to "improve" natural sites or to exploit them, even efficiently. They sought instead to have them set aside and preserved unspoiled in the form of national parks or national monuments. Beginning in 1872 with the creation of Yellowstone Park, Congress periodically endorsed this policy. After 1900 the preservationists grew in influence, riding the coattails of the more numerous conservationists.

Roosevelt was a combination of the preservationist and the conservationist. TR was a nature lover who reveled in the great outdoors. A hunter, camper, hiker, and erstwhile cowboy, his exuberant personality could expand and express itself in the wilderness. He cherished his Dakota ranching experience during the 1880s and regretted the passing of the free life of the cattleman's frontier. "We who ... felt that charm of the life [of the plains], and have exulted in its abounding vigor and its bold, restless freedom," he wrote, "must ... feel real sorrow that those who came after us are not to see ... what is perhaps the pleasantest, healthiest and most exciting phase of American existence." And as was usual with TR, his personal inclinations were reinforced by an improving cause: the battle against selfish, vested interests as exemplified by the mine owners, lumber men, and ranchers of the West who feared government regulation and tried to impede every effort to control laissez-faire exploitation of natural resources.

Roosevelt's inclinations were reinforced by the resolute devotion to conservation of the chief forester of the Department of Agriculture, Gifford Pinchot. Dedicated to scientific usage of the forests, rivers, and farmlands, Pinchot belongs to the group of progressives who, Samuel Hays has said, believed in the "gospel of efficiency." As Hays sees it, these leaders reflected less the humanitarianism of the day than its centralizing, rationalizing tendencies. Actually there is no necessary conflict between efficient, centralized decision making and the public welfare. Indeed the New Nationalism version of progressivism clearly advocated concentrating power in the federal government; yet even more than the neo-Jeffersonian liberalism of the Brandeis-Wilson type, it sought to protect the weak against the powerful. There is, then, no reason to doubt that Pinchot and Roosevelt were public-spirited men merely because they wished to exploit natural resources in a scientific, rational manner.

At all events Roosevelt always befriended conservation. In 1901 and 1902, he used his influence to secure passage of the Newlands Act, which set aside the proceeds of public land sales in sixteen Western states as a fund to finance irrigation projects in the arid areas of the country. A little later, at Pinchot's behest, he reserved areas in Nebraska for an experiment to determine whether trees would grow in a natural grassland region. In 1905 Roosevelt got the forest reserve transferred from the Department of the Interior, where a giveaway mood prevailed, to the Department of Agriculture, where as the Forest Service, it was under Pinchot's jurisdiction. In 1907 TR and Pinchot snatched from the hands of Western lumbering interests millions of acres of forest land and a number of important power sites that were put into forest preserves or designated as ranger stations to keep them from being privately exploited. During Roosevelt's two terms, five additional national parks were created, and Congress authorized a new type of preserve, the "national monument," to set aside for future generations smaller areas of unusual interest to the public.

Much remained to be done to round out the nation's conservation policies and much still had to be learned about the complex interrelations of climate, topography, plants, animals, and man before Americans could say that they had checked the deterioration of their natural environment. But by early 1909, as TR stepped down from office and prepared to go off to Africa to hunt big game,[3] he could feel satisfied that he had established a new commitment to use government to protect and preserve nature's unusually bountiful gift to the American people.

III

As TR and his son Kermit steamed off to East Africa, William Howard Taft, his ponderous successor, was beginning his duties as president. Taft was Roosevelt's choice and had pledged to continue his progressive program, but at heart he was a conservative man with the temperament of a judge, and an indolent judge at that. When it came to enforcing the antitrust acts, he was reasonably energetic, for the Sherman Act was the law and the president was entrusted unequivocally with the reponsibility to enforce the law. As many historians have pointed out, Taft actually instigated more suits against the trusts than either his predecessor or his successor. But when it came to implementing the spirit of progressivism by new initiatives, or even preserving those already laid out by his predecessor, that was quite another matter to a man who cherished peace and quiet above all.

Roosevelt had scarcely left the United States when the new president

[3]Roosevelt's attitude toward nature and the outdoors was paradoxical. On the one hand, he wished to preserve the natural environment; on the other, he was himself a ruthless hunter of big game. Perhaps the explanation of this apparent conflict lies in the fact that neither conservationists nor preservationists in this period were concerned much with the problem of wildlife but were more interested by far in the plant life and mineral resources of the natural environment. For Roosevelt, moreover, hunting represented a masculine testing of skill and endurance and was part of that cult of machismo, to use a recent term, that TR embraced with such great zeal.

managed to alienate these in the progressive wing of his party and drive them into angry opposition to his policies. The tug came over the tariff, an issue raised to national prominence by Taft himself when, in fulfillment of his campaign pledge in 1908, he called Congress into special session to consider a downward revision of customs rates.

The tariff question threw into sharp relief one of the most fundamental issues of the era, consumer vulnerability. The 1897 Dingley bill had established the highest duties in history. Its passage had coincided with the economy's rebound from the depressed levels of the early 1890s, but recovery had also brought higher prices for consumer goods. Each year following 1897, the household market basket had gotten more expensive so that by 1908 the "high cost of living" was an acute problem for millions of Americans.

Clearly something had to be done, consumer advocates insisted. Roosevelt himself had favored lower rates while in office, but feared that tampering with the existing schedules might split the party, and so had done nothing. Now, under Taft, Roosevelt's fears were realized spectacularly. In April 1909 a tariff measure modestly lowering duties passed the House in good order under the sponsorship of Sereno Payne of New York, chairman of the Ways and Means Committee. In the Senate, however, where Aldrich had charge of the bill, the House measure was amended out of recognition. Almost all the House schedules were raised, especially those on products made of textiles, iron and steel, and lumber; most of the free list for raw materials included in the House bill was cut out, as was the inheritance tax provision of the Payne measure that had been designed to offset the expected loss of revenue resulting from the lower rates.

Taft was dismayed by the Senate's action but not as much as a group of Midwestern progressive Republicans led by Beveridge, La Follette, Dolliver, Bristow, and Clapp. Dividing the various schedules among themselves, they studied the complex Aldrich bill closely and during the Senate debate each in turn rose to attack the portion of the measure he knew best. For three months during the near tropical heat of a Washington summer, the insurgent Republicans battled against Aldrich, Lodge, and the other regulars in the name of downward revision.

In the past tariff struggles had generally been between competing groups of businessmen and producers. Merchants had fought manufacturers; those manufacturers who relied on cheap foreign raw materials had battled against domestic raw material producers. Farmers had opposed industrialists. Now for the first time, the issue was primarily between producers and consumers with the progressives insisting that consumers must be protected against the power of big business. "There was a time," Clapp charged, "when ... we could say that a protective tariff ... was not a tax and was added to the price of the domestic commodity." That was when the tariff stimulated new industry at home and created new competition for the consumer's dollar. Now, however, the tariff merely encouraged trusts to impose higher prices on consumers. La Follette picked up the theme. The tariff, he insisted, was the mother of monopoly. "A single control commands business. . . . It does not ask it, because competitors have been driven from the field. Hence there is shoddy in everything we wear and adulteration in everything we eat." Beveridge took on the chief argument of the protectionists. The tariff advocates insisted that high duties were needed to protect American manufacturers and wage earners against the low costs and cheap labor of Europe. "Full regard," he admitted, "ought to be given to the wage-earner and to invested capital in manufacture; but it is high concern to both and to the prosperity of our people as a whole that a just and equal consideration should be shown the consuming public."

The plea for the consumer left the Aldrich forces cold. Lodge replied that no one could "draw a distinction between consumer and producer." Whatever the insurgents said, all Americans were one sort of producer or other, and whether industrialists or their employees, they needed high duties to fend off foreign competition. But besides, prices had risen since the late nineties all over the world, not just in the United States. Obviously the reason could not be the Dingley tariff. Rather, it was the tremendous increase in the world gold supply, a change that affected all nations equally.

In their battle for the American consumer, the insurgents at first believed that the president was with them, Taft having promised La Follette that if the final bill did not lower rates substantially he would veto it. But in the end he reneged. Indolent and fundamentally conservative, the president, unlike Roosevelt, was reluctant to appeal to the voters over the heads of the Senate leaders. Moreover, Aldrich had convinced him that the Senate bill represented.a statesmanlike effort to curb the still more protectionist demands of individual Republican senators. Rather than supporting the insurgents in their battle, Taft became increasingly annoyed at them for rocking the political boat and was soon calling them "pretty stupid," "rather forward," "self-centered," "self-absorbed," and "demagogues."

Taft's attitude appalled the congressional insurgents. Considering themselves the true heirs of TR, they saw the president's defection as an act of betrayal. He had been handpicked by Roosevelt as his successor, someone to carry on his policies, and as such they and other progressive Republicans had supported him in 1908. Now he was cozying up to Aldrich and the old guard, and the progressives felt that they had been deceived.

When the tariff bill came to a vote, ten progressive Republican senators voted against it but to no avail. When the measure emerged from the joint conference committee as the Payne-Aldrich Tariff, it represented no net improvement over the Dingley rates, and in some instances, it was even more protectionist, though Taft, true to his campaign pledge, had succeeded at the end in getting a few rates reduced. The insurgents' anger at the president was exacerbated at the signing ceremony when he called the bill "a sincere effort ... to make a downward revision. ..." Six weeks later at Winona, Minnesota, Taft further offended them when he praised the Payne-Aldrich bill as "the best tariff measure the Republican party has ever passed."

Already disenchanted with Taft's tariff performance, the insurgents broke into open revolt over the president's handling of the conservation issue. When he came to office, Taft had replaced the dedicated conservationist James Garfield, TR's secretary of the interior, with Richard Ballinger. Ballinger was not a conservationist as that term was understood by most progressives. As head of the Interior Department, he restored lands to public entry that Roosevelt had withdrawn. He also interfered in the operations of the Reclamation Service and canceled an agreement whereby the Forest Service had control over forest preserves on Indian lands. In each of these actions, he clashed with Pinchot, who remained as chief forester and who, somewhat self-righteously, considered himself the special guardian of the public against the selfish interests.

The argument between Ballinger and Pinchot came to a head over the patenting of government-owned coal lands in Alaska by a Morgan-Guggenheim syndicate. Pinchot believed this was a blatant giveaway of public resources, and he accused Secretary Ballinger of favoring the despoilers of the public domain. Rather than confining his criticism to office memos, Pinchot elevated it to a personal crusade and made speeches all over the country attacking his department chief. Pinchot also leaked information to the newspapers, which pilloried Ballinger and by inference condemned Taft himself. Eventually he clashed head-on with the president, who promptly fired Pinchot for insubordination and retained Ballinger.

The insurgent Republicans also clashed with Taft over congressional reorganization. Soon after Pinchot's dismissal, the long-standing feud between the congressional progressives and the conservative Speaker of the House, Joseph Cannon, came to a head when Cannon began to deprive the party insurgents in the House of committee chairmanships they had earned by seniority. Long aggrieved at Cannon's ruthless suppression of progressive legislation that he opposed, they resolved to break his power and turned to Taft for support. Taft admitted he disliked Cannon but declined to help the insurgents in their fight, claiming that the Speaker was too deeply entrenched to be ousted. The insurgents refused to give up. At the opening of the March 1910 congressional session, under the leadership of George Norris, a young Republican congressman from Nebraska, they combined with the Democrats to strip the Speaker of his power to appoint the members of the all-important Rules Committee and deprived him of his place on it. Some of the insurgents would have been happy if Cannon had also been deposed as Speaker of the House, but they had to be content with limiting his ability to undercut progressive legislation.

Meanwhile Roosevelt was exuberantly slaughtering lions and wild buffalo in East Africa. After almost a year of happy mayhem, he and his party moved on to Europe, where the ex-president enjoyed himself almost as much hobnobbing with the kaiser, the king and queen of Italy, Emperor Franz Joseph, and the scholars and students of the Sorbonne and Oxford. During this carefree period, Roosevelt was kept informed by his political friends back home of Taft's antiprogressive transgressions. In early April 1910, Pinchot met with Roosevelt in Italy and filled his ears with his successor's misdeeds. To support his case against Taft, Pinchot delivered a bundle of letters from Beveridge, Dolliver, and William Allen White attacking the president. Dolliver's note charged that Taft had snatched "the certificate of character which Mr. Roosevelt had given him and turned it over to the Senator [Aldrich] from Rhode Island." The president was "helplessly following the very men who took the field to crush Mr. Roosevelt in 1906." Beveridge noted that public opinion was "rapidly crystallizing into something like hatred" against the president. Taft presented his side of the story in a long letter emphasizing his support for such progressive measures as tougher railroad regulatory legislation, statehood for Arizona and New Mexico, and a postal savings system. Roosevelt answered his old friend sympathetically but returned to the United States convinced that he had been betrayed.

Yet for a while after his arrival in May, TR tried to keep up appearances. He received visiting delegations of progressives at his home at Oyster Bay, Long Island, but avoided an open break with the president and even attempted to smooth over party differences. Nevertheless, with the passing weeks, the party split widened. In the spring state and local primary contests, Republican voters chose progressive candidates over their old guard opponents, many of whom had received Taft's endorsement. In August Roosevelt set out on a campaign trip ostensibly to support Republican candidates in the fall election. Actually, he was testing his own popularity. Wherever he went, the ex-president was greeted by enormous crowds of well-wishers who cheered their hero in a frenzy of enthusiasm. TR spoke less about the virtues of Republican candidates than about his own views of national issues. By now Roosevelt sounded like the most advanced progressive in the land. Strongly influenced by Croly's *Promise of American Life*, which he had read soon after returning home, he criticized the federal courts for attempting to restrict federal jurisdiction and reiterated the absolute necessity for the federal government to use its power to advance the public good. At Osawatomie, Kansas, he told his listeners that "the man who wrongly holds that every human right is secondary to his profit must now give way to the advocate of human welfare, who rightly maintains that every man holds his property subject to the general rights of the community to regulate its use to whatever degree the public welfare may require it." Calling his program the New Nationalism, he endorsed income and inheritance taxes, workmen's compensation, laws restricting the labor of women and children, sharply reduced tariff rates and additional power for the Bureau of Corporations and the Interstate Commerce Commission.

The 1910 congressional elections were a repudiation of old-guard Republicanism. In the East, where the standpatters were in control, the party lost heavily to the Democrats, while in the Midwest and Far West, where the party was in the hands of the progressive wing, it did relatively well. The most important single result was the election of progressive Democrat Woodrow Wilson, former president of Princeton University, as governor of New Jersey. To TR the results seemed mixed. He was exhilarated by the enthusiasm of his audiences but also considered the outcome a disavowal of his efforts at party conciliation. Soon after the returns were in, he retired to his Long Island home to ponder the lessons of old-guard impotence and progressive vitality.

Yet as late as the following June, he was still in touch with Taft and the two were seen together at a public occasion in Baltimore, laughing and whispering like the old friends they were. But not for long. In the next few months, Roosevelt lost whatever trust he still felt in his successor, as Taft sought to get the United States to adopt a series of arbitration treaties that, as TR saw it, sacrificed American interests and sovereignty. This was followed by further revelations concerning Ballinger's role in the transfer of the Alaska coal lands. A final blow to the already strained relationship was the Justice Department charge in its antitrust suit against the United States Steel Company in 1911 that U.S. Steel had acquired illegally the Tennessee Coal and Iron Company four years before. This was during the 1907 panic, and the sale had been approved by Roosevelt, who had accepted Morgan's plea that unless it was allowed, a major New York brokerage firm would fail, further jolting the reeling stock market. Roosevelt had consulted Taft at the time and was now furious that his embarrassing dealings with the arch-monopolist Morgan were being paraded out in the open.

This personal estrangement coincided with the growing clamor of many progressives that TR personally challenge the president for the party nomination. From all over the country, insurgent Republicans wrote Roosevelt that he alone could carry progressive principles to victory. La Follette, though an estimable man, was a regional, not a national figure. Roosevelt alone could win national support, and he alone could be elected.

Still only fifty-four, full of energy, with a personality that craved the limelight, Roosevelt found these blandishments hard to resist. Yet he did not want to try for the nomination and fail. Both his likely opponents promised to be formidable. Taft could count on the party regulars, of course. These remained in control in most of the Northeast and in the South. In the West by this time, the strong grass roots progressive surge and the preferential primary had ousted the standpat party leaders and placed insurgents in control. But unfortunately for TR, his friends' encouraging statements notwithstanding, La Follette had strong support in the region. Many advanced Western progressives considered him a more reliable reformer than Roosevelt and also preferred him as a native son.

By 1911 the La Follette candidacy was far along and well organized. The Wisconsin senator had the backing of the newly formed National Progressive Republican League, a group of Republican progressives who had joined together to promote their principles and fight Taft. With offices in Washington and a staff of volunteer speakers and organizers all through the Midwest, the league was financed by such rich reformers as A. E. Filene, Joseph Fels, Charles Crane, and Rudolph Spreckels. In early October 1911, the La Follette leaders felt sufficiently confident of their cause to issue a call for a progressive Republican convention to meet later in the month and prepare the ground for the national party convention the following year. The momentum was to be maintained until La Follette was safely ensconced in the White House.

For the La Follette forces, the big stumbling block was the ex-president. La Follette and TR were not the best of friends. The Wisconsin senator did not trust Roosevelt and would later describe him as a trimmer who "sought to win approval from both . . . radicals and conservatives." Roosevelt, on his part, had once considered La Follette a dangerous agitator and professional radical. Historians have taken sides in the rivalry between the two, with many accepting the La Follette forces' view that TR was a stalking horse for a group of shrewd plutocrats, including the wealthy publisher Frank Munsey and George W. Perkins, a Morgan partner. The fact is that both men had some rich backers. La Follette's campaign efforts were underwritten by the rich men of the National Progressive League and the affluent Pinchots, who by mid-1911 were raising about $5,000 a month to put their candidate in the White House. If Perkins's support for TR stigmatizes his progressive credentials, the backing of Spreckles, Crane, and the other moneyed men on the National Progressive League board would seem to do the same for La Follette's. The truth is that reform does not become fraudulent just because it is taken up by a few rich men. Even Socialists and Communists have had their "angels," their wealthy supporters and contributors, and the phenomenon of the radical nobleman or banker has been part of every European revolutionary movement.

At all events, when the October conference met, its major act was to endorse La Follette for the Republican presidential nomination. In the next few months, the La Follette forces were encouraged as Roosevelt, uncertain whether to make a fight for the party nomination, dithered and wavered. Finally convinced that Taft could be beaten, TR acted decisively. On January 16, 1912, he wrote publisher Frank Munsey that he would run if the Republican nomination appeared to be a public draft rather than a matter of personal ambition. Fortunately for TR the La Follette boom began to deflate rapidly as it became increasingly clear that Battle Bob could not compete nationally in popularity with Roosevelt. On January 29, 1912, a group of La Follette lieutenants met with him at his Washington headquarters and urged the Wisconsin senator to withdraw in favor of TR. Several days later, tired and discouraged, La Follette spoke to the Periodical Publishers' Association at their annual dinner and gave a long, rambling, disjointed, and aggressive speech that infuriated the publishers and dismayed and embarrassed his friends. Intentionally or not, La Follette had deeply offended a powerful group of opinion makers, and thereafter the senator was virtually out of the race. Early in February TR's letter to Munsey was published. On February 25 Roosevelt replied directly to contrived letters of Governors William E. Glasscock of West Virginia and Herbert Hadley of Missouri urging him to run: "I will accept the nomination for President if it is tendered me, and I will adhere to this decision until the convention has expressed a preference." The old cowboy hat was finally in the ring!

The main event followed: a fierce battle for delegates between TR and Taft. At one point Roosevelt's cause seemed to falter when at Columbus, Ohio, he endorsed the "recall" of judges and of specific judicial decisions as a way to overcome the federal courts' conservative braking effect on progressive reform. Considered by moderates and conservatives a dangerous attack on the sanctity of the judiciary, the proposal drew outraged protests from many opinion leaders. Yet TR refused to withdraw his scheme and continued to defend it from other platforms.

Meanwhile, the early preconvention battles were being fought out with mixed results. As expected, Taft won all the delegates from the South and took most of those in the North controlled by the Republican state machines. In the Midwest La Follette won a number of primary states, but Roosevelt carried most of the rest, running up a delegate total by the eve of the convention only about 70 short of the majority needed for nomination. In addition, the Roosevelt supporters determined to challenge some 250 more delegate choices.

The Republican National Committee, meeting eleven days before the main event, heard the opposing claims and rejected practically all of the Roosevelt challenges. At the Chicago convention itself, passions ran high. By every preliminary count, the Taft forces had the votes to confirm the decision of the national committee. But perhaps enough committed Taft delegates could be induced to change their minds to swing the convention to TR. The Roosevelt forces put strong pressure on the 66 black delegates from the South to change their allegiances. The Taft leaders worked equally hard to keep them in line. Both sides charged fraud and corruption and hired detectives to insure that their opponents did not use bribery to change delegates' minds.

In the end the Taft majority held. Amid catcalls, hooting, and shouts of "liar," "thief," and "swindler" from the Roosevelt men, the Taft forces succeeded in gaining official control of the convention proceedings. Maybe if the Roosevelt and La Follette forces had combined, they might have stopped the conservatives, but by now La Follette detested Roosevelt almost as much as he did the party standpatters, and he and his followers refused to cooperate. As for the alternative of a compromise candidate such as the respected governor of Missouri, Herbert Hadley, TR was adamant: either he got the nomination himself or he would run on a separate ticket.

And so he did. On the evening of June 20, after the tumultuous convention had adjourned for the day, Roosevelt conferred with Frank Munsey and George Perkins. The two millionaires assured the colonel that they would find the money to mount an impressive third party campaign. The following afternoon TR announced that if he did not get the official Republican nomination, he would run anyway.

On Saturday, June 22, the convention formally renominated Taft, and after selecting James Sherman as his running mate, adjourned. That evening the Roosevelt rump met and resolved to organize a new party.

Early in August some two thousand men and women assembled in Chicago to launch the Progressive party and to nominate their hero. Composed of progressive office-holders, disgruntled Republican politicians, opportunists, and Roosevelt worshipers, as well as hundreds of distinguished reformers, the convention was more like a bible belt revival meeting than an assemblage of urban and sophisticated folk. Absent were the hoopla, claques, and brass bands of the major party conventions but in their stead were hymns and prayers for divine guidance.

On the first day, Beveridge gave the keynote address, emphasizing the need for a national policy of "social brotherhood as against savage individualism." He finished with the words "mine eyes have seen the glory of the coming of the Lord," and he was echoed by the delegates' singing of the "Battle Hymn of the Republic." On the following day, TR appeared to accept the nomination and give his "confession of faith." Blasting the two old parties, he demanded a majoritarian political system that repudiated almost totally the checks on the public will the Founding Fathers had written into the Constitution. This was followed by a list of specific demands that would have instantly established the modern welfare state. The United States, TR insisted, must enact women's suffrage, the initiative, referendum and recall, the recall of state judicial decisions, a minimum wage and maximum hours law, abolition of child labor, unemployment insurance, and old age pensions. At the end he spoke these ringing words: "Our cause is based on the eternal principles of righteousness; and even though we who now lead may for the first time fail, in the end the cause itself will triumph. . . . We stand at Armageddon, and we battle for the Lord."

TR's reference to possible failure was scarcely noticed by the frenzied delegates, but failure was a likelihood from the beginning. Ominously many progressives refused to support the Bull Moosers, as the new party was called.[4] Many could not bring themselves to desert their old party. Others did not like Roosevelt. Still others preferred the candidate that the Democrats had just nominated, Governor Woodrow Wilson of New Jersey.

At the time of the Democratic convention, Wilson was fresh from his successes as progressive governor of New Jersey. At Trenton he had defied the bosses, who had mistaken his politics and foolishly chosen him as their gubernatorial candidate for the purpose of heading off a progressive revolt within the party. In his first months in office, Wilson confounded the Democratic machine and electrified the nation by his attacks on corruption, his program of utility regulation, and his liberal social legislation. A conservative in 1910, by 1912 the scholarly former president of Princeton University had emerged as the most attractive progressive figure in the Democratic camp. After a hard fought battle with Champ Clark of Missouri, Speaker of the House of Representatives, Wilson won the Democratic presidential nomination and prepared to face Taft and Roosevelt in the election.

During the next months, Taft, Roosevelt, and Wilson fought the liveliest presidential election battle since 1896. To add to the excitement, Eugene V. Debs, nominee of the Socialist party, made a strong bid for working-class support that would win him 6 percent of the vote. By mid-August, the Taft campaign had come to seem hopeless, and the president exuded gloom. Wilson and Roosevelt, on the other hand, both smelling possible victory, went at one another with great gusto.[5]

The campaign brought out the conflicting ideologies of both front runners. TR predictably trumpeted his New Nationalism and the "confession of faith," sounding the more radical of the two. TR contrasted his program, which he insisted was designed realistically for the new urban-industrial era, with Wilson's "rural Toryism," better suited, he asserted, to an earlier, simpler age.

Deeply influenced by a brilliant Boston lawyer, Louis D. Brandeis, Wilson called his approach to the problems of the day the New Freedom. Government, he declared, could be oppressive as well as benevolent. It could help to solve current problems by policing the large corporations, but government paternalism of the sort that Roosevelt advocated also could be dangerous to the very groups it was intended to protect. Though the governor talked increasingly of social justice as the campaign wore on, today's perspective suggests that TR was the one actually speaking in the authentic voice of twentieth century liberalism as it would evolve under Franklin Roosevelt, Harry Truman, and Lyndon Johnson.

---

[4]Upon first arriving in Chicago for the Republican convention, TR remarked that he felt "as strong as a bull moose."

[5]Even an attempted assassination in Milwaukee could not dampen TR's spirits. Though badly wounded, he went on and finished his planned speech and thereafter scarcely paused in his campaign pace to allow the wound to heal.

In the end Wilson won a substantial majority over his nearest opponent. Though the public loved TR, and although by election day most Republican progressives supported him, his seemingly new-found radicalism also aroused some suspicion among advanced progressives, as did his connection with Perkins, who had become increasingly prominent in the campaign as a Bull Moose fund-raiser and the new party's adviser on business attitudes. More important probably was the simple fact that Wilson could count on the votes of traditional Democrats as well as the party's progressive wing. He received almost 6.3 million votes (433 electoral votes) to TR's 4.1 million (88 electoral votes). The hapless Taft followed with 3.5 million popular votes (8 electoral votes), while Debs received over 900,000 popular votes.

IV

Wilson noted in the concluding words of his brief inaugural address that he regarded the occasion of his assuming the presidency not as a moment of triumph but as one of dedication. But dedication to what? The Democrats were committed to a low tariff, and substantial tariff reductions were clearly in the cards. Wilson had campaigned on a platform of restoring competition, and obviously he would demand stronger antitrust legislation and more vigorous antitrust enforcement. The Democrats had been out of office for a decade and a half, and certainly a lot of new blood would enter the federal bureaucracy. In addition, the new president, a Southerner by birth himself, owed much to the South, and the South assuredly would have a greater voice than formerly in national affairs.

But beyond this: what? Did the New Freedom mean, for example, the return to a relatively passive federal government and a retiring, unassertive president? Anyone who knew Wilson's career would have few doubts of his activist temperament, the 1912 Democratic campaign slogans notwithstanding. As president of Princeton, Wilson had made some serious mistakes, but his attack on the elitist undergraduate eating clubs, which he believed diluted the university's educational experience, and his introduction of the preceptorial system demonstrated anything but weak leadership. As governor, too, he had instilled new vigor into New Jersey's executive branch. Now, as president of the United States, the ex-professor exhibited a great capacity for strong leadership.

Yet we must distinguish Wilson's version of leadership from Roosevelt's. The two men were endowed with very different personalities. Roosevelt was exuberant, playful, self-dramatizing, full of bonhomie and flashing egotism. Though he was literate and intelligent, he was not primarily a man of thought. Wilson was the classic intellectual in politics. Capable of great flights of eloquence in which he movingly expressed the finest ideals of the

American democratic tradition, he seldom evoked personal affection in either the masses or those who associated with him politically in the same way as TR.

Some of this can be ascribed to personal manner. Where Roosevelt was loud, Wilson was dignified; where Roosevelt was physical, Wilson was verbal. But it went deeper. Both men knew their minds, and both were stubborn in defending what they believed to be right, but Roosevelt tended to be a pragmatist who cared little for consistency, while Wilson tended to be an absolutist who often sanctimoniously insisted on consistency, even when it was inexpedient. Not that he always succeeded in being consistent. In fact, Wilson was as capable of bending with the wind as the best of them, but he seldom admitted to a change of heart, and at times his obstinate refusal to yield on minor matters seriously endangered major policies. As president of Princeton, Wilson's bullheaded need to get his way on the establishment of a graduate college integrated into the university led to a major defeat when Dean Andrew F. West's detached school was subsidized by some rich backers. Far more important was his refusal in 1919 to go along with those who had reservations about the Versailles Treaty and the League of Nations. A good case can be made for the contention that Wilson's stubbornness and his need to be right, whether this resulted from a personality defect or, as some have thought, was neurological in origin,[6] ensured the defeat of the league and the isolation of the United States from world affairs between the two world wars.

But at first few of the new president's defects as a leader were apparent. Wilson set the vigorous tone of his administration at the beginning by calling Congress into special session and appearing in person to deliver his message, thereby restoring the practice ended by Jefferson in 1801. The president's words were mostly about the tariff. The recent election, he told the assembled members of both houses, had been a mandate for tariff revision. For too long the tariff system had been an accommodation to the wishes of businessmen without regard to the public interest to the point where "consciously or unconsciously, we have built up a set of privileges and exemptions from competition behind which it was easy by any, even the crudest, forms of combination to organize monopoly; until at last nothing is normal, nothing is obliged to stand the tests of efficiency and economy, in our world of big business, but everything thrives by concerted arrangement." The structure of "privilege" and "artificial advantage" had to be destroyed, and American businessmen had to compete with the businessmen of the whole world.

---

[6]Edwin Weinstein, a neurologist, argued in 1970 that Wilson's irascible and obsessional public behavior may well have been due to a series of small strokes that he began to suffer about 1895. See Weinstein, "Woodrow Wilson's Neurological Illness," *Journal of American History* (September 1970): 324–51.

Wilson's determination to reduce the tariff was soon brought to bear on Oscar Underwood of Alabama, chairman of the House Ways and Means Committee, whose efforts to revise the tariff already had been frustrated on several occasions by Taft's vetoes. Now for the first time in many years, a low-tariff Democratic Congress would be working with a low-tariff Democratic president. If anything, Wilson was ahead of the congressional leadership and insisted that the basic Underwood bill be modified to reduce rates on wool and sugar. Since the result of the proposed measure would be to lower government income, the Ways and Means Committee, taking advantage of the recently adopted Sixteenth Amendment, also included a moderate income tax clause in the revised bill. In this form it passed the House on May 8, 1913. In the Senate, the more conservative chamber, the bill encountered stiffer opposition, as had earlier tariff revision measures. The Senate always had been more independent of presidential direction than the House. In the past it had also been composed of rich men close to the predominate business interests of their states. This situation was likely to be altered by the new Seventeenth Amendment, which provided for the popular election of United States senators; but as yet the reform had not changed the upper chamber, and for a time the tariff bill was in danger.

During the weeks that followed the submission of the Underwood bill, the Senate was beseiged by lobbyists, mostly from the West and mostly interested in protecting domestically produced raw materials. Outraged at this concerted effort to defeat the good work of the House, the president lashed out at those who connived to undermine the public interest for their private profit. His attack stung even the more progressive senators, and Albert Cummins proposed a full-scale investigation into the pressures being brought to bear on the Senate. This inquiry not only confirmed the president's charges concerning the lobbyists but also revealed that many senators had personal holdings in industries or other businesses that were likely to suffer injury by lower duties. Embarrassed by the results of their own inquiry, many senators dropped their opposition and even joined to improve on the reductions of the House bill. When the Underwood tariff was signed into law on October 3, 1913, it enacted substantial rate cuts for the first time in decades.

With this triumph for executive leadership now safely under his belt, Wilson's next order of business was the reform of the American financial system. Ever since the panic of 1907, the country's monetary and banking structures had been under particularly close scrutiny, although their acknowledged deficiencies went back to their very origins during the Civil War era. The complaints came from every quarter. Reformers charged that the banks were too much under the thumb of Wall Street. Farmers complained that the money supply did not adjust adequately to the extra burdens of making payments during the busy fall harvesting season. Bankers, businessmen, and economists noted that the money and credit supply had no give, no flexibility, through the fluctuations of the business cycle. Most serious of all, many intelligent people could see that the existing structures made no provision for fresh funds to meet periodic liquidity crises when, as during the recent panic, businessmen of all sorts needed immediate cash and no one could get it. Unfortunately, virtually no one, not even the most sophisticated financial experts, understood the heart of the problem—the need for a central bank not only capable of meeting seasonal emergencies but also capable of stimulating a declining economy or dampening an over-heated one.[7] But however inconsistent or ill-informed the businessmen, bankers, farmers, experts, politicians, and the educated public, all agreed that the existing financial structure had to be reformed if the country was to improve its economic health.

Congress's first response to the financial weaknesses spotlighted by the 1907 panic was the Aldrich-Vreeland Act (1908) which allowed the banks to issue emergency currency for short periods and established the National Monetary Commission to investigate the banking and currency systems and recommend remedial legislation. After lengthy hearings and extensive research by its staff, the commission issued a massive report containing much valuable historical information and a proposal for reform. The commission's reform scheme, written by the New York banker Paul Warburg, provided for a highly centralized federal bank that would hold member banks' reserves, buy and sell government securities on the open market in order to expand or contract the money supply, raise and lower interest rates, and, most controversial, issue a currency that would be the obligation of the central banks, not of the government. The system as a whole would be controlled by the private member banks.

The Warburg proposal was supported by Aldrich and other conservative Republicans and the Eastern bankers, but it offended other groups. Agrarians of the South and West objected to its confirmation of New York's existing banking control. Bryan, along with old Populists and many progressives, preferred a government-issued currency. Within the Democratic party, these differences caused great dissension. Carter Glass, a conservative Virginia congressman who nevertheless showed the traditional Southern suspicion of Wall Street, demanded a decentralized system. Glass and his allies rode a wave of public concern following the 1912–13 congressional investigations by the Pujo committee, which purported to show the tremendous power wielded by the investment bankers of New York and the Morgan firm in particular. The Pujo data seemed to be sober, documented

---

[7]This deficient understanding of the country's financial needs persisted despite the central banking functions exercised almost a century before by the Second Bank of the United States under Nicholas Biddle. It was only as the result of experience and trial and error that the Federal Reserve System eventually began to take a positive modern role in regulating and guiding the economy.

confirmation of the existence of a money trust. Agrarians, of course, had been making this claim for over a generation, and the public now demanded that something be done about it.

Wilson himself was not opposed to banking decentralization, but he wished to see some sort of overall supervision of the system by a government agency. The Democratic progressives and Bryan, now secretary of state, feared that the Glass proposal, even as modified by the president, would ignore federal control of the system as a whole and were particularly opposed to a bank-issued currency. They were disturbed also that no provision in the bill prohibited the kind of interlocking business directorates that the Pujo committee had revealed and that no arrangement provided for the discounting of farmers' notes by the new banks. At the behest of the advanced progressives, Bryan induced Wilson to support the discounting of agricultural notes and to promise further legislation to outlaw interlocking directorates. Eventually the president had to compromise all these opposing views, and in the end the Federal Reserve Act of 1913 reflected his successful efforts as reconciler of important intraparty differences.

As enacted, the Federal Reserve law established twelve Federal Reserve district banks located in twelve separate regions of the country. These banks would hold the reserves of the member banks. All the national banks were required to join the system as member banks and deposit their reserves with the district banks; state banks might join if they wished. Each district bank was to be governed by a board composed of bankers, businessmen, farmers, and the general public. They could adjust the credit of their areas by raising or lowering the rate at which they would lend money to member banks or by buying and selling government securities on the "open market," an operation which worked like a sponge to sop up credit or squeeze it out again, depending on public need. The twelve district banks also would issue the currency of the nation. This currency, which would supersede the old national bank notes, took the form of new Federal Reserve notes. Backed partially by gold and partially by commercial paper (that is, by the IOUs that were created whenever a businessman borrowed money), the new notes presumably would expand and contract to suit the seasonal cash needs of business. At the apex of the whole system was the Federal Reserve Board, located in Washington and appointed by the president.

Time would show that the new structure had serious flaws that would have to be modified. In its original form it did not fully satisfy any group. Bankers objected to the principle of government control as exemplified by the Federal Reserve Board. The measure, declared one San Antonio banker before the bill even passed, contained "a communistic idea that is sought to be written into the financial statutes of the nation." Agrarians and progressives, on the other hand, complained about the private control of the twelve district banks and were disappointed that the new system made little provision for expanded agricultural credit. Nevertheless, the bill was a triumph for Wilson's version of moderate reform, and most contemporaries considered it a major breakthrough in an area of the nation's economic life that had been troublesome for two generations.

The Underwood tariff and the Federal Reserve Act were the two major accomplishments of Wilson's first term. Both were increments to the New Freedom that Wilson had proclaimed during the presidential campaign; neither was an advanced progressive measure for social justice. During the remainder of his first four years in office, several important social justice bills passed, including the measure to restrict the hours of working women in the District of Columbia (the La Follette–Peters Eight Hour Act, 1914), a law to improve the lot of American merchant seamen (the Seamen's Act, 1915), and the provision of the Clayton Antitrust Act (1914) designed to exempt labor unions from antitrust prosecution. Wilson supported these measures, but their initiative came from Congress, not the president.

Several other favored measures of the advanced progressives—including a women's suffrage amendment, a rural credits bill, and, the boldest constitutional departure of all, a child labor bill forbidding the production and sale of goods produced by children that entered into interstate commerce—failed because Wilson would not support them. The president had good reasons, he believed, to oppose each of these measures. Women's suffrage was a matter to be left to the individual states; the rural credits scheme was "unwise and unjustifiable"; the child labor bill was unconstitutional.

In still another area of social concern, Negro rights, Wilson actually played a reactionary role. In the 1912 presidential campaign, Wilson had vied for the black vote, then normally Republican, and for a Democrat had won an unusually large proportion of it. Several Negro delegations had visited Wilson before the election to see where he stood on racial issues and had come away with the impression that blacks would get their fair share of federal jobs from a Democratic administration. The candidate also told Oswald Garrison Villard of the NAACP that as president he would oppose racial discrimination and take a public stand against lynching. Once actually in office, however, Wilson dismayed black leaders and many white progressives by acquiescing in a deliberate effort by his subordinates to reduce the number of blacks in federal jobs and apply the then universal Southern system of race segregation to the remaining black federal employees. A Southerner by birth, although at times he preferred to ignore the fact, Wilson headed a cabinet and a party strongly Southern in personnel. The president was scarcely a vulgar racist, but he felt little affinity for blacks and was largely indifferent to their aspirations and hopes.

The Democratic administration's racial policies produced a loud outcry in parts of the North. Northern black Democrats, anxious to expand their base with the growing number of Northern Negro voters, complained that Wilson was hurting them politically. White progressives like Villard felt betrayed. The NAACP bitterly attacked the changes in Washington. Even

Booker T. Washington, who had seen Wilson's election as promising great things for his race, noted in August 1913 that since the Democrats' accession to office he had "never seen the colored people [of the nation's capital] so discouraged and bitter as they are at the present time." Despite the outcry Wilson did little at first to interfere with the policies of his subordinates, notably Albert Burleson, the postmaster general, and William McAdoo, secretary of the treasury. By 1913, however, protests from the North and Midwest grew so vociferous that Wilson slowed the pace of segregation in the federal government. But the damage was done, and in the end, the Wilson administration helped to make Washington, D.C., even more of a Southern city than it had been in the past.

If Wilson let the progressives down on children and women's rights, rural credits, and racial justice, he did not disappoint them on the trust issue. Early in the new administration, the Justice Department under Attorney General James McReynolds instituted a number of important antitrust suits against such corporate giants as the American Telephone and Telegraph Company and the New York, New Haven, and Hartford Railroad as well as carrying to a conclusion a number of cases begun under Taft. The administration also sought to strengthen the basic antitrust law, the Sherman Act, by new, tighter legislation that among other things would close up the loophole that the Supreme Court had recently opened in the 1890 law by the so-called "rule of reason." This pinciple declared that the Sherman law had forbidden only direct and "unreasonable" restraints of trade, not those that followed unintentionally from normal business arrangements. Announced in the Standard Oil and American Tobacco decisions of 1911, the rule of reason threatened to emasculate the whole federal antitrust policy.

The bill that emerged from Congress under the prodding of the administration and its congressional supporters strengthened the Sherman Act in a number of important ways. It prohibited price discrimination if such favoritism tended to encourage monopoly; it forbade contracts requiring buyers not to do business with sellers' competitors; it declared illegal interlocking directorates in businesses capitalized at $1 million or more; it restricted corporate acquisition of stock in other firms where such acquisition tended to lessen competition. Businessmen convicted of committing any of these acts could be held individually responsible for violating federal statutes and punished. The law was to be administered by the recently established Federal Trade Commission (Federal Trade Commission Act of September 1914), which could issue cease-and-desist orders against firms held to be violating the law.[8]

One controversial provision of the Clayton Act, passed October 1914,

---

[8]The Federal Trade Commission superseded the Bureau of Corporations and had some of the same investigatory functions as the older body—along with its enlarged powers.

exempted labor and farm organizations from prosecution under the antitrust laws and restrained the power of the courts to issue labor injunctions. Both the injunction and the Sherman Act had been employed effectively against unions. In the Danbury Hatters case of 1908, the Supreme Court declared that a secondary boycott[9] by the unions was a violation of the antitrust laws. At the level of the lower federal courts, the use of the Sherman Act against unions in the next few years was even more sweeping. Actually, organized labor wanted total exemption from antitrust prosecution, though they did not expect, of course, that unions or union leaders would be free from prosecution for criminal acts in the course of labor disputes. But all Wilson would concede was that unions as such should not be considered combinations in restraint of trade. He and the Democratic congressional leaders refused to exempt specific union acts from consideration as illegal restraints on trade. Presumably the courts would decide legality in particular cases. The effect of this omission was predictable. Eventually the courts emasculated the labor clause of the Clayton Act and in fact later used the law effectively against unions. But this was in the future. For the moment Gompers and organized labor as a whole professed to see the bill as labor's Magna Carta.

The Federal Trade Commission and Clayton Acts temporarily exhausted the reform energies of the Wilson administration. Increasingly the president was forced to turn his attention to foreign affairs as the whole of Europe and then the world erupted into a gigantic conflagration such as mankind had not experienced in a century (see Chapter 6). During the months that Wilson was struggling to define America's role in a world at war, domestic legislation took a back seat, in part because the president was otherwise occupied, in part because he feared the effects on business—already shaken by the European war—of further reform, and in part, finally, because he had come to the end of his own rather limited commitment to reform. During this period Wilson talked of "a time of healing" following the recent legislative battles, chose conservative men for the Federal Trade Commission and the Federal Reserve Board, and generally dismayed the advanced social justice progressives.

But his reform impulses revived as the 1916 presidential election approached. Wilson's reelection problem was formidable. The Democrats were the minority party in normal years. Wilson had won in 1912 with less than half of the popular vote. In 1916 he could not count on another split among his opponents. Roosevelt by this time was fast back-peddling toward the Republican party, having convinced himself that he alone could lead the

---

[9]A secondary boycott was an arrangement by which a union not itself engaged in a labor dispute supported a strike by another union by promising that its members would not patronize the struck employer.

nation away from the wishy-washy foreign policy that he accused Wilson of pursuing. Wilson and the Democrats, TR insisted, were appeasing Germany and its allies and deserved to be thrown out of office. Roosevelt was still titular head of the Bull Moosers, but he clearly preferred the endorsement of his old party, without which, he now recognized, he could not expect to exercise power. The president recognized that a united opposition, whether under Roosevelt or some other candidate, was sure to give the Democrats a difficult fight. The dangers already had been demonstrated amply by the Republican resurgence in the 1914 congressional elections, when they had reduced the Democratic House majority from a comfortable seventy-three to a thin twenty-five.

With Roosevelt sounding increasingly jingoistic and conservative, Wilson might have concluded that he could count willy-nilly on the progressive vote. Where else, after all, could the liberals who had voted for TR in 1912—not to speak of those who had voted Democratic—go, except to him? But the president hedged his bet. Hitherto, Wilson's kind of reform, true to his New Freedom principles, had emphasized the restoration of free competition by use of federal power to break up combinations. There had been little of the social welfare legislation that represented a real expansion of federal power. Brandeis, with his laissez-faire attitude, rather than Herbert Croly, with his governmental paternalism, had been the administration's ideological guide.

Now Wilson shifted ground. Yet his first move in the new dispensation, paradoxically, was to nominate Brandeis, the high priest of New Freedom progressivism, to the Supreme Court. The "peoples' lawyer," whose brief in *Muller* v. *Oregon* had first employed social data to defend the legality of social legislation (the Brandeis Brief), Brandeis was also one of Wilson's closest advisers. A man of great learning and deep social sympathies, his elevation to the Supreme Court represented an opportunity to modify the narrowly legalistic approach of the Court which, despite the appointment of Oliver Wendell Holmes, Jr., in 1902, had time and again struck down much progressive state social legislation.

From today's perspective, the Brandeis nomination seems scarcely startling. A liberal president was appointing a close liberal adviser who was also acknowledged to be an outstanding legal mind. But the nomination shocked and outraged conservatives. Ex-president Taft called Brandeis a "muckraker, an emotionalist for his own purposes, a socialist, prompted by jealousy, a hypocrite, a man who has certain high ideals in his imagination, but who is utterly unscrupulous in method in reaching them, a man of infinite cunning ... and, in my judgment, of much power for evil." Other critics, including Elihu Root and Moorfield Storey, signed a statement which declared that "taking into view the reputation, character, and professional career of Mr. Louis D. Brandeis, he is not a fit person to be a member of the Supreme Court of the United States." Running through the attacks of many of Brandeis's enemies was an ugly undertone of anti-Semitism.

At first reluctant to intrude into the extended confirmation deliberations of the Senate Judiciary Committee for fear of offending the touchy senators, Wilson eventually used cajolery, flattery, and patronage to get his way. On June 1, 1916, by a strict party vote of forty-seven to twenty-two, the Senate finally confirmed the appointment.

The Brandeis nomination was soon followed by a flock of New Nationalism–type legislative proposals. The first measure in the new mode was the Federal Farm Loan Act of 1916, followed a few months later by the Warehouse Act. Although Wilson had earlier accepted the agrarian demand that the new Federal Reserve banks be permitted to lend money on farm mortgages, he was reluctant to go much further. In 1914 he had attacked the principle of direct government support for farm loans on the grounds that such a law would be "class legislation." The principle of cheap government-supported rural credits had not been abandoned by its friends, however, and in the spring of 1916, Wilson finally gave the pending legislation his endorsement. The Farm Loan Act, as passed, established the Farm Loan Board and twelve Farm Loan banks, the capital of which was to be subscribed jointly by the government and the public. The new banks could lend money to farmers who joined certain farm loan associations on the security of mortgages at rates no greater than 6 percent on a long-term repayment plan. The Warehouse Act, reminiscent of the old Populist subtreasury scheme, permitted farmers to deposit certain nonperishable crops in authorized warehouses and to use the crop receipts issued against these deposits as collateral for loans. Under these two measures, especially the first, millions of dollars of credit would eventually be made available to farmers at low rates of interest.

Wilson also promoted two measures that incorporated views long advocated by the advanced urban progressives. The more important of these was the Keating-Owen Child Labor Bill. This measure followed years of agitation and propaganda against the child labor evil by the National Child Labor Committee, a group consisting of such advanced progressives as Felix Adler, Florence Kelley, Lillian Wald, Edgar Gardner Murphy, and Jane Addams. In Congress the outstanding champion of child labor legislation was Senator Beveridge, whose eloquence and dogged determination had at first been wasted on his senatorial colleagues. Beveridge hoped to use the commerce clause of the Constitution to outlaw child labor, a strategy that struck strict constructionists as mistaken. Even labor leaders and a portion of the National Child Labor Committee were skeptical of the institutionality of the child labor bill that Beveridge introduced in 1906. Roosevelt, too, had refused to support the measure, and it had died a quiet death.

Now in 1916, in the climate of revived advanced progressivism, the proposal came up again, this time sponsored by Senator Robert Owen of

Oklahoma and Congressman Edward Keating of Colorado.[10] The Keating-Owen bill, modeled on the Beveridge proposal, passed the House of Representatives in February. But when it came to the Senate, it was sidetracked by the opposition of the National Association of Manufacturers. Also held up in the Senate was the Kern-McGillicuddy bill establishing a system for workmen's compensation under federal auspices. At this point, A. J. McKelway of the Child Labor Committee and Secretary of the Navy Josephus Daniels urged Wilson to intervene. Daniels warned the president that if these bills failed, the Democrats might lose the 1916 election. The Republican nominee was planning to support a comprehensive social justice program, and besides, he pointed out, women, who were particularly sensitive to social justice issues, now had the vote in many crucial states. In mid-July Wilson went to the Capitol, called in the members of the Democratic senatorial steering committee, and demanded that the Senate act on the two stalled bills. Common justice required it, he declared, but so did political expediency. Within a month both were enacted into law.[11]

These new laws represented the capstone of social justice progressivism, bringing to a conclusion more than a decade of reform agitation. However effective in improving the quality of American life, they served their immediate political purpose well. Although the Republicans had nominated a progressive as their presidential candidate, on election day Wilson attracted enough votes from former Bull Moosers to beat out Governor Charles Evans Hughes of New York by a narrow margin. Whether it was this last burst of liberal energies or the slogan "He kept us out of war!" that put Wilson over the top is difficult to say; yet from the number of former TR supporters who openly endorsed the Democratic candidate, it seems likely that Wilson's leftward turn of 1916 made a significant difference in November. After midsummer 1916 the domestic phase of the progressive movement was over, not to be resurrected for another decade and a half. Meanwhile, the United States was about to embark on a crusade to make the whole world safe for the kind of liberal society that for a dozen years the progressives had been demanding at home.

---

[10]By now Beveridge was out of office, retired by a Democratic Indiana legislature in 1910 when United States senators were still chosen by state legislatures.

[11]The child labor law was declared unconstitutional in May 1922 in *Hammer v. Dagenhart* on the grounds that the law was not truly designed to regulate commerce but only to regulate the labor of children. Such regulation was beyond the powers of the federal government, the Supreme Court stated, and had to be left to the jurisdiction of the states.

Chapter Six

An Era Ends: World War I

Where is Sarajevo? Americans wondered as they scanned the headlines of their morning newspapers on June 29, 1914. The lead stories told them that the strange sounding city was the capital of Bosnia, a Balkan province inhabited by South Slavs that had been recently annexed by the Austro-Hungarian empire. There a young Serbian student, Gavrilo Princip, enraged at Austria's annexation of provinces that Serbia considered rightly hers, had assassinated Archduke Francis Ferdinand, heir to the Austrian throne. Most readers dismissed the murder as just another incident in the Balkan troubles that had come thick and fast since the first Balkan War in 1912. Many, no doubt, sympathized with the tragedy-prone Hapsburg family and the venerable Emperor Franz Joseph. In Washington, officials and diplomats recognized the seriousness of the assassination but could not believe that Europe, which had been threatening war for so long, was about to be sucked into a tragic international confrontation.

As the summer wore on, people were dismayed to find that the worst had indeed finally happened. On July 23, the Austrian government, hoping to end once and for all the continual anti-Austrian agitation of Serbian nationalists, sent an ultimatum to Serbia that threatened its national sovereignty. The Serbs appealed to the Russians, their Slavic big brothers, to help out. The Austrians in turn asked the German kaiser for support against the Russians and got what amounted to a blank check: if they invaded Serbia and the Russians intervened, Germany would back them up.

On July 28 Austria declared war on Serbia. Four days later Germany declared war on Russia. Two days after that, the Germans, expecting the French to rush to the aid of their Russian allies, attacked France. That same day the German armies swept into Belgium. Frightened by German encroachment on the English Channel coast, Britain now honored her recent alliance with France and Russia and joined the fight. By mid-August 1914, the greatest war in history was on; a century of peace had been shattered by a fanatic's bullet in the obscure town of Sarajevo.

Americans were confused and disheartened by the rush of events in Europe, but virtually to a man they were determined to keep out of the war. An almost universal reaction in the late summer of 1914 was relief at being so far from Europe. The *Literary Digest* polled newspapers all over the nation and concluded, "Our isolated position and freedom from entangling alliances inspire our press with the cheering assurance that we are in no peril of being drawn into the European quarrel."

Unfortunately, the press's conclusions were naive. Americans were not as far removed emotionally from Europe's problems and disputes as it seemed. Millions of citizens had been born in one or another of the belligerent nations and were ready-made partisans of their homelands. The many Americans of English, Scotch, and Welsh ancestry, especially recent arrivals, supported the Triple Entente, or Allies, as they came to be called. Millions of German-born Americans upheld the *Vaterland.* In the case of the polyglot empires of Russia and Austria-Hungary, the picture was more complicated. Americans who derived from the suppressed nationalities of Austria-Hungary generally wished to see the Hapsburg Empire defeated. Thousands of Czechs, Slovaks, and Croatians hoped for an Allied victory to free their compatriots from alien rule. Americans derived from nationalities under the Russian thumb—Poles, Lithuanians, Finns, and Jews, for example—had no reason to wish the czarist empire well. The Irish further complicated this tangle of confused responses, since they detested Britain as the age-old oppressor of Ireland. Irish-Americans supported Irish home rule and hoped that England's troubles would be Ireland's opportunity. Prominent in politics, they formed an influential bloc of American citizens skeptical of the Allied cause.

This jumble of conflicting attitudes among the "hyphenates," to use a contemporary term for the unassimilated mass of foreign-born and second-generation stock, produced a cacophonous babble of voices in communities all over America. One patron of a barbershop caught the discordant chorus in a witty jingle printed in the *New York Sun:*

> The barber to the right of me was hoching for the Kaiser.
> The barber to the left of me was hacking for the Czar.
> A gentleman from Greece was shearing off my fleece,
> While very near a swart Italian stropped his scimitar.
> And when presently discussion, polyglot and fervid,
> On political conditions burst about my chair,
> I left the place unshaven—I hope I'm not a craven,
> But I sort of like to wear a head beneath my hair!

Not all old-stock Americans thought the continued attachments and commitments of the hyphenates so amusing. To many it suggested the feeble loyalty of the newcomers to their adopted land. But even native Americans took sides. A small but prestigious group of educators and intellectuals respected German culture and intellectual accomplishment and supported the Central Powers, as Imperial Germany and its allies were called. Most native Americans, however, found themselves at least moderately pro-British and pro-French.

The reasons for this bias were complex. Ever since the unpleasant Venezuela affair, Britain's fear of expanding German power had made it eager to court America. During the Spanish-American War England was among the few European nations that supported the United States. Thereafter it had yielded readily to American demands over the Panama Canal and in 1903 had induced the Canadians to accept the American position on the disputed Canadian-Alaska boundary. These concessions did much to quiet the anti-British feelings stirred up by the Venezuela incident.

Yet even when American anglophobia was at its worst, it was highly qualified. Old-stock Americans, particularly, had always felt a kinship and at least a begrudging admiration for England and English culture. Americans read the classics of English literature and admired English law and parliamentary institutions. By the early twentieth century, among the prosperous and educated classes, respect for all things British was more general than at any previous time in our history. France, too, was regarded with affection. Old-fashioned, churchgoing Americans were inclined to associate France and the French with bohemianism, sexual laxity, and pleasure seeking. Other Americans, however, remembered French aid during the American Revolution, while sophisticated folk, including many of the country's opinion makers, were fascinated with French fashions, art, food, and thought and felt strong sympathy for *la belle France* in its plight. As a Philadelphia paper expressed it: "... the stirring thing is that France the frivolous, France the debonair, France the carefree and laughter-loving, has met the supreme ordeal of her existence in a manner to teach the whole world lessons of steadiness, of sobriety, of dogged courage, of concentrated efficiency and of uncomplaining sacrifice."

But beyond the ties of culture, aesthetic preference, and sentiment, both England and France were democracies which shared with the United States a common bond of liberalism and egalitarianism. This natural political sympathy for France and England was to some extent offset by the hostile feeling toward tyrannical and backward czarist Russia. But Russia was very far away and seemed, at most, a junior partner of the Allies.

On the other side, Kaiser Wilhelm's imperial Germany was the senior partner of the Central Powers, and Germany was generally disliked for its conservatism, its saber-rattling militarism, and its Prussian arrogance. Many Americans, remembering the German threat to the Philippines and other incidents, also feared Germany's imperialist ambitions, which under Wilhelm had swollen to gigantic proportions. The conclusion seemed obvious: American interests would best be served by an Allied victory which would preserve the European balance of power and check Germany's expansionist and aggressive designs. As Secretary of State Robert Lansing wrote in early 1916:

> It is my opinion that the military oligarchy which rules Germany is a bitter enemy to democracy in every form; that, if that oligarchy triumphs over the liberal governments of Great Britain and France, it will then turn upon us as its next obstacle to imperial rule over the world; and that it is safer and surer and wiser for us to be one of many enemies than to be in the future alone against a victorious Germany.

How valid was American fear of a German victory? It is hard to see how Wilhelmine Germany could have threatened the populous and economically potent United States, ensconced as it was behind its Atlantic moat. Yet it would be a mistake to dismiss the German danger out of hand. We now know that the Kaiser's Reich was indeed an aggressively expansionist power. The work of recent German scholarship has shown that Wilhelm and his advisers, in the event of victory, planned to replace Britain as the dominant world power. If the Germans had had their way in 1914–18, a *Pax Germania* would have succeeded the *Pax Brittanica* that had for so long provided the roughly defined outer limits of relations in the non-European world.[1] The United States doubtless would have found the world a more problematical place than it had been.

Wilson and his advisers, of course, did not have the modern historians' access to secret memorandms, diplomatic notes, and foreign office documents, but in some general way they understood that Allied defeat would endanger America's long-range interests. The United States and Britain had reached a modus vivendi on spheres of international influence, on foreign trade, and on naval policy. A German triumph, given the unreliability and notorious truculence of Wilhelm's government, was certain to disturb these arrangements and place the United States in a defensive position in the world. Even on the level of the informed man in the street, Germany was regarded with suspicion. Lansing regretted that the public was not more alert to the German danger, but according to Daniel Smith, the "decade before World War I witnessed a slowly maturing conviction . . . that Germany was a potential enemy and Great Britain a natural ally of the United States."[2] Behind the whole sequence of fateful events for America that followed Sarajevo, this conviction that Germany represented a menace could be found in one form or another.

---

[1]Fritz Fischer, *Germany's Aims in the First World War* (New York: W. W. Norton and Company, 1967).

[2]Daniel Smith, "National Interest and American Intervention, 1917: An Historical Appraisal," *Journal of American History* (June 1965):10.

II

But this was in the future. At the beginning of his administration, Wilson's desire to make his mark as a reformer far outweighed his interest in international problems. When he took office, he had expected to devote much of his energies to tariff revision, financial reform, and stricter control of the trusts. Although the world was relatively peaceful in March 1913, he feared that foreign policy problems might overwhelm his domestic programs and told a friend shortly before his inauguration that it would be ironic if he had to spend most of his time as president on foreign affairs.

As it turned out, foreign relations did indeed occupy an enormous amount of the president's time. Two principles governed Wilson's view of international relations. One was national interest. The United States had to protect itself against bullying and had to guarantee that its vital concerns were not endangered or impinged upon. The other was mission. This country was not like other great powers. Founded on the premises of liberty and justice, the United States owed a debt to mankind. It had to be an example and a guide, and insofar as it lay within its powers, it had to lead the world toward peace and light.

Wilson, at least in public, spoke more about America's mission than about its self-interest. The son of a Presbyterian minister, he saw international affairs as a confrontation of good and evil in which America was a force for world morality and for liberal values. There seemed nothing self-serving in this; nor was it simple altruism. Wilson had no doubt that a world order constructed out of the materials of liberal and progressive American capitalism would be a far better alternative for the United States than one based on either rightist autocracy or leftist socialism. It would also be, he was certain, a better and happier world for all mankind.

Foreigners were not so certain. To Europeans and Latin Americans Wilson's incessant preaching often seemed sanctimonious, and they found his constant advice to the rest of the world irritating. It also seemed insincere: the American president was merely excusing his country's meddling in other nations' concerns. Though at times Wilson's words expressed the fondest hopes and aspirations of men and women everywhere, at other times they created the impression that the United States was a nation of moralistic hypocrites.

Wilson's choice of Bryan as his first secretary of state, in recognition of his importance in the Democratic party, was a congenial one. Bryan was always a tireless, if naive, laborer in the cause of peace, sharing Wilson's ideas about America's liberal mission in the world. The earnest secretary often seemed an object of fun to skeptical European diplomats. Sir Cecil Spring Rice, British ambassador to the United States, commented on one encounter with the secretary of state soon after World War I broke out:

Bryan spoke to me about peace as he always does. He sighs for the Nobel [Peace] Prize, and besides that he is a really convinced peaceman. He has just given me a sword beaten into a ploughshare six inches long to serve as a paperweight. It is adorned with quotations from Isaiah and himself. No one doubts his sincerity, but that is rather embarrassing for us at the present moment, because he is always at us with peace propositions.

Bryan's first efforts for peace were in 1913 and 1914, before Sarajevo, when he attempted to negotiate conciliation treaties with some thirty different nations. These treaties stipulated that all disputes between signatory countries would be submitted to a permanent investigatory commission and that the contending nations would agree to delay for a period of one year before taking unilateral action. Great Britain, France, and Italy went along with Bryan's pet project, but the German government, insensitive as always to world opinion or perhaps less given to hypocrisy, declined to sign one of the secretary's treaties.

The principled and idealistic side of the Wilson-Bryan foreign policy revealed itself in other ways, too. The two men opposed the more blatant forms of Dollar Diplomacy. They refused, for example, to underwrite American bankers' participation in the Six Power Consortium, which had been formed during Taft's administration to aid in the construction of a railroad in China, on the grounds that it might undermine China's fragile sovereignty. They also induced Congress to repeal a 1912 law exempting American vessels from the tolls at the Panama Canal as a measure of justice toward the British, who had vociferously protested the exemption on the grounds that the Hay-Pauncefote Treaty[3] had promised equal rates for all nations.

But the Wilson-Bryan attempt to forge a virtuous and liberal foreign policy broke down in relations with the Latin American nations, particularly Nicaragua, Haiti, and the Dominican Republic. In these cases, where the most immediate political and economic interests of the United States seemed to be threatened and the risks involved seemed minor, *realpolitik* took precedence over ideals.

Our intervention in the Caribbean had become an annual event by 1914. In that year the Bryan-Chamorro Treaty, which paid the Nicaraguan government $3 million in return for giving the United States exclusive right to construct a new Atlantic-Pacific canal, made that Central American nation into a virtual American protectorate. In 1915 the United States sent a naval force to restore order in Haiti after Haitian president Vilbrun G. Sam was hacked to pieces by an angry mob in reprisal for Sam's execution of 160

---

[3]As one of its features, the Hay-Pauncefote Treaty provided that while the United States could build, control, and fortify the proposed isthmian canal, it would be free and open to ships of all countries on equal terms. This seemed to require the United States to charge equal tolls to all users regardless of nationality.

political prisoners. The State Department supported the election of the pro-American Sudre Dartiguenave as president of Haiti and then forced him to sign a treaty that surrendered much of his country's sovereignty to the United States. In 1916, United States marines landed at Santo Domingo, capital of the Dominican Republic, to crush an impending revolution, and established a virtual dictatorship which lasted until 1924. The American military occupation brought improved material conditions and political stability to the troubled Caribbean republic but deeply offended Dominican patriots.

Bryan and Wilson argued that American intervention in the Caribbean was intended to help our sister republics solve their financial difficulties and establish politically stable regimes. In reality the United States was defending its strategic and economic interests. Wilson was afraid, like Roosevelt and Taft before him, that the continued turmoil in these countries would invite European, particularly German, intervention. American concern for Latin American stability and fear of German expansionism was not entirely invalid. Unfortunately, American attitudes were cloaked in sanctimony. Perhaps if the United States had been less self-deceived about its interests and less noisy in proclaiming its virtue, it would have offended Latin Americans less.

The inconsistencies of Wilsonian foreign policy were most evident in our treatment of Mexico. Aside from Europe, Wilson was forced to pay more attention to Mexico than to any other part of the world. While Taft was still president, a revolution overthrew Porfirio Diaz, the Mexican strongman who had been the country's virtual dictator for three decades. During Diaz's long reign, American investors had poured a billion dollars into Mexican mines, oil wells, and railroads. By 1913 over fifty thousand Americans were living in that country, serving as mining engineers, geologists, and businessmen. In some ways Mexico benefited from this influx of American capital and expertise. Some Mexicans grew rich under Diaz's regime, and the nation acquired much-needed railroads, factories, and urban amenities. But foreign investment did not improve the lot of the ordinary Mexican. Most still lived as half-free peons as they had for centuries, steeped in ignorance and poverty and toiling under conditions akin to those of black sharecroppers in the American South. Equally discontented, though perhaps not equally exploited, were the country's intellectuals and members of the small, liberal middle class. These people hated the brutal and undemocratic rule of Diaz, and they deplored the extent to which he had given away Mexico's resources to foreigners.

In 1911 Diaz's enemies, under Francisco Madero, a gentleman farmer, spiritualist, and homeopathic physician, launched a revolt against the dictator that quickly overthrew him. The Taft administration recognized the Madero government and embargoed munitions shipments to Madero's foes. Unfortunately, these foes proved too strong. Madero tried to effect sweeping reforms which aroused the hostility of the Mexican aristocracy, the army, and the Church. For a brief time, he managed to hold on to office, but his power steadily weakened, and in 1913 he was murdered in a coup d'état mounted by Victoriano Huerta, his chief military advisor.

Taft left the question of recognizing the Huerta government to his successor, and Wilson found the problem almost the first order of business in 1913. Certain groups in the United States favored recognition. Businessmen with investments in Mexico preferred Huerta, since he was clearly more friendly to foreign capital than the Mexican liberals. The American Catholic Church also favored the general because the liberals were anticlerical and hostile to the Catholic Church in Mexico. Finally, precedent favored Huerta. The United States traditionally had recognized established governments, as had the other major nations of the world, no matter what methods they had used to gain power or what their internal policies had been. Diplomatic recognition had not implied approval but merely an acceptance of international realities. State Department specialists pointed out this precedent to Wilson, noting that the Huerta regime was the only effective government that Mexico had.

But Wilson refused to be pushed into a course he considered morally contemptible. Huerta's accession to power was based on murder and did not represent the will of the "eighty-five percent" of the Mexican people who were "now struggling toward liberty." He would not, the president remarked to a friend, "recognize a government of butchers."

Wilson soon translated this attitude into action. On March 11, 1913, he proclaimed a new policy toward revolutionary regimes in Latin America. Recognition of such governments was possible, he declared,

> only when supported at every turn by the orderly processes of just government based upon law, not upon arbitrary or irregular force. We hold, as I am sure all thoughtful leaders of republican governments everywhere hold, that just government rests always upon the consent of the governed, and that there can be no freedom without order based upon law and upon the public conscience and approval. We shall look to make these principles the basis of mutual intercourse, respect and helpfulness between our sister republics and ourselves.

Wilson's announced reasons for nonrecognition, then, were mainly ethical, but he could also claim that Huerta's government was not securely established. Almost on the very day that Huerta took power, a new liberal revolution broke out in northern Mexico under the leadership of Venustiano Carranza, a self-proclaimed "constitutionalist." It now looked as if Mexico was in for a long period of civil war and disorder with the final outcome uncertain. To recognize Huerta might leave the United States foolishly holding the bag.

The likelihood of an extended period of trouble south of the border disturbed many Americans. Businessmen feared damage to their property.

Other citizens worried about the possible loss of American lives. Despite the gloomy prospects, Wilson waited to see what would happen in Mexico before committing himself to a definite plan of action. The president called this policy "watchful waiting," but his critics were annoyed at what they considered his feckless wavering. One skeptic likened Wilson's policies in Mexico to a new ballroom dance. The "Wilson tango" was "one step forward, two steps backward, sidestep, hesitate."

The president eventually lost patience and intervened in the chaotic Mexican situation. In August 1913 he sent an American representative, John Lind, former governor of Minnesota, to demand assurances from Huerta that he would hold an early national election. Huerta himself could not be a candidate and had to promise to accept the results. Such an agreement, Wilson believed, would enable Mexico to return to constitutional processes and allow the Mexican people to express their political wishes freely. Although by now severely pressed by Carranza's forces, Huerta announced that he would oppose with arms any attempt by the United States to intrude into Mexico's domestic affairs. Soon after, he imprisoned 110 of his opponents in the Mexican Chamber of Deputies and set up a full-fledged military dictatorship.

This turn of events further incensed Wilson. In November 1913 he informed Sir William Tyrrell, representative of the British foreign secretary, that he was going to "teach the South American [sic] republics to elect good men." For a time he considered blockading the major Mexican ports. He soon reconsidered and settled for trying to quarantine Huerta diplomatically and putting pressure on England and other powers to withdraw their recognition. Assured by Wilson that both countries could work together towards establishing a new government in Mexico that would guarantee the safety of foreign lives and property, the British yielded to Wilson, withdrew their recognition, and advised Huerta to cooperate with the United States. Huerta refused, and Wilson now determined to force him out of office.

The president contacted the Carranza people and offered to aid them in overthrowing Huerta in exchange for promises of free elections when they were victorious. The offer created a dilemma for Huerta's opponents. American help was not to be lightly rejected, but what would it entail? Fearing that it meant American troops on Mexican soil, they turned down Wilson's offer, stating that they wanted only American recognition as Mexico's legal government. Despite this rebuff Wilson persisted in pressing American cooperation on the Carranza constitutionalists. This only made them more wary of the Yankees, whose importuning seemed merely to strengthen Huerta by bringing to his side Mexicans who were outraged by United States intervention. Meanwhile, months passed, and the detested dictatorship remained in power.

Suddenly the tense situation exploded. In April 1914 some crew members of an American naval vessel docked at the port of Tampico went ashore to purchase supplies. They were arrested by a Huertista officer. Although they were soon released, the hot-headed American naval commander, Admiral Henry T. Mayo, sent an ultimatum to the Mexican general in Tampico demanding that he punish the guilty Mexican officer and order a twenty-one gun salute to the American flag. The Mexican commander apologized and promised that disciplinary actions would be taken against his aggressive subordinate, but he refused to salute the American flag.

Although Mayo's demands were unauthorized, the American public considered this refusal insulting, and Congress gave Wilson the power to intervene militarily. Meanwhile, the State Department learned that some German merchants were about to land munitions at the Atlantic port of Vera Cruz. To forestall this move the American naval commander attacked the city. The Mexicans resisted, and in the fighting that followed, over a hundred Mexicans lost their lives.

War with Mexico now seemed likely unless Wilson was willing to risk humiliation by withdrawing American troops. The president was dismayed at this unexpected turn of events. At home the country refused to back him. Roosevelt predictably threatened to return from a European trip and raise a brigade of cavalry to fight as in 1898, but church groups, labor leaders, anti-imperialists, and even bankers expressed dismay at the possibility of war. Abroad the reaction was still more negative. In Mexico, thousands volunteered to fight the American invaders, and mobs burned a number of United States consulates. Elsewhere in Latin America, the Americans were fiercely attacked in the press as brutal imperialists.

Wilson tried to explain his actions in Mexico. He did not wish to injure the Mexican people, he stated. Indeed, he had nothing but sympathy for them and hoped to see Mexico establish a new order based on "human liberty and human rights." The new system he envisaged would allow foreign investment but would not condone foreign economic exploitation. Mexico, he agreed, must undertake fundamental change, especially land redistribution, but "by constitutional means" that would compensate landlords.

These remarks reveal Wilson's decency and understanding, but they also expose his limitations. His solution for Mexico's problems was stamped with an Anglo-Saxon label. It suited a society whose class differences and ideological disputes were reconcilable. That it made practical sense in a nation like Mexico, deeply divided by class, caste, belief, and race, was dubious. His inability to see that America's answers often were unsuitable for other countries was a persistent fault in Wilson's foreign policy and caused much mischief and grief in the years to come.

Fortunately for the president, this time he was rescued from the consequences of his own limitations and his subordinates' overreaction. In late

April 1914, Argentina, Brazil, and Chile (the so-called ABC powers) offered to mediate between Mexico and the United States, and Wilson, glad to save face, immediately accepted. On the other side, Huerta was pressured into agreeing to mediation by England, France, and Germany. In May the United States, Mexico, and the ABC powers met at Niagara Falls, Canada, and the two neighbors thrashed out an agreement that settled their outstanding differences. This accord, however, turned out to be irrelevant. The Niagara Falls agreement was negotiated with Huerta, but by this time, Huerta's power had almost disintegrated; on July 15 he resigned, turning over the presidency to a temporary successor, who then turned it over to Carranza.

The American government had worked hard for Huerta's fall, but ironically the United States soon came close to war with the new Mexican regime. This strange situation was brought about by Francisco ("Pancho") Villa, a former supporter of Carranza, who in September 1914 broke with his chief and attempted to establish himself as an independent leader in the divided nation. Driven northward to the American border by the Carranza forces, Villa tried to goad the United States into some overt action against Mexico which he could then use to his advantage. In January 1916 at Santa Ysabel in Chihuahua, his forces boarded a train and crying "Viva Villa!" and "Death to the Gringos!" shot at every American in sight. Eighteen Americans died at Santa Ysabel and seventeen more at Columbus, New Mexico, two months later, when Villa crossed the border and shot up the town.

Villa almost succeeded in his plan. Under great pressure from Congress to avenge the cold-blooded killings, in March Wilson ordered General John J. Pershing to cross into Mexico with six thousand troops to capture Villa. The wily Mexican leader eluded the American army, however, while drawing it deeper and deeper into Mexico's northern states. Carranza, who had agreed to permit the Americans to cross into Mexico to pursue Villa, had not contemplated an invasion on this scale, and he denounced Pershing's incursion as a violation of Mexican sovereignty. Before long, actual skirmishes between the Mexican and American military forces were taking place deep within Mexico.

War seemed certain. But at the last minute a surge of peace sentiment among the American people made Wilson realize the enormity of attacking America's weaker neighbor. In January 1917, with the country about to intervene in Europe, Wilson ordered Pershing back to his Texas base. The next month the president sent Ambassador Henry P. Fletcher to Mexico and in effect finally recognized the Carranza regime as Mexico's legitimate government. The Mexican revolution had not run its course, and in the decades ahead, relations between the two American republics often were troubled. But the worst had been avoided: America had been spared the trauma and disgrace of another Mexican war.

III

Months before the problems to the south came to a head, the United States had become deeply entangled in European affairs. Since the outbreak of hostilities, Americans had been trying to avoid active involvement. They might take sides, but only as spectators at a football game; few at first favored rushing onto the field to help one team smash the other. No matter how many citizens feared Germany or, alternately, detested Britain, most would have accepted defeat for the side they favored if the war could have been kept at arm's length.

Unfortunately, it could not. As in 1812, the United States was the only important neutral in a world at war. In peace time, American vessels and American goods traveled to every part of the world. Now, more than ever, the United States was a vital source of food, fiber, raw materials, and manufactured goods. Neither side could ignore that fact. Each had to try to keep the sea lanes open for its own use while denying the American cornucopia to its enemies. But the task was not a symmetrical one. The Allied navies controlled the surface sea routes to Europe. They could easily blockade the Central Powers while ensuring their own access to American goods. Germany and Austria could never hope to get more than a trickle through the British blockade, but their raiders could make the sea lanes risky for Allied commerce and so reduce the impact of American supplies.

Blockades and commerce raids unfortunately directly challenged the rights of neutral traders and raised serious issues of international law. Today we may find the whole concept of neutral rights and limited war rather elusive. We live in a period of undeclared wars, mass killings of civilians, terrorism, genocide, saturation bombing, and other brutally unrestrained crimes against human beings in the name of ideology or national interest. The world seems to have given up the idea that even countries at war must limit their behavior. How can we understand the elaborate rules that governed the dealings of belligerents with one another and with neutral nations before our time? But men did take these rules seriously in 1914 and were even ready to go to war to uphold them. Of course, war between major powers, horrible though it was, did not then threaten total world annihilation as it does today.

At beginning of World War I, the United States expected European belligerents to observe the commercial rights it believed due to a neutral nation. Under American definition vessels owned by neutrals had the right to carry all goods except contraband ("free ships make free goods"). Contraband in turn was to be strictly defined as arms and munitions, with such items as food, textiles, and naval stores excluded from the list. Neutrals could trade freely with all the belligerents, subject only to recognized rules of blockade. Under these rules belligerents had the right to establish a naval blockade off an enemy's coast to keep that enemy from receiving war

material (that is, contraband) from other countries. Under a blockade belligerents were entitled to stop vessels, inspect them for this material, and
confiscate ships or cargoes if contraband was found. Even a naval blockade
had to be conducted in certain specific ways, however. The blockading
power was required to have enough ships to mount effective guard outside
enemy harbors to stop incoming ships to inspect them for illegal goods in
an orderly manner. It could not merely declare a "paper blockade," that is,
one not backed by a substantial naval force, and use this as an excuse to
confiscate the property of suspected violators on a catch-as-catch-can basis.
In addition, the blockading power had to provide for the safety of the
passengers and crews of whatever vessels it detained.

To Wilson the right of a neutral citizen to go wherever he pleased, sell
whatever he pleased to whomever he pleased, subject only to recognized
rules of war, was more than a mere legal abstraction. It was also more than
a matter of simple profit. What was at stake, he believed, was the fundamental structure of the international order. This had to be based on well-defined,
inviolable rules which in turn had to be derived from basic ethical principles.
Not only was this inherently right and just, it was to America's advantage
as well, since American prosperity and American interests could be served
best by a world order respectful of international law.

It is easy enough to be cynical of this view. The United States, as the
major trading neutral, had much to gain materially by as broad a definition
of neutral rights as possible. Yet in the president's view, immediate profits
from munitions sales and the carrying trade were far less important than the
gains to America of a stable system of acceptable international morality.
The president hoped to serve long-range American interests rather than
immediate ones, but he had little doubt that such a system was also best for
the world as a whole.

Until 1917 these views tended to reinforce Wilson's desire for peace. If
such a system was to prevail, the United States had to set an example for
the rest of the world. America had to remain at peace so that it could exert
its moral force to end the fighting quickly. After peace was achieved, it
would be possible to establish a new international regime based on disarmament, arbitration, and international justice. America, Wilson declared,
"should show herself in this time of peculiar trial a nation fit beyond others
to exhibit the fine poise of undisturbed judgment, the dignity of self-control,
the efficiency of dispassionate action; a nation that neither sits in judgment
upon others nor is disturbed in her own counsels and which keeps herself
fit and free to do what is honest and disinterested and truly serviceable for
the peace of the world."

Unfortunately, Wilson's hope of simultaneously protecting traditional
American commercial rights, keeping the United States in a position to
mediate impartially among the belligerents, and reforming the world was
impractical and unrealistic. Both the Allies and the Central Powers fought

for victory. Certainly neither side shared Wilson's view that a neutral America might be the instrument by which to forge a better international regime. The Allies hoped to shake the Americans out of their neutral position into full-fledged participation against the Central Powers. The Germans were anxious to preserve American neutrality but were skeptical of Wilson's altruism and were not interested, as German chancellor Theobald Bethmann-Hollweg admitted, in a utopian postwar order.

Neither side could leave American relations to chance, and they were soon engaged in a titanic tug-of-war to manipulate American opinion. From the outset the Allies had the advantage. Besides the natural sympathies of many Americans for the Western democracies, the British and French proved masters at what the *New York Times* would call the "first press agents' war." Allied propaganda superiority was established almost immediately when the British cut the cable lines connecting Germany with the United States, forcing the Germans to rely on the uncertain and roundabout mails or the still imperfect wireless to get their side of the story before the American public. This was, however, only part of the problem. For years American newspaper readers had relied on the British news services for information about Europe, and this practice continued after the outbreak of war. The bias inherent in this arrangement was amplified by the fact that American foreign correspondents on the various battle fronts usually traveled with the Allied troops, since the British and French controlled the cable lines. Only in this way could the American newsmen be sure their dispatches home would arrive safely.

Even if the Allies had not completely dominated the channels of information, they would have outdistanced their opponents. The Germans were incredibly inept in dealing with world opinion. The rulers of imperial Germany, although they were not the uncivilized savages the Allies depicted, were scarcely humane democrats. Arrogant, jingoistic, and abrasive, they were incapable of disguising their true attitudes, and their war propaganda generally ended up arousing revulsion and distaste. The "Hymn of Hate Against England" by Ernest Lissauer, a poem that was handed out to German soldiers, typified much of what the Americans found repugnant about German propaganda:

> You we will hate with a lasting hate,
> We will never forego our hate,
> Hate by water and hate by land,
> Hate of the head and hate of the hand,
> Hate of the hammer and hate of the crown,
> Hate of seventy millions choking down.
> We love as one, we hate as one,
> We have one foe and one alone—
>   ENGLAND!

Even more important in repelling Americans than German words were

German deeds. The German invasion of Belgium placed every American friend of the Central Powers at a disadvantage. The invasion itself directly violated a solemn international agreement dating from the early nineteenth century that guaranteed Belgium's frontiers, and the outrageousness of the act was exacerbated by the German chancellor's contemptuous reference to the treaty as a "scrap of paper." The occupation that followed made matters still worse. The patriotic Belgians refused to accept meekly their German conquerors and soon were defying the occupation authorities. Eventually Belgian patriots attacked German troops. The Germans retaliated by executing scores of Belgian civilians and by burning the university town of Louvain. The kaiser only aroused fresh outrage at Germany when he clumsily sought to justify the desecration of the beautiful old city.

However awful the reality, the Allies undoubtedly used Belgium's plight for their own propaganda advantage. In 1915 the British government issued an official report depicting the outrages committed by the Germans in Belgium. Signed by James Bryce, a distinguished historian and respected former British ambassador to Washington, it described in gruesome detail the torture, mutilation, and murder of Belgian civilians. Many of the atrocity tales were unsubstantiated; others were exaggerated. But the Bryce report convinced many Americans that the Germans were savage "Huns," who deserved the condemnation of the whole civilized world.

Still another advantage of Britain and France was the pro-Ally sympathies of the men in strategic foreign policy positions in the Wilson administration. Colonel Edward House, the president's closest adviser and personal emissary for many years, repeatedly urged Wilson to enter the war on the Allied side. The American ambassador to Britain, Walter Hines Page, was a confirmed anglophile who worked regularly with Sir Edward Grey, the British foreign secretary, to soften the impact of Anglo-American clashes. Another pro-Ally Wilson adviser was Robert Lansing, who became secretary of state when Bryan resigned in protest over what he considered an excessively strong note to the German government following the sinking of the *Lusitania.* Former counselor of the State Department, Lansing believed that the United States would and should eventually enter the war on the Allied side. In his memoirs he later described his efforts to talk the American people into accepting war with the Central Powers. "It was necessary to analyze American public opinion without prejudice and to determine upon a general course of action which would not abruptly challenge that opinion but guide it in the right direction." The Wilson administration, he wrote, had to show that "everything had been done to avoid war in order to arouse a public demand for it." Lansing tried to encourage Wilson to admit his own pro-Ally sympathies and, like House, urged him to be tolerant of the British and the French.

Finally, there was the president himself. Although Wilson sincerely tried to be neutral "in fact as well as name," his sympathies were irrefutably on the side of the Allies. A great admirer of British political institutions, he had set out to prove in his first book, *Congressional Government*, that the British parliamentary system was superior to his own country's. Like a virtuous man struggling against worldly temptations, Wilson attempted to prevent his feelings about the Allies and the Central Powers from influencing his course of action. He was not always successful. At one point he told Spring Rice that "everything I love most in the world is at stake. . . . If they [the Germans] succeed, we shall be forced to take such measures of defence here as would be fatal to our form of Government and American ideals."

Allied propaganda and official American anglophilia contributed significantly to pushing the American republic into the war, but they are not enough to explain the drift to belligerency. America also had a material stake in Allied victory. During the 1930s revisionist historians claimed that economic motives lay behind American entrance into World War I. The war, they insisted, was foisted on the country by a cabal of "merchants of death"—the munitions makers, ship builders, armor plate manufacturers, bankers, and other businessmen who made good dividends out of the belligerents' needs. These men had an interest in Allied victory not shared by other Americans, and their power and influence proved the undoing of neutrality.

Without question America's economic interests worked in favor of the Allies, though we do not have to accept so exaggerated an interpretation. The American economy had been depressed in 1913–14. The international crisis of late summer 1914 made things worse for a while. But then war orders began to pour in for guns, ammunition, motor vehicles, horses, wheat, flour, and cotton. At first the Allies were able to pay for these supplies by liquidating their American investments, converting the American bonds and stocks held by their citizens into guns and supplies. But as these funds were used up, Britain, France, and later Italy appealed to American bankers for loans.

Soon after the war started, J. P. Morgan was asked by the French government to privately lend it $100 million. Morgan in turn asked the State Department whether he would be permitted to do this. Distracted by the death of his first wife, Wilson left the answer entirely to Secretary of State Bryan, who refused on the grounds that loans to belligerents violated the essence of neutrality. As the secretary told the president, "money is the worst of all contrabands—it commands all other things."

But as Allied cash began to give out, President Wilson countermanded the State Department, and in October 1914, Bryan announced that the government would permit bankers to advance commercial credits. By August 1916 this policy was extended to permit outright loans. By April 1917 American private citizens and bankers had lent the Allies some $2.3 billion, while the Germans were able to raise only $27 million in the same period.

The recession of 1913–14 soon gave way to exuberant prosperity. Fueled by war orders, the American economy bounded upward. Unemployment evaporated, and wages and profits shot up. Good times normally inspire national confidence, but Americans remained insecure. Prosperity seemed to depend on continued Allied war orders. In addition, with so much credit extended to Britain and France, could the United States afford to let Germany win?

Keenly aware of how vital American aid was to their enemies, the Germans complained bitterly about the growing trans-Atlantic trade in munitions. On numerous occasions the German government accused the United States of prolonging the struggle by supplying the Allies with indispensable war materiel. In the United States itself, *The Fatherland,* a pro-German newspaper published in New York,[4] exclaimed in fury: "We [Americans] prattle about humanity, while we manufacture poisoned shrapnel and picric acid for profit. Ten thousand German widows, ten thousand graves bear the legend 'Made in America.'" The State Department answered the complaints of the Central Powers by insisting that it was perfectly legal for private firms in a neutral country to sell munitions to belligerents. Moreover, an embargo would so strongly favor the better-prepared Germans that it would merely constitute an unneutral act on the other side of the scale.

Notwithstanding the State Department's rationalization, there was truth in the charges of unneutrality toward the Central Powers. Allied dependence on American munitions gave Wilson the leverage he needed to force major trade concessions out of the British. An embargo on American arms exports might have hurt the American economy temporarily, but it would have been a disaster for the British and French. It is hard to imagine that, faced with such a prospect, they would not have yielded to virtually all American demands. Wilson either failed to see what weapon he had or refused to use it, and in actual fact, Allied war orders merely tied the American economy to the Allied war effort and helped commit the United States to the Allied cause.

Although propaganda, official anglophilia, and economic dependence all tilted the balance against Germany, the neutral rights issue ultimately proved crucial. From the beginning of the war, the British and the Germans were both guilty of violating American neutrality. The British were actually the first to anger the United States when they refused Bryan's request in August 1914 to abide by the Declaration of London. This agreement attempted to codify the rules of naval warfare in a way that would have weakened traditional British naval superiority. It was never ratified, but the United States hoped that the warring nations would accept it during the

---

[4]*The Fatherland* was a propaganda sheet subsidized by the German government and edited by George Sylvester Viereck.

conflict. The Central Powers, with navies inferior to Britain's, were happy to agree, but England refused.

This marked only the beginning of Anglo-American differences. Trying to avoid offending Southerners, who counted on large German cotton purchases to lift them out of the 1913–14 economic doldrums, the British at first excluded cotton from their list of absolute contraband.[5] Then in August 1915, they reversed themselves. Southern congressmen, fearful of yet another year of depression, protested and demanded that Washington take action against the British. To allay Southern anger and prevent American retaliation, the British government unofficially negotiated an agreement with the Federal Reserve Board to buy enough cotton to maintain its price.

The British also infuriated the United States by disregarding the traditional rules concerning detention and search of neutral ships. In the past under international law, a belligerent could stop a neutral merchant ship on the seas and search it for contraband but, if none were found, had to permit it to resume its voyage. The British now insisted on bringing neutral vessels into port and detaining them until they could be thoroughly inspected, a practice that resulted in long delays and serious losses for the merchants involved.

They also insisted on the doctrine of "continuous voyage," by which a neutral vessel en route to a neutral port might be detained if the British had reason to think that its cargo was destined ultimately for the Central Powers. As the Allied governments saw it, the American claim that such trade with neutrals was inviolable, ignored the fact that it had become a subterfuge for indirectly supplying their enemies with much-needed commodities and constituted a serious leak in their blockade.

The British used still other means to impede neutral commerce. They planted mines in the North Sea, forcing vessels routed through the area to stop at English ports to get directions for safe passage. They opened neutral mail on the grounds that it might contain information useful to the Central Powers. They set up blacklists of American firms suspected of trading with Germany through such European neutrals as Holland and Denmark. In each of these cases, British motives are understandable: Britain was fighting for its life, it believed, and could not afford to comply with the niceties of international law. But these actions outraged American businessmen, who demanded that the American government intervene to stop them.

The State Department in fact complained about each violation of American rights. Periodically it shot off notes protesting policies that illegally interfered with American trade. But the messages seldom got through in-

---

[5]Absolute contraband was distinguished from provisional contraband. The latter could be sold to the enemy if the British felt it would not hurt them; the former was interdicted totally.

tact. At times the Department's intentions were frustrated by its own representatives abroad. At one point Ambassador Page told Sir Edward Grey that he did not agree with a strongly worded State Department dispatch and would help the foreign secretary compose an acceptable answer to it! But the protests themselves were often half-hearted. Pro-Ally sentiment was so strong in American government circles that Washington could not bring itself to force a showdown.

Yet the complaints were not entirely ineffective. We have already noted the British effort to uphold Southern cotton prices after declaring cotton contraband. At various times, moreover, the British promised to compensate Americans for economic losses after the war. In fact, broadly speaking, the British were able to adhere to the traditional practices of warfare on the high seas because they controlled the ocean surface with their incomparable navy. They certainly stretched these practices, but they managed nevertheless to stay roughly within the bounds of traditional international law.

The British-French performance looked all the better when contrasted with the German. The chief German naval weapon was the small, fragile U-boat (*unterseeboot*), a submarine armed with torpedoes and one small deck gun. The major advantage of the U-boat was its ability to creep up on its target unseen and sink it without warning. These tactics were perfectly legal under international law when employed against enemy warships but were enjoined against merchant vessels. The rules of naval war, as developed in the era of the surface cruiser, forbade attacks on civilians, even those traveling on enemy ships. They also required, as we have seen, that commercial vessels be stopped and their cargoes inspected for contraband before being seized or sunk. But how could the submarine do this? The thin-skinned U-boats were highly vulnerable to an armed ship's guns and could not risk coming to the surface to go through the inspection procedure. In any case, by arming freighters and liners, the Germans contended, the British were converting them into naval vessels which could be rightfully attacked without warning. But legality aside, the submarine was obviously most effective when used for hit-and-run attacks on all shipping that came within a particular zone, whether naval or merchant, enemy or neutral.

Such a shoot-on-sight policy was strongly favored by the German navy and by the more militaristic groups in German political life. The German chancellor, Theobald Bethmann-Hollweg, who foresaw that it would lead to serious problems with the United States, resisted it, though he believed it morally justified by Britain's blockade. Bethmann-Hollweg was forced to yield. In February 1915 the German government announced that it was setting up a war zone around the British Isles and would authorize its U-boats to sink all neutral or enemy ships found within it. Recognizing the probable American response, the German chancellor defended the new policy on the grounds that Britain's purpose was to starve Germany's civilian population, not merely attack its government's ability to wage war.

Regretfully, he noted, neutrals aboard these ships might be killed inadver-tently.

Americans were outraged by the February 1915 order. The State Depart-ment immediately drafted a note to the German government warning that if these "unprecedented" tactics were actually employed and American lives were lost, then the Imperial German government would be held to "a strict accountability for such acts of their naval authorities" and the United States would "take any steps it might be necessary to take to safeguard lives and property and to secure to American citizens the full enjoyment of their acknowledged rights on the high seas. . . ." To take some of the sting out of this brusque threat, the State Department tried to talk the British into removing food and other articles from their contraband list but did not prod them when they refused.

The crisis soon worsened. In March 1915 the Germans sank the British steamer *Falaba*. Drowned in the attack was Leon Thrasher, the first Ameri-can casualty of the war. The American government was divided over the proper course of action to take in protesting the *Falaba* incident. Bryan did not wish to take too hard a line with the Germans. Thrasher, he believed, should not have been traveling on a British ship in the first place, and in any case, Americans who sailed on belligerent vessels were guilty of "con-tributory negligence." Lansing, then State Department counselor, on the other hand, felt that the German attack was a serious departure from inter-national law and that to keep Americans from going wherever and however they wished was unthinkable. Bryan, in effect, was willing to forego an established "right" by forbidding all Americans to travel in the war zone, while Lansing insisted that free movement was a matter of principle. We should protest the incident, the latter wrote, "not on the loss of this single man's life but in the interests of mankind which are involved . . . ; on the manifest impropriety of a single nation essaying to alter the understandings of nations. . . ."

Wilson basically agreed with Counselor Lansing, but while he was agoniz-ing over what to do, the Germans struck again. On May 8 off the Irish coast, a German submarine sank an unarmed British Cunard luxury liner, the *Lusitania*, with one torpedo. Nearly two thousand persons died when the vessel went down in a matter of minutes. One hundred twenty-eight of the dead were United States citizens.

The German government had taken the unusual step before the liner sailed of placing a notice in the New York papers warning Americans not to travel on belligerent ships. The 200 Americans aboard the *Lusitania* had chosen to ignore the warning. Nevertheless, the sinking was a profound shock. Newspapers for days afterward carried accounts of the bravery and suffering of the survivors, and editorials denounced the attack as "crimi-nal," "bestial," "uncivilized," and "barbarous." "The torpedo that sank the *Lusitania* also sank Germany in the opinion of mankind," declared *The Nation*.

In the first excited days following the sinking, there was much talk of war with Germany. But once the furor died down, most Americans were willing to settle for firm words instead. Wilson sent a note to the German government demanding an apology for the brutal act, a promise that they would never use these tactics again, and reparations for the lives lost. This note also officially asserted for the first time the unrestricted right of Americans to travel on belligerent ships. The German reply expressed regret at the American dead but maintained that the sinking was in self-defense. The *Lusitania*, it insisted, carried arms,[6] and these would have been used eventually against German soldiers. In a second and stronger note, which caused Bryan to resign in protest, Wilson demanded that the Germans abandon submarine warfare altogether, and in a third note sent at the beginning of the summer, he threatened a break in diplomatic relations if the Germans continued to attack passenger ships.

Meanwhile, as notes passed between Berlin and Washington, the *Arabic*, another unarmed British passenger liner sailing westbound without contraband, was sent to the bottom. Two Americans were among the forty-four persons killed. The *Arabic* sinking brought to a climax the battle within the German government between the extremists, who wanted to continue unrestricted submarine warfare at all costs, and the Bethmann-Hollweg moderates, who were fearful of active American intervention. Siding with Bethmann-Hollweg, the kaiser pledged that his government would stop sinking passenger ships without warning and in the future would make provision for the safety of passengers and crews. The German promise was actually limited in extent, applying only to passenger liners, leaving unresolved the question of attacks on freighters, particularly those that were armed. Nevertheless, the German government for a while virtually suspended submarine warfare.

IV

Following the *Arabic* pledge, the submarine issue receded but not hostility to the kaiser's government. By this time many Americans were not only convinced that Germany was a brutal bully but that it was directly meddling in American domestic affairs. Shortly before the *Arabic* sinking, an American secret service agent managed to acquire a briefcase carelessly left by a German national on a streetcar in New York City. The briefcase belonged to Doctor Heinrich F. Albert, and its contents revealed him as the head of a covert German operation in the United States that contemplated sabotage

---

[6]The *Lusitania* did in fact carry a shipment of small arms, and no doubt these were destined for the western front.

of munitions factories and other facilities that were producing war materiel for the Allies. At about the same time, the British published captured documents that disclosed German-Austrian plans to foment strikes at American munitions plants. Meanwhile, two German attachés stationed in America were found to be involved in spying and sabotage and were sent home.

Americans predictably were infuriated at these machinations. The *New York World*, which published Dr. Albert's papers, asserted:

> German propaganda in the United States has become a political conspiracy against the government and people of the United States. This conspiracy is directed from Berlin and is financed by the German government. It has been organized with all the amazing thoroughness and efficiency that characterizes all German military activity, and it is as much a part of the German campaigns as the operations of armies in the field. The German government is subsidizing sedition throughout the United States.

From the distance of two generations, it is difficult to blame the Central Powers for trying to neutralize the American munitions industry. By the end of 1915, it had become an important arm of the Allied war effort. On the other hand, it is easy to see why the espionage and sabotage operations outraged Americans and why these actions further alienated them from the Central Powers.

By 1915, many Americans had concluded that the country would almost certainly be forced to enter the war. In the last months of 1914, this conviction already had led a small group of pro-Ally Americans to launch a preparedness movement. In December the preparedness people established a National Security League, which promptly announced that it foresaw war with Germany and declared that the United States must prepare itself to fight.

At first the public ignored or scoffed at the preparedness advocates. The small American army with its antiquated equipment was no doubt unready for war, but we had a wide ocean between us and any potential enemy, so why worry? Then came the sinkings of the *Lusitania* and the *Arabic* and the exposure of the German spying and sabotage network. This was followed in late 1915 by the torpedoing by the Austrians of two more unarmed passenger liners, resulting in the deaths of more Americans and in apparent disregard of the *Arabic* pledge. These events tipped the balance. At the very least, it now seemed that preparedness was an unpleasant necessity. In midsummer 1915 Wilson, who had been loath to undertake such action, asked Congress to prepare measures for expanded national security. In November 1915 he formally endorsed increased military spending and urged Congress to appropriate hundreds of millions of dollars for new ships and new army units.

Yet even now not all Americans favored preparedness. Bitterly opposed to the preparedness groups were pacifists of various kinds. Aside from pure pacifists, such as the Quakers and members of the other traditional peace churches, the opponents of preparedness included many liberals and radicals. Many progressives, convinced that war benefited only big business and the munitions makers, also feared that domestic reform would be forgotten if the country became embroiled in war. In a naive analysis of international politics that has also proven popular in more recent times, they called for Americans to solve their own domestic problems and let Europeans solve theirs. When the United States had achieved political amity, democracy, and social justice at home, Europeans would notice its accomplishments, be impressed by them, and follow its example. War would cease, and peace would reign unchallenged. Organized into the League to Limit Armaments and the Women's Peace Party, many progressives, including Jane Addams, Carrie Chapman Catt, Oswald Garrison Villard, George Foster Peabody, and Lillian Wald, resisted the preparedness advocates.

Not all progressives were pacifists, however. Many were willing to go along with Wilson's preparedness programs, feeling that a strong defense was necessary in case America inadvertently became embroiled in the European war. Preparedness need not lead to militarism, said William Borah and George Norris, and it was the only way that America could fend off Germany, which was an enemy of peace and democracy and which would, if victorious, extinguish America as a beacon light. Theodore Roosevelt, of course, supported preparedness. Indeed, TR was an outright interventionist and in his usual intemperate way attacked his antipreparedness opponents, particularly Wilson (before he changed his mind), as cowards and "abject creatures."

If anything, Socialists were still more intensely opposed to preparedness than were progressives. American Socialists considered the war in Europe a battle between rival capitalist imperialists in which the world's working classes had no vital interest. The European Socialist parties, with few exceptions, had denied their own precepts and had voted for war with the same patriotic fervor as members of the bourgeois parties. American Socialists, they insisted, must refuse to follow their European brothers and must refuse to cooperate with the capitalist war makers. As the war dragged on and Americans began to take sides against the Central Powers, some Socialists joined with the preparedness advocates. A few even supported intervention on the side of the Allies. But the Socialist party as a whole maintained its pacifist position even after America had declared war on Germany.

V

By mid-1915 Wilson's mood was becoming more militant and more pro-Ally. He still preferred peace, if possible, and was willing to try every conceivable means to avoid war. Early in the year, the president had sent

Colonel House to Europe to see if he could bring the belligerents together around a peace table. House was ignored. In January 1916 the colonel went back to Europe to talk with both sides about the possibility of a negotiated peace. Once again his mission achieved little. In Britain, France, and Germany, House discovered, the politicians wanted no part of any peace except on their own terms. Despite the stubbornness of both the Allied and German leaders, House made some vague promises to Britain and France. In talks with Sir Edward Grey, he gave the impression that the United States would join the Allies if Germany refused to accept a peace conference. In the words of the House-Grey memorandum as recorded by Grey:

> Colonel House told me that President Wilson was ready, on hearing from France and England that the moment was opportune, to propose that a Conference be summoned to put an end to the war. Should the Allies accept this proposal, and should Germany refuse it, the United States would probably enter the war against Germany.

If this conference met and peace could not be secured, "the United States would [probably] leave the Conference as a belligerent on the side of the Allies, if Germany was unreasonable."[7]

Meanwhile, the problem of neutral rights on the seas revived to plague America's relations with the belligerents. One of the German justifications for its shoot-on-sight policy was, as we have seen, the fragility of the U-boat and its vulnerability to even armed merchant vessels. To deal with this problem, in early 1916 Lansing proposed a modus vivendi: if the Allies agreed to disarm their merchant ships, the Germans would agree to the principle, suspended but not yet formally acknowledged, that their submarines would not attack such vessels without warning and without protecting the safety of civilians. In effect, the submarine would function as a surface cruiser and observe the humane rules of naval warfare laid down in past years.

Unwilling to surrender what they considered a well-established right to arm surface vessels in exchange for a German concession to abide by existing international law, the British rejected the proposal immediately. Faced with this hostile response, Lansing quickly dropped the modus vivendi proposal. Unfortunately, he had opened a Pandora's box. In explaining it to the German government, Lansing had implied that the American government regarded Allied armed merchant vessels as warships. This had been the German position all along, and they eagerly seized on the opening the Americans had created. On February 10 the kaiser's government informed the American State Department that beginning on February 29, German U-boats would resume their attacks on *armed* merchant vessels

---

[7]When Wilson received this memorandum, he cautiously added the second "probably" (the one in brackets).

without prior warning. In effect, the truce ushered in by the *Arabic* pledge was over.

The sequence of events alarmed the pacifists and the isolationists. The Wilson administration, by dropping the modus vivendi, seemed to be saying that it accepted the British position that armed merchant vessels were not warships. If this were so, then by the administration's interpretation, Americans would have the right to travel on such vessels. Since the Germans now intended to attack them on sight, Wilson was almost guaranteeing a collision with Germany. Hoping to head off such a confrontation, Representative Jeff McLemore of Texas and Senator Thomas P. Gore of Oklahoma introduced resolutions forbidding American travel on armed or contraband-carrying ships. Wilson interpreted this as a challenge to his leadership in foreign affairs and a cowardly surrender of American rights. "For my own part," he wrote the chairman of the Senate Foreign Relations Committee, "I cannot consent to any abridgement of the rights of American citizens in any respect. . . . Once accept a single abatement of rights, and many other humiliations would certainly follow, and the whole fine fabric of international law might crumble under our hands piece by piece." Congress backed down under the president's pressure and tabled the Gore-McLemore resolutions.

Wilson's victory over Congress and the peace groups marked the further drift to war. With each passing week, American intervention seemed to approach closer. Then on March 25, 1916, a U-boat torpedoed an unarmed French channel steamer, the *Sussex*, carrying a number of American passengers. Although the vessel remained afloat, eighty lives were lost and a number of Americans were injured. Secretary Lansing advised severing relations with Germany immediately. Realizing that the public was still opposed to war and feeling that it was the wrong time for a complete break, Wilson vetoed this course of action. Instead, he sent a curt warning (the *Sussex* note) to the German government that unless it surrendered its unrestricted submarine warfare against all passenger- and freight-carrying ships, the United States would break off diplomatic relations.

Luckily, the moderates, led by Bethmann-Hollweg, were still in control in Berlin. On May 8, 1916, the German government gave the pledge required by Wilson: Germany would abandon its claim to shoot on sight in all cases except those involving actual units of the enemy navy. There was one qualifier, however. It would accept the American terms only if the United States also compelled the Allies to abide by the rules of international law. Wilson chose to accept the *Sussex* pledge, even though he knew it would be impossible to extract the guarantees the Germans wanted. The Germans themselves, he realized, would abide by their promise only as long as it was militarily expedient for them to do so. But for the time being, peace was preserved, and that was enough.

For some months after the *Sussex* pledge, the Germans desisted from illegal submarine warfare. Meanwhile, the British intensified their efforts to stifle the German economy. It was during this period that they refused to permit American ship owners to use their coaling facilities unless they obeyed strict British orders for operating their vessels, seized packages and parcels from the United States to look for contraband, and opened and read letters to and from America. This last practice, businessmen complained, enabled the British to steal American trade secrets.

Anglo-American relations in 1916 were further strained by British tactics in suppressing the Easter Rebellion in Ireland. In April, under the leadership of the Irish Republican Brotherhood, a German-aided revolt against England erupted in Dublin. British troops smashed the uprising, executed its leaders, and put Ireland under martial law. The affair revolted many Americans, especially Irish-Americans, who accused Britain of hypocrisy in parading before the world as a champion of democracy while treating Ireland tyrannically.

British-American relations reached their low point in the summer of 1916, a few months after the Easter Rebellion, when the British established their economic blacklist of American private firms suspected of aiding the Central Powers. Americans found this measure the most nettlesome and punitive of all British regulations. Not only did the blacklisted firms lose their British customers, they also lost business at home since many American firms, fearful of being blacklisted themselves, ceased to do business with them as well. Britain was probably within its rights in issuing the blacklist, but in antagonizing American businessmen, it was committing a grave blunder. Already annoyed at its truculent behavior in Ireland, many influential Americans now concluded that Britain had become totally indifferent to opinion on this side of the Atlantic. In a letter to Colonel House, Wilson expressed the anger of many of his countrymen:

> I am, I must admit, about at the end of my patience with Great Britain and the Allies. This blacklist business is the last straw. I have told Spring Rice so, and he sees the reasons very clearly. Both he and Jusserand [Jean Jules Jusserand, French Ambassador to the United States] think it is a stupid blunder. I am seriously considering asking Congress to authorize me to prohibit loans and restrict exportations to the Allies. . . . Polk [Frank L. Polk, Lansing's successor as counselor of the State Department] and I are compounding a very sharp note. I may feel obliged to make it as sharp as the one to Germany on the submarine. . . . Can we any longer endure their intolerable course?

The note actually sent was strong, and although the British did not formally rescind the blacklist, they realized that they had blundered and slowly retreated.

For the next few months, foreign affairs took a back seat to the 1916 presidential election. Yet the issue of war or peace could not be ignored during the campaign. The Republicans nominated Supreme Court Justice Charles Evans Hughes, while the Democrats renominated Wilson by acclamation. The war in Europe created a quandary for Hughes, the former progressive governor of New York. His chief task, obviously, was to win the votes of those who were dissatisfied with Wilson's policies, both foreign and domestic. Domestically, Hughes was a liberal. Wilson made him out to be a conservative, however, and the Republican candidate had to establish his liberal credentials anew without antagonizing the conservative wing of the party. In foreign policy he had to win over German- and Irish-Americans without appearing to those Republicans like Roosevelt and Henry Cabot Lodge, who were either neutral or partisans of the Allies, too friendly to the Central Powers. The effect of this straddling stance was to make Hughes seem inconsistent and evasive.

Wilson, on the other hand, not only had the advantage of being the incumbent but his supporters could truthfully say, "he kept us out of war" without specifying what Wilson would do in the future. Democratic strategy was to reiterate Wilson's successful avoidance of war over and over. A typical paid Democratic advertisement in the *New York Times* stated:

You are Working;
   —Not Fighting!
Alive and Happy:
   —Not Cannon Fodder!
Wilson and Peace with Honor?
   or
Hughes with Roosevelt and War?

As news of the first election returns trickled in on the evening of November 7, 1916, it seemed that Hughes had won by a landslide. But when the results arrived from the Middle and Far West, where isolationism was stronger, Wilson moved ahead and in the end won by a close margin. The final vote gave Wilson slightly over 9 million votes, to Hughes's 8.5 million.

The election made it clear that although Americans had strong sympathies in the war, they still very much wanted to keep out of it, and in the wake of his victory, Wilson decided to make one last effort to secure peace between the Allies and the Central Powers. On December 18 he sent notes to the belligerents asking them to state their war aims and offering once again to mediate. Neither side was willing to stop fighting, and although they tried to disguise their true attitudes by diplomatic evasion, both proved hostile to Wilson's request. In a speech to Congress really meant for the belligerents, Wilson responded to this rebuff on January 22, 1917. To guarantee world peace, he said, the countries of the world must establish a league of nations and must seek "peace without victory." He warned the belligerents that:

Victory would mean peace forced upon the loser, a victor's terms imposed upon the vanquished. It would be accepted in humiliation under duress, at an intolerable sacrifice, and would leave a sting, a resentment, a bitter memory upon which terms of peace would rest, not permanently, but only as upon quicksand. Only a peace between equals can last, only a peace the very principle of which is equality and a common participation in a common benefit. The right state of mind, the right feeling between nations, is as necessary for a lasting peace as is the just settlement of vexed questions of territory or of racial and national allegiance.

The president's words were prophetic.

VI

Wilson did not know at this point that fateful changes had been taking place in Germany. By the end of 1916, the persistent military stalemate on the European war fronts had decisively shifted the balance of power in Germany from the civilian leaders to the military commanders. The kaiser was now merely a figurehead for a virtual military dictatorship. At a momentous conference in January 1917, the military leaders told Wilhelm that the United States could never send enough men to Europe in time to make a military difference. And since America was already providing the Allies with as much war materiel and financial aid as it could, actual war with the United States would not change the military situation significantly. Unrestricted submarine warfare, on the other hand, might knock Britain out of the war in short order.

The emperor could do little but accept the view of his military advisers. On January 31, 1917, less than two weeks after Wilson's peace without victory appeal, the German ambassador in Washington, Count Johann von Bernstorff, informed Secretary Lansing that Germany would direct its U-boats to sink all ships, both neutral and belligerent, without warning in a specified zone around Great Britain, France, Italy, and in the eastern Mediterranean.

Wilson was utterly dismayed by this move. Relations with Germany since May had been better than those with the Allies. The new German order totally repudiated the *Sussex* pledge, and Wilson was faced with the prospect of breaking with Germany or admitting that the United States would not defend its stand on unrestricted U-boat warfare. On February 3, 1917, Wilson appeared before Congress and announced the severing of diplomatic relations with Germany. Most Americans, even many of Wilson's critics, supported his decision. Volunteers began to show up at army enlistment centers.

But war was still some distance away. Wilson hoped that a showdown could yet be avoided if the Germans exercised restraint. His prayers went unanswered. In January British intelligence intercepted a sensational note from the German foreign secretary, Alfred Zimmermann, to the German minister to Mexico. The communication was turned over to the American ambassador in England, sent to Wilson, and then published in the American press. The note said:

> We intend to begin . . . unrestricted submarine warfare. We shall endeavor in spite of this to keep the United States of America neutral. In the event of this not succeeding, we make Mexico a proposal of alliance on the following basis: make war together, make peace together, generous financial support and an understanding on our part that Mexico is to reconquer the lost territory in Texas, New Mexico and Arizona. You will inform the President [of Mexico] of the above most secretly as soon as the outbreak of war with the United States of America is certain and add the suggestion that he should, on his own initiative, invite Japan to immediate adherence and at the same time mediate between Japan [which was at this point at war with Germany] and ourselves. Please call the President's attention to the fact that the ruthless employment of our submarines now offers the prospect of compelling England in a few months to make peace.

The Zimmermann telegram was a shocker! Southerners and Southwesterners felt threatened by the possible loss of their territory to Mexico. Westerners, barraged for years by propaganda about the "Yellow Peril," were startled by the idea of a Japanese attack in the Pacific. Anti-German feelings, already intense, engulfed the United States. Events now moved quickly. Wilson already had proposed that Congress allow him to permit the arming of American merchant vessels sailing to the war zones. When the isolationists in the Senate filibustered the measure to death, Wilson proceeded to arm the vessels by executive order after denouncing the obstructionists as a "little group of willful men." In rapid succession there now followed a series of sinkings of American ships. In March 1917 one of the remaining "moral" reasons for avoiding war was eliminated when the autocratic czarist government in Russia was overthrown by a liberal revolution. Now more than ever the Allied cause could be labeled the cause of democracy.

On the evening of April 2, 1917, the president reluctantly appeared before a joint session of Congress to ask for a declaration of war. It was, Bernard Baruch recalled forty years later, a solemn and impressive occasion. Sitting in the Senate gallery with other distinguished visitors, many carrying small American flags, Baruch noted the tenseness in the stately hall and how he and the others in the gallery strained forward to hear the president's words. Still morally opposed to belligerency, Wilson declared that Germany's contempt for American rights and American lives allowed him no other course. The president was earnest and eloquent. The tall, slender man briefly recounted the circumstances leading up to his appearance before Congress. Wilson put the blame for war squarely on the submarine policy of Germany, especially the unrestricted attacks begun on February 1.

> The new policy has swept every restriction aside. Vessels of every kind, whatever their flag, their character, their cargo, their destination, their errand, have been

ruthlessly sent to the bottom without warning and without thought of help or mercy for those on board, the vessels of friendly neutrals along with those of belligerents. Even hospital ships and ships carrying relief to the sorely bereaved and stricken people of Belgium ... have been sunk with the same reckless lack of compassion or of principle. . . .

Wilson denied that his country would be fighting for itself alone. Germany's attacks were directed against all neutrals, not solely against the United States. We would fight, he said, for all mankind, for "the vindication of right, of human right" against "autocratic governments backed by organized force. . . ." The president concluded with a stirring peroration that summarized America's hopes for the war's outcome:

It is a distressing and oppressive duty, Gentlemen of the Congress, which I have performed in addressing you. There are, it may be, many months of fiery trial and sacrifice ahead of us. It is a fearful thing to lead this great peaceful people into war, into the most terrible and disastrous of all wars, civilization itself seeming to be in the balance. But the right is more precious than peace, and we shall fight for the things which have always carried nearest our hearts—for democracy, for the right of those who submit to authority to have a voice in their own Governments, for the rights and liberties of small nations, for a universal dominion of rights by a concert of free peoples as shall bring peace and safety to all nations and make the world itself at last free. To such a task we can dedicate our lives and our fortunes, everything that we are and everything that we have, with the pride of those who know that the day has come when America is privileged to spend her blood and her might for the principles that gave her birth and happiness and the peace which she has treasured. God helping her, she can do no other.

America was finally in! In London, Paris, and Rome, crowds cheered the news. Sagging Allied spirits soared. At home the war was generally popular. Socialists and progressive isolationists opposed it, and among German-Americans there was some dissent and grumbling. But on the whole, the American people embraced the war and its sacrifices enthusiastically. Part of this, no doubt, had to do with old-fashioned patriotism. In this simpler, less sophisticated age, Americans were inclined to believe the adage "My country right or wrong." And beyond this that generation of Americans believed that war might actually serve to end international injustices and create a new and better international order.

This hope for a better world was the emotional foundation of the whole progressive era, and it proved to be one of the most potent instruments for whipping up enthusiasm for the war. In his war message, Wilson already had suggested that he considered our entry an opportunity to establish a more ethical and democratic international system. As time passed Wilson and the very effective Committee on Public Information under George Creel helped to convince the American people that the struggle was indeed designed to "make the world safe for democracy."

The most powerful expression of the president's hopes for the future was contained in his famous Fourteen Points issued in January 1918. Several of the points were concerned with reversing German gains since the war. These included the evacuation of France, Belgium, and Russia by German troops and the return to France of its lost provinces of Alsace and Lorraine. Another group of points emphasized the right of self-determination for the submerged peoples of the Austro-Hungarian, Turkish, and German empires. All these subject peoples finally were to be given their autonomy.

More important than these specific territorial provisions, the document laid down a number of general principles for constructing a new world system. The president wanted the nations of the world to accept "open covenants, openly arrived at," a blow against secret agreements among governments that vitally affected millions but were arrived at without consulting them. Wilson also wanted freedom of the seas, both in time of war and time of peace. He wanted to reduce trade barriers between nations. He wanted general disarmament. He wanted conflicting claims of the colonial powers settled with regard for the wishes of the colonial peoples. Finally, as the capstone of the whole structure, the president wanted "a general association of nations . . . for the purpose of affording mutual guarantees of political independence and territorial integrity to great and small states alike."

VII

The Fourteen Points and the League of Nations in many ways were the finest expressions of the progressive spirit as projected onto a world screen. As historians have noted more than once, Wilson's war aims represented a logical extension of progressive values, hopes, and attitudes to the international order. In recent years Wilson's international moralism has been attacked as naive, hypocritical, self-serving, and muddled. No doubt it was all of these. It certainly did not lead to an international paradise. And yet like progressivism itself, it failed not because of its inherent defects but because it demanded too much of men in the way of dedication and vigilance. In the end the American people repudiated both domestic reform and Wilsonian internationalism, not because they were foolish, naive, or insincere, but because they demanded more than the American people were willing to give them. The return to isolation and to privatism after 1919 expressed as much the exhaustion of the American will as the exhaustion of the progressive vision.

This change in the public mood would prove disastrous. During the 1920s the United States, for all its wealth and power, became an unlovely nation. Prosperous as never before, it was disfigured by greater extremes of wealth and poverty than in the past and by deep and ugly class, cultural, and religious differences. Gone or muted were the voices that had pleaded for social justice for all regardless of race, sex, nationality, or economic condition. George Norris, La Follette and other older progressives continued to be active in national politics, but others followed most of their fellow countrymen into the headlong pursuit of money, pleasure, and personal fulfillment.

A few historians have discerned a flourishing progressivism in the 1920s. But the progressivism of the 1920s was a different phenomenon from its predecessor. The regulatory agencies that reformers had painfully constructed to protect the weak and unorganized against the power of the mighty quickly slipped into the hands of the very groups they were intended to control. Organized labor, temporarily strengthened by a friendly government, was weakened cumulatively by the hostile courts that twisted the Clayton Act to suit the needs of management. The settlement movement in the cities receded in the face of indifference or, worse, a growing hostility to immigrants and blacks, their chief clientele. Politics once more settled into the divisive mold of pietist versus ritualist. The only progressive reform that seemed to retain the allegiance of any substantial part of the American people during the new decade was its most ambiguous one, Prohibition, and by this time, the generosity and social concern had largely disappeared from temperance reform, reducing it to little more than a weapon of old-stock, evangelical Protestants against Catholics and ethnic minorities.

In the realm of foreign relations, the exhaustion of the progressive impulse was still more obvious. In 1920 the United States Senate conclusively rejected the Versailles Treaty incorporating Wilson's League of Nations, and the country retreated into international irresponsibility that, as the world's major creditor nation, it could afford even less than in the past. Refusing to share in the inconveniences of collective security, we allowed our former allies, enfeebled morally and economically by the war, to face the problems of communism and then fascism and nazism, alone. Indeed, not only did we fail to contribute positively to a better world order, but by insisting on collecting outstanding war debts, and by refusing at the same time to allow the debtor nations to sell freely in the American market, we actively hampered European recovery and made more difficult the reestablishment of a stable European political system. The war to make the world safe for democracy ultimately ended by almost making the world safe for totalitarianism.

And yet it need not have been so. No matter how flawed and simplistic the progressive image of a more just society and a world governed by peaceful arbitration, it was far better, as events would soon demonstrate, than a nation and a world governed by unchecked laissez-faire and unqualified national sovereignty. The progressive vision was ultimately the better one, and this truth would have to be discovered once again a generation later.